Dearest Lenny

Dearest Lenny

Letters from Japan and the Making of the World Maestro

MARI YOSHIHARA

OXFORD
UNIVERSITY PRESS

Oxford University Press is a department of the University of Oxford. It furthers
the University's objective of excellence in research, scholarship, and education
by publishing worldwide. Oxford is a registered trade mark of Oxford University
Press in the UK and certain other countries.

Published in the United States of America by Oxford University Press
198 Madison Avenue, New York, NY 10016, United States of America.

Library of Congress Cataloging-in-Publication Data
Names: Yoshihara, Mari, 1968– author.
Title: Dearest Lenny : letters from Japan and the making of the world maestro / Mari
Yoshihara.
Description: New York, NY : Oxford University Press, [2019] | Includes bibliographical
references and index.
Identifiers: LCCN 2018054954 (print) | LCCN 2018056310 (ebook) |
ISBN 9780190465797 (updf) | ISBN 9780190465803 (epub) |
ISBN 9780190465780 (hardcover : alk. paper)
Subjects: LCSH: Bernstein, Leonard, 1918–1990—Appreciation—Japan. | Bernstein, Leonard,
1918–1990—Travel—Japan. | Bernstein, Leonard, 1918–1990—Correspondence. |
Hashimoto, Kunihiko—Correspondence. | Amano, Kazuko, 1929—Correspondence |
Musicians—United States—Correspondence. | Musicians—Japan—Correspondence.
Classification: LCC ML410.B566 (ebook) | LCC ML410.B566 Y67 2019 (print) |
DDC 780.92—dc23
LC record available at https://lccn.loc.gov/2018054954

9 8 7 6 5 4 3 2 1

Printed by Sheridan Books, Inc., United States of America

Letters by Kunihiko Hashimoto, Kazuko Amano, and Kikuko Amano are used by their
permission.

Writings by Leonard Bernstein and Felicia Montealegre Bernstein are copyrighted and used
by permission of The Leonard Bernstein Office, Inc. Correspondence from individuals
writing in their capacity as employees of Amberson Enterprises used by permission of The
Leonard Bernstein Office, Inc.

Other writings and images that are not in the public domain are used with the permissions of
the respective rights holder.

In memory of Steve Dinion

Contents

Dearest Lenny

Introduction

LEONARD BERNSTEIN—INDISPUTABLY ONE of the most iconic figures of twentieth-century American music—was a man with an insatiable thirst for love. His love of music, people, and life overflowed not only in his compositions and writings but also in the form of his dancelike moves on the podium and the tight hugs and wet kisses he bestowed upon men and women, both young and old. He poured his heart and soul into everything he did—composing, conducting, teaching, writing, speaking, organizing, smoking, and drinking.

Bernstein's overflowing nature is evident not only in his recordings, compositions, books, and lectures but also in the vast archives of his unpublished materials. The Leonard Bernstein Collection at the Library of Congress, still being processed, is comprised of over 1,700 boxes containing around four hundred thousand items, including manuscripts, correspondence, datebooks, and business records. Bernstein was extremely productive in everything he did, and he and his staff seem to have saved just about everything.

His personal correspondence was always touching, intriguing, amusing, and enlightening. Bernstein's mentor Serge Koussevitzky chastised him for insisting on performing his own composition as a guest conductor: "May I ask you: do you think that your composition is worthy of the Boston Symphony Orchestra and the Boston organization? Can it be placed on the same level as Beethoven, Schubert, Brahms, Stravinsky, Prokofieff, Bartok or Copland?"[1] Enclosing a check for $1.37 owed from a game of gin rummy, Isaac Stern instructed Bernstein not to spend it rashly, as money doesn't grow on trees.[2] In a holiday greeting card, ten-year-old Yo-Yo Ma reported on the three concerti he learned that year and the joint recital that he and his sister were giving the following month.[3]

The many and diverse letters Bernstein wrote and received paint a vivid picture of the man and his life.[4]

While looking through the Leonard Bernstein Collection's finding aid, I stumbled upon two unfamiliar Japanese names: Kazuko Amano and Kunihiko Hashimoto. I had expected to see Japanese names such as conductor Seiji Ozawa, violinist Midori, composer Toru Takemitsu, or Sony CEOs Akio Morita and Norio Ohga—all of whom had professional relationships with Bernstein—but I had never heard of these two.

The finding aid showed hefty amounts of their correspondences. Those with close personal relationships with Bernstein typically had several folders in a box at most. His wife Felicia's letters to him comprise three folders, his letters to Felicia another three; Aaron Copland also has three folders. But Amano too was listed with three folders, and Hashimoto with more than two entire boxes. I wondered who these two Japanese people were to the maestro.

Going back to the many biographies of Bernstein did not yield much information. Even the most comprehensive one, by Humphrey Burton, simply described Amano as "a former piano student in Paris who had been writing fan letters to him since 1947." Hashimoto was briefly mentioned toward the end as "[Bernstein's] Japanese liaison officer and friend."[5]

I requested to see the letters. I started with Hashimoto's, intrigued by the sheer volume of his correspondence.

What filled the boxes were love letters from a young Japanese man— young enough to be Bernstein's son.[6] The letters were written over the course of eleven years, starting in the summer of 1979, right after Bernstein's departure from Tokyo, where he was on tour with the New York Philharmonic, and continued until the summer of 1990, a few months before Bernstein's death. There are over 350 letters, most of which are handwritten on stationery, others on greeting cards with artwork on the cover or postcards from different cities. They are passionate, tender, and sometimes heartbreaking. Hashimoto's writing is also perceptive and self-reflexive, revealing his intelligence and sensitivity. Together, the many letters tell a moving story of his growing and deepening love for Bernstein.

Kazuko Amano's correspondence was no less moving and intriguing. Her letters span the course of four decades, from the late 1940s to 1990. They are written in longhand, in beautiful penmanship on carefully selected stationery, in elegant English sometimes mixed with French. Like Hashimoto's, her writing is at once passionate and articulate. The letters convey the deeply personal meanings Bernstein and his music had for her throughout various stages of her life. More vividly than many reviews by music critics and journalists, her writing illuminates how Bernstein's compositions, recordings, and performances touched his audiences. Her letters also reveal the evolving nature of her love for, and relationship with, "Mr. Bernstein," "Dear Leonard," and "Beloved Lenny."

Immersing myself in Amano's and Hashimoto's letters, I was quickly drawn into their close and lasting relationships with the maestro. By piecing together clues from their letters, I gradually painted portraits of these two unique individuals in my mind. I also began to trace the stories of their very different but equally special relationships to Bernstein. Further research soon made it clear that Amano and Hashimoto occupied a precious place in Bernstein's heart and mind as well.

After Bernstein replied to Kazuko's first letter, the two corresponded a number of times before they met in person for the first time during his first Japan tour in 1961. During his subsequent visits to Japan, Bernstein made sure to spend private time with her and her family amidst his packed schedule. While traveling, he sent her his photographs, programs, and news clippings. Later in life, Bernstein welcomed her to his home in New York, invited her to his seventieth birthday celebration, and treated her as an important guest while touring Japan. Amano described herself as Bernstein's oldest and most loyal Japanese fan, but he obviously thought of her as much more than that.

Hashimoto's relationship with Bernstein began much later than Amano's, yet it was equally, if not more, intense. While the two men did have a physical relationship, they were bonded by far more than sexual intimacy. It was commonly known that Bernstein was attracted to men, and, concurrent with his relationship with Hashimoto, he had many other male lovers, some of whom he surely saw much more frequently. At the same time, it is evident that Hashimoto was not just one of Bernstein's dalliances. Bernstein took time amidst his jet-setting travels to write or call him, and on two occasions he brought him to Europe to spend time with him. From the mid-1980s, Hashimoto became professionally involved in Bernstein's work and played a key role in some of the most important projects in the last stage of Bernstein's career.

There is no denying that Amano and Hashimoto lived in completely different worlds from that of Bernstein. For much of her adult life, Amano was a full-time housewife raising two children in Japan. When Hashimoto first met Bernstein, he was what the Japanese call a "salaryman," working for an insurance company in Tokyo. Meanwhile, Bernstein was a man of tremendous fame, fortune, and influence. In addition to having achieved international acclaim as a composer, conductor, pianist, and media personality, he was involved in various political causes such as civil rights and nuclear disarmament. He also had a strong Jewish heritage and worked closely with the Israel Philharmonic Orchestra throughout his career. He had a busy and happy family life. His exceptionally vibrant career and colorful social life were utterly different from Amano's or Hashimoto's.

What drove these two Japanese individuals to write, with such passion, diligence, and persistence, to this international celebrity so distant from their everyday reality? What was the nature of their love for, and relationships with, Bernstein? And why did Bernstein cherish these relationships so dearly?

These curiosities about their personal relationships led me to questions about the meaning of Bernstein's relationship with Japan. Was it purely coincidental that these two individuals were Japanese? Or were there specific factors that brought Bernstein and these Japanese individuals together? Why did one of the last major projects of Bernstein's career—founding and directing the Pacific Music Festival—take place in Japan?

Beyond Japan, why did Bernstein have such an impact—a deeply personal and life-changing one—on so many around the world? How did Bernstein, a quintessential American in so many ways, become the world maestro who reached and communicated so powerfully across borders?

Amano's and Hashimoto's letters to and relationships with Bernstein are moving first and foremost because of the depth of their devotion. Tracing how their love emerged, endured, and evolved takes one on a rich emotional journey. The letters also speak eloquently to the power of music and human will in history and society. Neither Amano's nor Hashimoto's relationship with Bernstein was determined by historical, political, and economic conditions, nor did they directly discuss such issues in their letters. They were writing fan letters and love letters, expressing their innermost thoughts and emotions as individuals, not as representatives of their culture, nation, class, gender, or sexual orientation. Nonetheless, trying to understand how these relationships were formed and grew allowed me to see how the personal intersects with the historical, political, economic, and social to make meaning in individual lives.

Since Bernstein's sensational debut with the New York Philharmonic in 1943, the nature of his stardom changed from that of an American icon in the 1950s to a globally revered maestro in the 1980s. It is widely understood that as Bernstein turned more of his professional energies to

Europe later in his career, he became not merely a world-class conductor but the maestro of the world. Yet that story often tends to be told in terms of Bernstein's reach across the Atlantic, focusing on his work in Europe as well as Israel. In contrast, Amano's and Hashimoto's relationships with Bernstein tell a story of the world maestro that looks east. The period when Bernstein's relationship with Amano and Hashimoto unfolded was one during which Japan's place in the world and its relationship to the United States changed dramatically. Those changes shaped Bernstein's relationship to the world in important ways and were reflected in his relationship to the two individuals. The focus on Japan and these two individuals allows for a broader understanding of the global Bernstein.

In tracing Bernstein's worldwide reach through the decades, *Dearest Lenny* looks at many forms of relationships—not only between Bernstein and Amano and Hashimoto but also between art and life, the United States and the world, culture and commerce, artists and the state, the private and the public, conventions and transgressions, dreams and realities. Some of the most difficult challenges Bernstein faced in his life and career lay in these relationships. Yet his greatest achievements as an artist and a human being were also born out of his uncompromising grappling with them. Amano's and Hashimoto's stories provide a unique window into these relationships, as well as the deep, intimate bond each of them built with their beloved maestro.

PART I

1

An American Icon Crosses the Pacific

LEONARD BERNSTEIN'S DRAMATIC debut with the New York Philharmonic conveyed his extraordinary star power. On November 14, 1943, he filled in at the last minute for an ill Bruno Walter and conducted the Philharmonic's subscription concert without a rehearsal. The concert was also broadcast on CBS radio network. At the age of twenty-five, Bernstein was the youngest man to step onto the podium of Carnegie Hall with the nation's oldest symphonic orchestra and one of the few US-born conductors to do so.

The morning after the concert, the *New York Times* reported Bernstein's sensational debut on the front page. The placement of this news item in the paper shows the global backdrop against which this American star was born. The headline, "Young Aide Leads Philharmonic, Steps In when Bruno Walter Is Ill" was printed in the same size and font as "Japanese Plane Transport Sunk as Our Submarines Bag 7 Ships." The rest of the front page was filled with reports of war from both the European and Pacific theaters. The top headline of the day was "Berlin Reports Russian Break-Through by 30 Divisions within the Dnieper Bend; Bitter Fighting Checks Allies in Italy." Other news included the United Nations Relief and Rehabilitation Administration's plans for postwar relief and rehabilitation programs, reports of the heaviest aerial assault ever inflicted on the Japanese in New Guinea, and a fierce battle between the British defenders and the German invaders on the island of Leros.[1]

Shortly after his Philharmonic debut, Bernstein achieved major success as a composer for the ballet *Fancy Free* and the musical *On the Town*, distinctively American works in both musical and narrative content that premiered in 1944. Bernstein's music mixed classical and jazz elements and "high" and "popular" styles, which became a signature of his compositions. Both works depict stories of three sailors who arrive in New York City on shore leave, seeking adventure and female companionship. Despite the benign romantic plot, the performance of these works, especially *On the Town*, delivered a bold political message in the midst of the war. Dancer Sono Osato, a daughter of a Japanese immigrant father and a white American mother, played the starring role of all-American heroine Ivy Smith; African American Everett Lee served as concertmaster and conductor. Such figures on the stage and in the pit were highly significant in light of Jim Crow segregation and Japanese internment.[2]

As it became safer to travel overseas after the end of the war, Bernstein made his international debut conducting the Czech Philharmonic in Prague and the European premiere of *Fancy Free* in London. He made his first trip to Palestine in 1947, then a British protectorate seeking to form an independent Jewish state. During this visit, he gave his first concerts with the Palestine Symphony Orchestra, many of whose members were Holocaust survivors, performing his own Symphony no. 1 *Jeremiah*, Ravel's Piano Concerto, and Schumann's Symphony no. 2. The following spring, Bernstein conducted an orchestra composed of the survivors of sixteen concentration camps in Germany. Later that year, Bernstein arrived in Israel in the midst of the War of Independence and performed forty concerts in sixty days amidst artillery explosions and air raids. These travels—during which he witnessed the aftermath of the Holocaust and the violent process of the establishment of Israel—decidedly shaped Bernstein's Jewish identity and his worldview. This was the beginning of his lifelong commitment to working with the Palestine Symphony, later renamed the Israel Philharmonic Orchestra, which he would continue to conduct for free for the rest of his career.[3]

The early career of this American star was thus shaped by his deep interest in the world beyond the United States, his understanding of war, and his dedication to world peace. But it was not only Bernstein's own political and moral commitment that led to his global reach.

In many ways, Bernstein was an ideal poster child for the American dream: he came from a relatively humble Jewish background; his compositions used uniquely American language, while incorporating elements from diverse cultures, mixing classical and modern idioms; he was both a serious intellectual and a popular entertainer; he was charismatic, charming, and communicative; and perhaps most importantly, he was the first American-born maestro to achieve international recognition.

It was no surprise that the US government actively tried to take advantage of Bernstein's background, qualities, and success both in its war effort and in postwar public relations.

Even in the 1940s, when the FBI and others suspicious of Bernstein's leftist political activities were closely monitoring him, he was also being watched by those in the US government seeking to win hearts and minds abroad. Toward the end of the war, the Office of War Information (OWI)— precursor to the United States Information Services, Office of Strategic Services, and the CIA—interviewed Bernstein in one of their radio broadcasts for overseas civilian listeners. Both *On the Town* and his up-coming performance with the New York Philharmonic were considered effective tools on the cultural front of the war.[4]

Amidst the rising fervor of the investigations of the House Un-American Activities Committee of the postwar years, Bernstein was blacklisted as a Communist, bringing his career to an abrupt halt. In 1953 he went through what he called a "ghastly and humiliating experience" of signing an affidavit disavowing his associations with unpatriotic organizations and denying any Communist affiliations.[5] Yet even during this same period, the State Department made numerous requests for Bernstein to participate in events dedicated to cultural exchange, write for foreign publications, appear in foreign broadcasts, and give lectures in cultural centers abroad. The language of such invitations sums up the state interests in cultural diplomacy: "The objective in assigning such persons [as visiting lecturers] is to promote further a better understanding on the part of the people of these countries of United States cultural life and social progress in our country and to acquaint them with the organizations and institutions in the United States which are devoted to such purposes."[6]

While Bernstein's early international endeavors were focused mostly in Europe, Israel, and the Soviet Union, his influence was beginning to reach across the Pacific as well. It was the convergence of Bernstein's own commitment to peace and the US state objectives during and after World War II that shaped his rising international fame and also created the setting for the making of Japan's earliest and most loyal fan of Bernstein.

* * *

CONSIDERING THE COMPREHENSIVENESS of the Leonard Bernstein Collection, it is curious that the very first letter from his self-proclaimed most dedicated follower in Japan—sent to wish him a happy birthday on August 25, 1947—is missing from the archives. While the contents of the letter that launched a precious, decades-long friendship are unknown, later letters and other sources illuminate how it came to be written.

Kazuko Ueno was born in January 1929 in Nagoya and raised in Tokyo, where she began studying the piano. When she was six, her father's appointment as an executive of a major Japanese trading corporation took the family to Paris, where she was enrolled in the Paris Conservatory. Although she continued her musical studies for a while after the Nazi invasion of France, the worsening war conditions forced the Uenos to leave Paris in late 1940. The family traveled through southern France and Spain, sailed across the Atlantic to New York, crossed the continent by rail, and boarded a ship from San Francisco to Japan via Honolulu, arriving in Yokohama in early 1941. Kazuko continued her piano lessons back home after the opening of the war between the United States and Japan and sometimes performed in concerts for soldiers departing for war. Yet Japan's wartime social climate stifled young Kazuko, who temporarily moved outside of Tokyo with her family to escape the US air raids.

After Japan's surrender, Kazuko feared that her dreams of a musical career would never be realized. That was when, at age eighteen, she chanced upon Bernstein's essay "The Essence of Musical Study" while browsing through *The Etude* magazine at the Civil Information and Education (CIE) Library in Tokyo.

The library was established as part of the cultural policy of the US-led Allied occupation of Japan in 1945–1952. Along with a wide variety of information control and cultural programs—such as rigid press code enforced on the media, sweeping educational reform geared toward democratization, restrictions on culture and the arts, and scholarships for study in the United States—the CIE libraries were a tool for turning the hated enemy into the United States' junior ally. During the occupation, the CIE set up twenty-three libraries in cities throughout Japan, lending books, journals, pamphlets, records, and musical scores for free, as well as offering film screenings, exhibitions, lectures, workshops, concerts, and English language classes.[7] At the CIE libraries, many young Japanese men, especially those in science and engineering, eagerly read the latest English-language academic journals, while many housewives and female students perused American fashion magazines. Those interested in culture and the arts attended the lectures and performances. For a generation of Japanese who had been forbidden to practice or consume many forms of Western, especially American, culture during the war years, the CIE libraries provided access to knowledge and ideas they had craved.

Kazuko was among those Japanese youths who frequented the CIE library in Tokyo. In 1947, the library was one of the few places where a young woman could satisfy her appetite for music and the arts. As a returned expatriate fluent in French and a diligent student of English, she was also eager to read English-language materials. The library felt like a haven where she could forget the devastation and poverty that filled the city. Browsing through magazines and books, she could let her imagination wander into the world she had known beyond Japan's borders.

Although Bernstein was quickly climbing the ladder to stardom in 1947, he was not yet an internationally known celebrity. Thus it is all the more remarkable that Kazuko paid attention to the short essay by this emerging artist. She was moved by his belief that a student of music "studies and learns and works and thinks to develop oneself as an intelligent, sensitive, and aware human being; and out of the always-increasing resources of intelligence, sensitivity, and awareness, the human being makes music."[8] His humanistic approach to music particularly resonated with Kazuko, who had felt suffocated by the nationalist teachings of the war years after having been educated in Paris. Having had her musical pursuits cut short, she had her passion reawakened by the acute intellect and ambitious attitude toward music evident in Bernstein's writing. She looked for his recordings at the CIE library and found a record of Serge Koussevitzky conducting the New York Philharmonic in which Bernstein made a guest appearance. As she listened to it, she was immediately entranced.

Convinced that this young conductor would go on to become a truly great maestro, she decided to send him a fan letter. She chose a postcard with a handmade woodblock print of the Daimonji Festival in Kyoto. In this annual festival, giant bonfires are lit on mountains to guide the souls of the ancestors making their yearly visit back to heaven. The most symbolic of the bonfires is in the shape of the character *dai*, meaning "large" or "great." Kazuko deliberately chose this postcard to convey her admiration for the magnificent, burning spirit that she sensed Bernstein to be.[9] She looked up his birthday in a reference book at the library and timed the sending of the letter for it. Not knowing his address, she sent it to the editor of the *Musical America* magazine, asking him to forward the letter to the maestro. She was not sure if the editor would do so and certainly never expected to receive a reply.

Between the slow sea mail—the standard medium for international mail at the time—and Bernstein's travels in 1947 and 1948, it probably took several months for her letter to reach Bernstein. To her surprise, he wrote back, likely after his tour of Palestine in October 1948, and enclosed a photo with his autograph.

As a rising star who was receiving many letters from adoring fans from around the world, he could not possibly have written back to everyone. Why, then, did Bernstein bother to send her a reply?

Surely Kazuko's eloquent and heartfelt words must have touched Bernstein. But it is also likely that his experiences in the preceding years made him especially sensitive to Kazuko's gesture. Having worked with Sono Osato—whose immigrant Japanese father was interned and whose brother joined the famed 442nd Regimental Combat Team of the US army—in *On the Town*, he must have had some understanding of the complex turmoil of Japanese and Japanese American families during the war.[10] Infuriated by the destruction wreaked by the atomic bombs in Hiroshima and Nagasaki, he became an advocate for nuclear disarmament, a cause he

FIGURES I.IA & I.IB Letter from Kazuko Ueno to Leonard Bernstein, February 10, 1949.

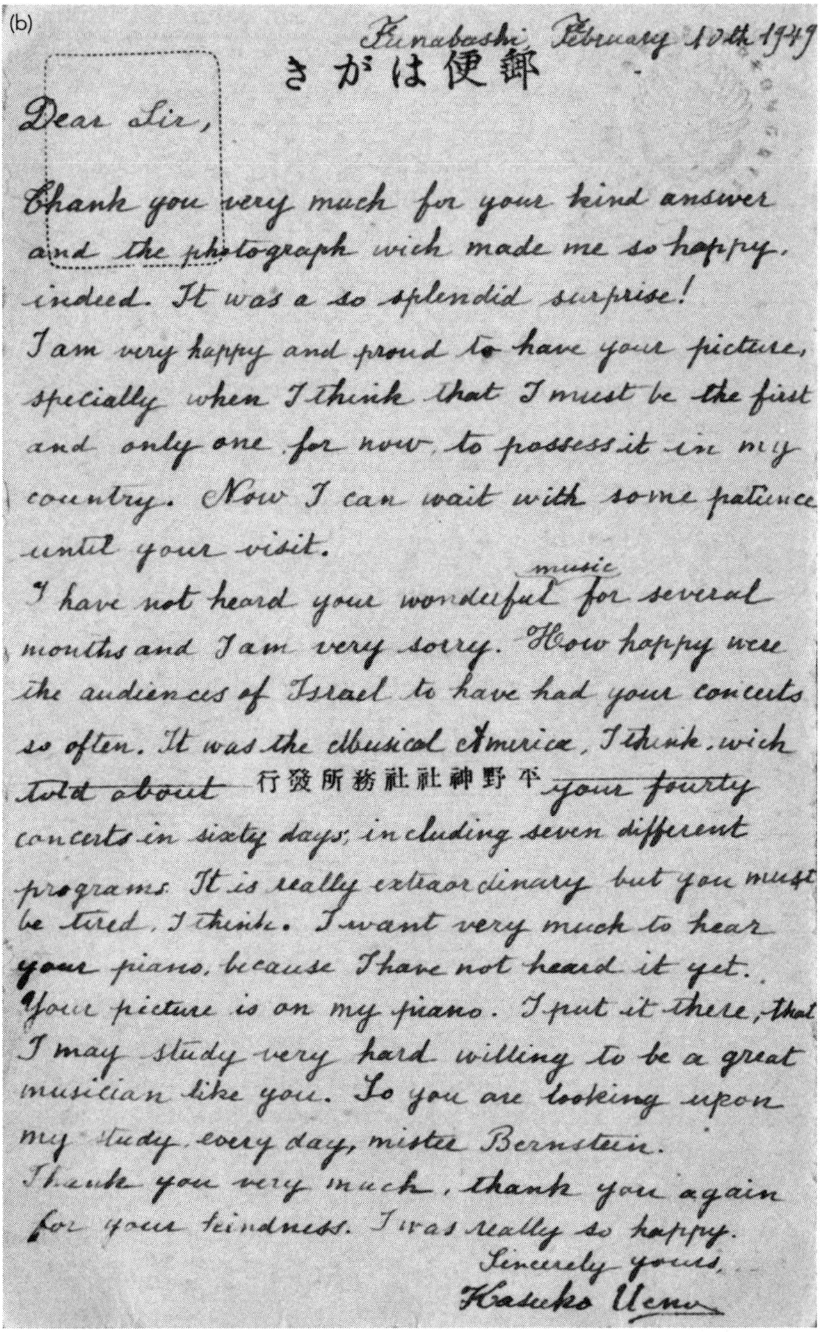

(b)

Funabashi, February 10th 1949

きがは便郵

Dear Sir,

Thank you very much for your kind answer
and the photograph wich made me so happy
indeed. It was a so splendid surprise!
I am very happy and proud to have your picture,
specially when I think that I must be the first
and only one, for now, to possess it in my
country. Now I can wait with some patience
until your visit.
                                    music
I have not heard your wonderful for several
months and I am very sorry. How happy were
the audiences of Israel to have had your concerts
so often. It was the Musical America, I think. wich
told about 平野神社社務所發行 your fourty
concerts in sixty days; including seven different
programs. It is really extraordinary but you must
be tired, I think. I want very much to hear
your piano, because I have not heard it yet.
Your picture is on my piano. I put it there, that
I may study very hard willing to be a great
musician like you. So you are looking upon
my study every day, mister Bernstein.
Thank you very much, thank you again
for your kindness. I was really so happy.
                         Sincerely yours,
                         Kazuko Ueno

FIGURES. I.IA & I.IB Continued

dedicated himself to for the rest of his life. Conducting the orchestras of Holocaust survivors and traveling and performing through the newly established state of Israel had solidified his commitment to peace everywhere in the world.

Of course, the wartime circumstances of Japanese nationals and Japanese Americans were entirely different. The conditions of newly established Israel and postwar Japan were also incomparable. Nonetheless, receiving a sincere, passionate letter from a young woman in Japan—which was still suffering from wartime devastation—must have made an impression on Bernstein, then barely thirty years old. Her letter must have reinforced his convictions about the power of music to transcend borders and work toward peace.

Kazuko's second correspondence, dated February 10, 1949, was written on a postcard with a watercolor painting of a cherry blossom festival. She wrote in response to Bernstein's reply. She formally addressed him as "Dear Sir":

Thank you very much for your kind answer and the photograph which made me so happy indeed. It was a splendid surprise!

I am very happy and proud to have your picture, especially when I think that I must be the first and only one, for now, to possess it in my country. Now I can wait with some patience until your visit.

I have not heard your wonderful music for several months and I am very sorry. How happy were the audiences of Israel to have had your concerts so often. It was *Musical America*, I think, which told about your forty concerts in sixty days, including seven different programs. It is really extraordinary, but you must be tired, I think. I want very much to hear your piano, because I have not heard it yet. Your picture is on my piano. I put it there, so that I may study very hard willing to be a great musician like you. So you are looking upon my study, every day, Mister Bernstein.

Thank you very much, thank you again for your kindness. I was really so happy.

Sincerely yours,
Kazuko Ueno[11]

The letter suggests that in the year and a half since her first letter, she had not only been reading magazines to follow Bernstein's career but also listening to many of his recordings. Kazuko's growing knowledge of his music reflects the critical role of the recording technology and industry in establishing Bernstein's stardom. Bernstein rose to fame just as Columbia Records became a leader in the development of twelve-inch, 33 1/3 rpm hi-fi long-playing (LP) vinyl records, and audio equipment manufacturers competed to produce high-fidelity stereo sounds for the mass market. The sales of LP records—with a longer recording time and wide frequency response, all sounds reproduced at equal levels, wide dynamic levels, and low distortion—were dominated by classical and Broadway music, making it a prime medium for Bernstein.[12] Signing his first exclusive contract with Columbia Records in 1949, Bernstein made his recording debut with his own Symphony no. 2 *The Age of Anxiety* with the New York Philharmonic.[13] This launched his extraordinary long and successful career as a recording artist. The wide distribution of the Columbia recordings expanded Bernstein's fame and delivered his music far beyond the concert halls and across national borders.

During Kazuko's visits to the CIE library, she befriended Y. Ernest Satow, who worked for the CIE as a music critic and lecturer during the occupation.[14] The son of a Japanese father and American mother, he played a key role in introducing contemporary American music, including Bernstein's compositions and performances, to the Japanese audience.[15] Kazuko and Satow shared their love of Bernstein and listened to his recordings together at the library.

After she received a reply from Bernstein, Kazuko's admiration for the maestro reached a whole new level of intensity. Placing his photograph on her piano for inspiration and motivation, she was beginning to make Bernstein an important part of her life and psyche. In subsequent years, Kazuko wrote long, thoughtful letters, filling each piece of stationery with beautiful, confident penmanship and smooth, eloquent English prose—sometimes mixed with French—revealing her cosmopolitan upbringing and education.

Her early letters depict the growing Japanese interest in Bernstein's music. Kazuko gave detailed accounts of concerts and radio broadcasts of Bernstein's compositions, often listing the names of performers. In March 1950, she reported that Bernstein's works—Sonata for Clarinet and Piano and *Four Anniversaries* for solo piano—were performed in Japan in a concert sponsored by the Association of Modern Music with the cooperation of the CIE. She confessed: "My little ambition was to be the first Japanese player of your *Anniversaries* and I've asked my American friend to send me the score. But I see there was [a pianist who performed it] earlier than me and I was a little disappointed. Nevertheless it was very good that your music was performed so early in Japan and I am glad for you."[16]

(a)

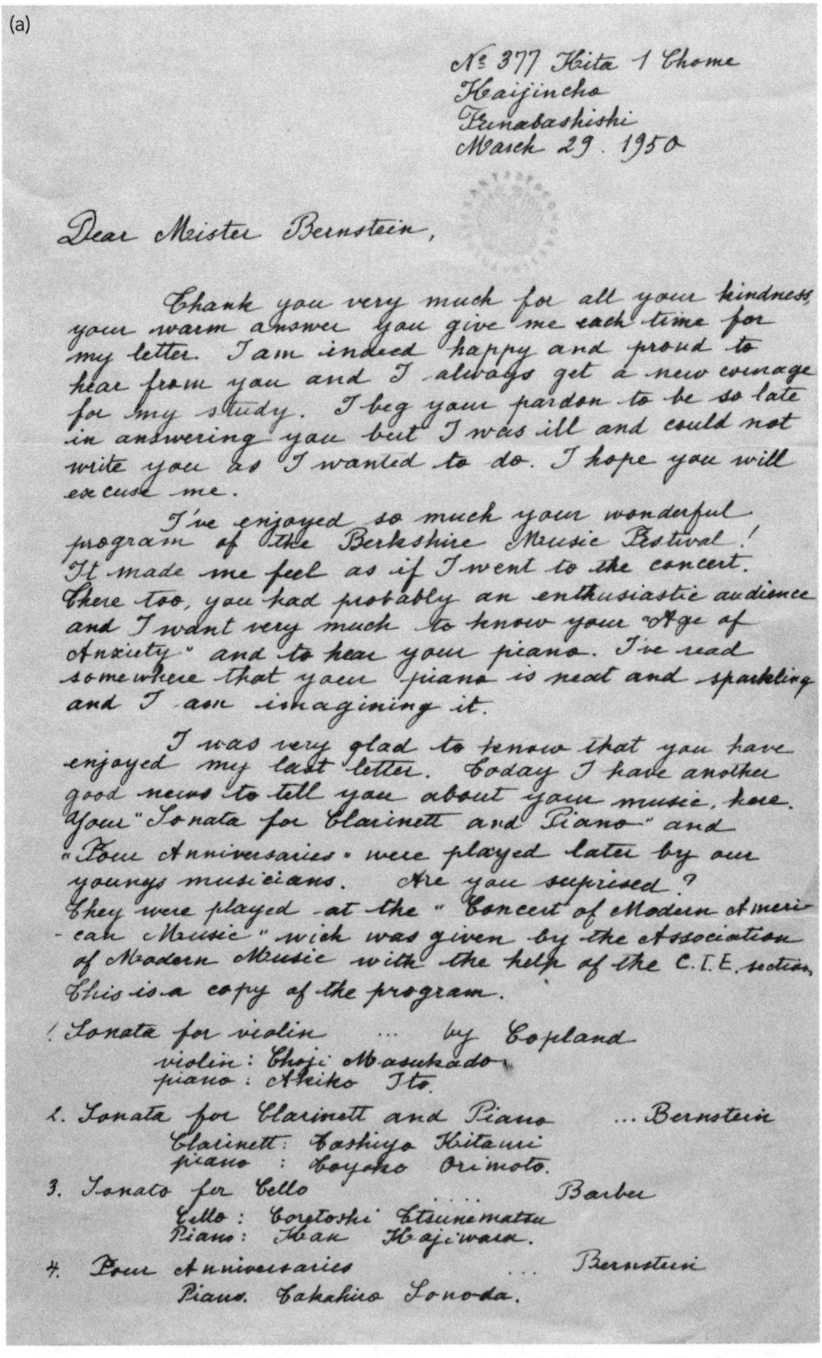

No 377 Kita 1 Chome
Kaijincho
Funabashishi
March 29. 1950

Dear Mister Bernstein,

Thank you very much for all your kindness, your warm answer you give me each time for my letter. I am indeed happy and proud to hear from you and I always get a new courage for my study. I beg your pardon to be so late in answering you but I was ill and could not write you as I wanted to do. I hope you will excuse me.

I've enjoyed so much your wonderful program of the Berkshire Music Festival! It made me feel as if I went to the concert. There too, you had probably an enthusiastic audience and I want very much to know your "Age of Anxiety" and to hear your piano. I've read somewhere that your piano is neat and sparkling and I am imagining it.

I was very glad to know that you have enjoyed my last letter. Today I have another good news to tell you about your music, here. Your "Sonata for Clarinett and Piano" and "Four Anniversaries" were played later by our youngs musicians. Are you surprised? They were played at the "Concert of Modern American Music" wich was given by the Association of Modern Music with the help of the C.I.E. section. This is a copy of the program.

1. Sonata for violin ... by Copland
   violin: Choji Masukado.
   piano: Akiko Ito.
2. Sonata for Clarinett and Piano ... Bernstein
   Clarinett: Toshiyo Kitami
   piano: Toyoko Orimoto.
3. Sonato for Cello ... Barber
   Cello: Koretoshi Tsunematsu
   Piano: Hean Kajiwara.
4. Four Anniversaries ... Bernstein
   Piano. Takahiro Sonoda.

FIGURES I.2A & I.2B Letter from Kazuko Ueno to Leonard Bernstein, March 29, 1950.

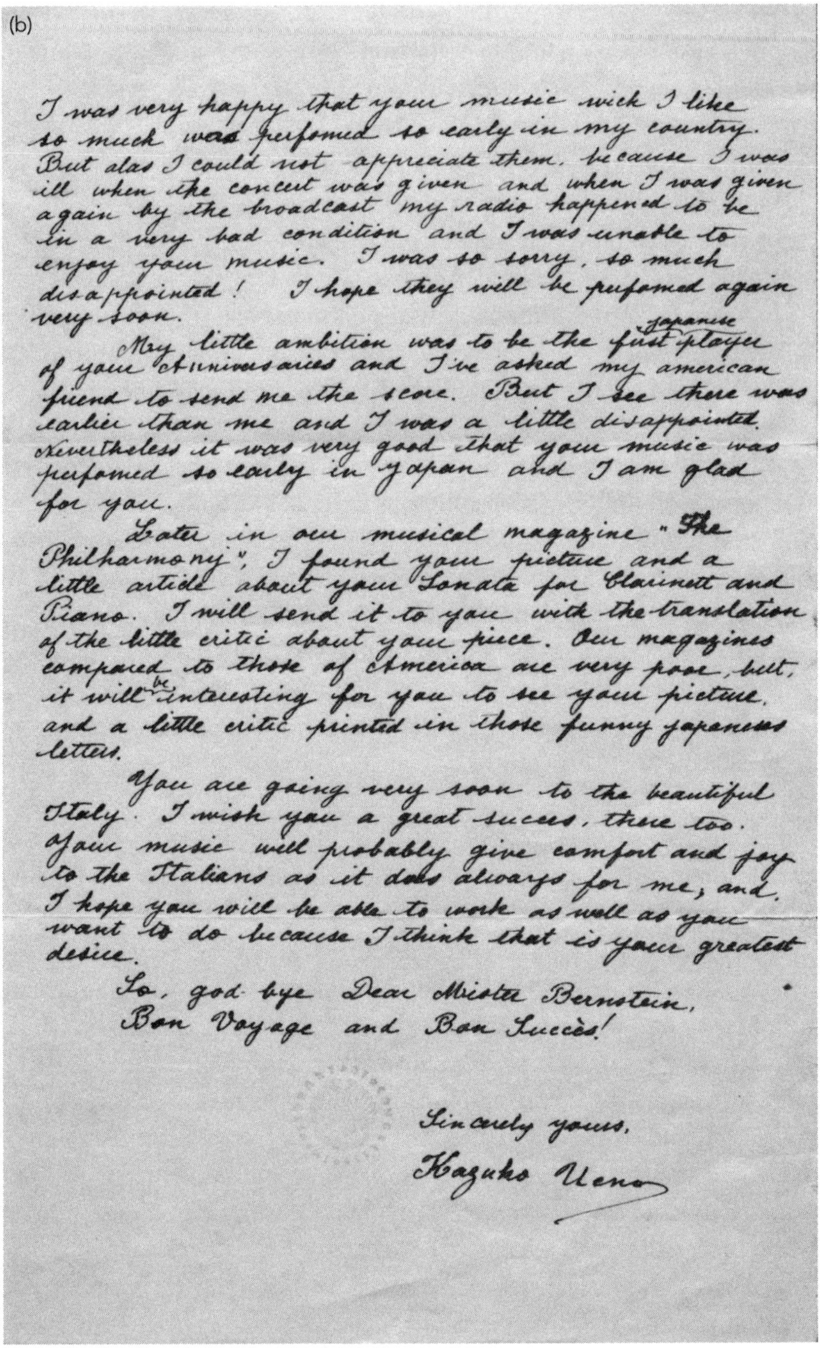

I was very happy that your music wick I like so much was performed so early in my country. But alas I could not appreciate them, because I was ill when the concert was given and when I was given again by the broadcast my radio happened to be in a very bad condition and I was unable to enjoy your music. I was so sorry, so much disappointed! I hope they will be performed again very soon.

My little ambition was to be the first japanese player of your Anniversaries and I've asked my american friend to send me the score. But I see there was earlier than me and I was a little disappointed. nevertheless it was very good that your music was performed so early in japan and I am glad for you.

Later in our musical magazine "The Philharmony", I found your picture and a little article about your Sonata for Clarinett and Piano. I will send it to you with the translation of the little critic about your piece. Our magazines compared to those of America are very poor, but, it will be interesting for you to see your picture, and a little critic printed in those funny japaneses letters.

You are going very soon to the beautiful Italy. I wish you a great success, there too. your music will probably give comfort and joy to the Italians as it does always for me, and, I hope you will be able to work as well as you want to do because I think that is your greatest desire.

So, god-bye Dear Mister Bernstein, Bon Voyage and Bon Succès!

Sincerely yours,

Kazuko Ueno

FIGURES. I.2A & I.2B Continued

In a letter written on Bernstein's birthday in 1950, she vividly described the identification that she and the Japanese audience felt with Bernstein's music:

> Your wonderful music which I like so much is getting more and more known and familiar to us every year, and it is indeed surprising to see how your music can take possession of our hearts of us all, in such a short time. As I told you [before] the Japanese are not very familiar with modern music and may be for that reason, they are not very much interested. There is something very far from them which they cannot understand. But your music is different, so beautiful, so warm, near to our hearts and easy to understand! We can really feel our hearts beat with yours and give a hearty appreciation for all the crescendos and diminuendos of your sentiments. You sing the song, a human one that all the people have in their hearts with such a beautiful expression never heard before. Hearing your music, we do not think that it is "your music" but the music of "ourselves," a sincere song of our souls. We are so happy when we have such a wonderful time . . . to hear the song we want to sing in a such nice expression. Mister Bernstein, will you please permit us to call you "our Musician"?[17]

Although she uses the pronoun "they" in the sentence about the lack of familiarity and interest with modern music among the Japanese, she then uses the first person plural—"we," "our hearts," "ourselves," "our souls"— to describe the Japanese audiences' responses to Bernstein's music.

Her subsequent letters reflect her growing closeness to and familiarity with Bernstein. They also display the typical qualities of fandom, in which admirers express not simply their love of but also their commitment to, pride in, and identification with the artist through their knowledge of the artist's life and work, acquisition and collection of goods and paraphernalia, and loyal participation in the artist's events. As with many committed fans of any artist, Kazuko's fandom for Bernstein became a way for her to process her own life and to relate to the world.[18]

Kazuko's enthusiasm for the talented and charismatic maestro was probably tinged with romantic attraction as well. Although she must have read about his marriage to Felicia in 1951, she never mentioned it in her letters. Perhaps she was a little sad, or jealous, even as she fully understood the irrationality of harboring such feelings for a man she had never even met. But upon reading the news of the birth of their daughter in 1952, she sent a toy dog, a traditional gift given to Japanese babies for their first visit to the temple. The letter, addressed to "Dear pretty little baby," reads: "I wish I could call you by your name but alas I don't know it! But I know that you are a most lovely baby and I love you."[19] In referring to the baby in the second person and declaring her love for her, she almost seems to be asserting her place in Bernstein's—and by extension, his family's—life.

* * *

DURING THIS PERIOD, Bernstein experienced a phenomenal rise to become an American icon. The unprecedented hit of *West Side Story* cemented his status as the unrivaled star of American music of his generation. After the show's Broadway opening in September 1957 and the release of the film in 1961, *West Side Story*'s soundtrack sat at the top of the Billboard charts for fifty-four weeks and had the longest run at no. 1 of any album in history.

In the same year *West Side Story* opened, Bernstein was also appointed the music director of the New York Philharmonic, becoming the first American to hold this preeminent classical music post. A consummate conductor, he intimately understood and maximized the power of the symphonic form. He introduced composers and works unfamiliar to many American audiences and even to the orchestra. He was especially instrumental in making Mahler's symphonies—which had been neglected not only in the United States but also in Europe—part of the standard repertoire. His energy, charm, and charisma and his tremendous success in conceiving, writing, and hosting the nationally televised *Young People's Concerts* series broadened his fan base far beyond the walls of the concert hall.[20]

Bernstein also proved to be a remarkable success as a recording artist. In 1959, Schuyler Chapin, recently appointed the director of Masterworks at Columbia Records, persuaded Bernstein to renew his contract for twenty years, with the right to record any repertoire of his choice at any time, plus a guarantee of $45,000 annual royalties, in addition to income from existing Columbia recordings. Such a generous contract was unprecedented in the industry and reflected Bernstein's status and Columbia's determination to retain him. Bernstein's recording output was astonishing. During the tenure of his contract with Columbia/CBS, he went on to make well over two hundred records. Along with Austrian conductor Herbert von Karajan, who commanded the Berlin Philharmonic for decades, Bernstein was indisputably the star of classical recordings of the LP era. Columbia's statement for Bernstein recording shows that the total royalties earned in 1960 was $60,217 (worth approximately $512,638 in 2018). The earnings steadily grew in the coming year, reaching $85,010 in 1964 (approximately $691,019 in 2018).[21]

The ever expanding scope and diversity of Bernstein's work necessitated a drastic change in the management of his business affairs. During the early stage of his career, his business was handled by Helen Coates, his former piano teacher turned secretary. Coates moved from Massachusetts to New York and served Bernstein with the loyalty of a dedicated admirer, close friend, and trusted confidante, and essentially became part of the Bernstein family. Coates was the one who had initially received Kazuko's letter to Bernstein and encouraged him to reply. But the small-scale operation of Bernstein's business by Coates and his accountant Gordon Freeman was no longer tenable as the scale of his work multiplied exponentially.

In 1959, Bernstein established Amberson Enterprises, Inc., to manage his business. Although using a corporate organization to run the business of individual artists would later become more common, especially among artists in the popular genres, it was a bold move for a classical musician and, according to his biographer Humphrey Burton, "prompted a few private sneers."[22] Yet Bernstein's foresight in taking this step proved tremendously important for protecting his artistic integrity, maximizing his commercial interests, and taking advantage of the technological and financial resources of the industry for the remainder of his life.

* * *

KAZUKO'S LIFE WAS changing dramatically as well.

The letter sent in November 1957 is the first in which she signs with her new family name, Amano, although none of her extant letters mentions the news of her marriage in the fall of 1955 or the birth of her first child the following year.

Why did Kazuko not write to Bernstein about her marriage and motherhood?

Perhaps she was simply too busy with the wedding, moving, and the birth of her son. Or she might have felt that such matters of her personal life would not be of interest to Bernstein. But there may have been other factors as well. Having expressed such strong adoration of the maestro who had occupied a central place in her psyche, she may not have known how to relate her everyday life—emotional, sexual, familial—to her love for Bernstein. Perhaps it was just easier for her to report these events to Bernstein after the fact.

Beginning with this same letter, she starts to address "Dear Leonard," whereas her earlier letters opened with "Dear Sir" and "Dear Mister Bernstein." Until then, her love for Bernstein seemed to have combined admiration for a great artist, a girlish fandom for a rising star, and a hint of romantic attraction. Perhaps with her own marriage, she felt that she was in a safe enough emotional space that she could strengthen her ties to Bernstein without exposing herself to vulnerability or public censure. In thanking him for sending her the recording of his analysis of symphonies and writing how much she enjoyed finally hearing his voice, she also reported, "I must tell you that my baby likes it very much! He is in a very happy mood when your analysis is on the record player."[23] She gradually merged her love for Bernstein with her love for his family, and her own family life with his.

In December 1960, after more than a decade of correspondence, Kazuko—now the mother of two children, living in the central city of Gifu, where her husband, Reiji, a civil engineer specializing in tunnel construction, worked—received the news of Bernstein's first Japan tour with the New York Philharmonic scheduled in the following year. She wrote excitedly, offering to help in any way to make his trip a pleasant and fruitful one. Bernstein must have written her that he did not want to trouble her amidst her busy domestic life, as she wrote:

Please don't mention about my being a busy housewife. I have many friends who can help me with their good tastes and skills and it wouldn't trouble me at all. On the contrary I shall be so happy to do something for you. It's such a joy to finally have you in my country and be able to meet you.[24]

2

Mr. Bernstein Goes to Tokyo

BERNSTEIN'S FIRST JAPAN tour in 1961—during which he performed ten concerts with the New York Philharmonic in Tokyo, Shizuoka, Nagoya, Osaka, Kobe, and Hitachi between April 24 and May 9—was shaped by the politics of the Cold War. As the needs of the government agencies fighting the cultural Cold War—including the State Department and the CIA—prevailed over those of the agencies and vigilante groups such as the FBI, House Un-American Activities Committee, and McCarthyite forces, Bernstein became a powerful advertisement for free, democratic America. The rise of his international fame and influence was propelled by the US investment in Cold War cultural diplomacy. During his years as the music director of the New York Philharmonic, Bernstein went on international tours under the State Department's Cultural Presentations Program, including the 1958 tour of Latin America, the 1959 tour of Europe and the Near East, and the 1968 tour of Europe and Israel. The New York Philharmonic also participated in the Berlin Cultural Festival in 1960 with the support of the United States Information Agency (USIA) and the State Department and the sponsorship of Ford Motor Company.[1]

In the context of the Cold War, of particular interest were programs related to the Soviet Union. In 1959, Bernstein led the New York Philharmonic on a tour of seventeen European and Near East countries, including two weeks in the Soviet Union. The same year, the Advisory Committee on the Arts for the Special Assistant to the Secretary of State requested Bernstein's input on the effectiveness of American presentations in the visual and performing arts in Moscow.[2] Bernstein was also invited to participate in the State Department–sponsored conference on US-Soviet cultural relations held at Harvard University in April 1960, along with such figures as statesman George Kennan, journalist Walter Lippmann, and leaders of major universities and foundations.[3] The USIA, formed under the Eisenhower administration to understand, inform, and influence foreign publics in promotion of US interest, similarly engaged Bernstein in various projects.[4] In 1959, it recruited him to give a lecture titled "The Conductor's Role" for a Voice of America radio program, designed "to establish a nexus between America's foremost academic and cultural figures and institutions and their counterparts abroad, to highlight current American trends and developments in the arts and sciences, and to gain added appreciation and respect for American intellectual achievement by displaying its best products."[5] In this spirit, Bernstein often agreed to speak on broadcasts, write essays or allow reprinting of his published writings, send comments for various events, and make recommendations on contemporary American music. The government's recognition of Bernstein's appeal was also evident in his relationship to the White House. The day after Bernstein was invited to perform with the New York Philharmonic at Eisenhower's White House in April 1960, Vice President Nixon wrote to him: "I can say without qualification that in all the times I have been in that room I have never heard more sustained or enthusiastic applause."[6]

Bernstein's 1961 Japan tour was part of the East-West Music Encounter, an international conference and festival "conceived to demonstrate the irresistible affinity between performers and composers of the Eastern and Western worlds." According to the event brochure, Japan was selected for the event because it "is the only country in the world where both Eastern and Western music have reached a high degree of development simultaneously."[7] Opening with a gagaku ceremony, the program included a solo recital by violinist Isaac Stern, a concert of "Oriental [Indian and Thai] music and dance," the Juilliard String Quartet, the Japan Philharmonic Symphony Orchestra, a kabuki performance, a concert of contemporary Japanese traditional music, and a concert of the NHK Symphony Orchestra. The festival was ponsored by the city of Tokyo, the Society for International Cultural Exchange (a Japanese foundation established in 1959 with the support of prominent businessmen and corporations), and the Congress for Cultural Freedom (CCF). Although the US State Department was sponsoring artists abroad under its Cultural Presentations program, it did not provide funds for the Philharmonic tour, as it had just funded the Boston Symphony Orchestra tour the previous year. Thus the remaining expenses of the tour—approximately $350,000—were covered by Columbia Broadcasting Company, John D. Rockefeller III, and two of the directors of the Philharmonic.[8]

The sponsorship of the East-West Music Encounter by the CCF—which later dissolved after revelations that it was secretly funded by the CIA—clearly signaled the US government's objectives in supporting such events. Japan had recently experienced mass, often violent, protests against the 1960 revision of the US-Japan Security Treaty (Anpo), resulting in the cancellation of President Eisenhower's scheduled visit to the country. Japanese leftists protested that the festival was organized by composer Nicolas Nabokov, an allegedly virulent anti-Communist, sponsored by a foundation that symbolized American capital, and had no representation of music and musicians from the socialist nations.[9] Prominent music critic Ginji Yamane published a harshly worded op-ed in the country's largest newspaper, *Yomiuri Shimbun*, asserting that the festival was designed primarily for the management organizations rather than the musicians. The organizers made little effort to integrate or feature local Japanese musicians, he pointed out, and so they failed to contribute to the growth of the local musical culture. Furthermore, he argued, the event was controlled by foreign interests despite the considerable funds coming from Tokyo taxpayers.[10] Incidentally, CBS Radio reported at the end of the tour that "the importance of the Orchestra's presence in Tokyo was underscored by the fact that, on the same day, the Gewandhaus Orchestra of Leipzig (East Germany) also began a series of concerts in the Japanese capital, resulting in a minor musical 'cold war.'"[11]

It was not only the US government that was invested in Bernstein's tour. The Tokyo concerts took place at Tokyo Bunka Kaikan, completed just a few weeks earlier to commemorate the five hundredth anniversary of the city. The hall is located inside Ueno Park, an area featuring a number of cultural institutions symbolizing Japan's civilization and Westernization: the Tokyo National Museum and the National Museum of Nature and Science, both founded amidst the modernization effort of the Meiji government; the Tokyo University of Fine Arts, the nation's most prestigious school for music and visual arts; the Sōgakudō Concert Hall, the oldest Western-style concert hall in Japan; and the new National Museum of Western Art, whose building was designed by Le Corbusier. For the Japanese hosts, Bernstein's tour with the Philharmonic was an occasion to showcase the nation's modernity and the rise of its economic and cultural power. Indeed, the Philharmonic members and executives were so impressed by the acoustics of Tokyo Bunka Kaikan that the controller asked for the architectural drawings so they could be studied by the acoustics consultants of Lincoln Center then under construction.[12]

The musical programming involved a different sort of politics. Just a year earlier, the Boston Symphony Orchestra's Japan tour caused the

Japanese presenters to feel "pushed around like in the days of the occupation."[13] This made the organizers of the New York Philharmonic tour particularly sensitive to the diplomatic aspects of the programming. They took extra care in consulting with the Japanese orgnizers and the local advisors before determining each concert program. Judging that "for diplomatic reasons, . . . it would be better if performers avoided performing their own music," Bernstein's *Jeremiah* Symphony was not performed as part of the festival but rather at the Tokyo Gymnasium and in Osaka.[14] Nabokov had suggested Henry Cowell's *On Gaku*, a quintessentially Orientalist piece using the pentatonic scale and other supposedly Asian musical elements, but later advised Bernstein in a telegram: "Advance Japanese reaction to proposed Cowell piece [Ongaku] but not to other Cowell music very bad. Japanese consider this piece condescending. Strongly urge its elimination. Another Cowell piece perfectly acceptable."[15] Bernstein decided to take Cowell off the program altogether, and after considering several suggested works of Japanese composers, he chose Toshiro Mayuzumi's *Bacchanale* for the May 5 concert.[16] Featuring Mayuzumi—a composer interested in amalgamating Western musical techniques with aspects of traditional Japanese music—was an especially apt choice for this cross-cultural festival and a meaningful gesture to the Japanese audience.[17]

What made this tour particularly meaningful for the Japanese audiences was the presence of Seiji Ozawa as an assistant conductor. After studying under Hideo Saito at the Toho School of Music in Tokyo, Ozawa left for Europe in 1959 and won first prize in the International Besançon Competition for Young Conductors, which put him on the map of emerging classical musicians.[18] When he won the Koussevitzky Prize at the Berkshire Music Center in Massachusetts, Ozawa caught Bernstein's attention and was assigned to be one of his three assistant conductors for the following season.[19]

At the time of the tour, Ozawa was still a twenty-five-year-old conductor largely unknown to Japanese or world audiences. It was Bernstein's faith in Ozawa's talent and promise that enabled his homecoming and major debut in his homeland. Ozawa's success bolstered nationalist pride in the midst of Japan's rapid economic growth and reentry onto the world stage. Japanese critics enthusiastically reviewed Ozawa's performance, stating that "with his unique performance style, he embodies a new type of conductor we have not seen among the Japanese thus far, and we have much to expect from him in the future. His performance with the Japan Philharmonic persuaded us of his superb sensibilities and grandeur."[20] Ozawa's memoir, published in Japanese a year after the 1961 tour, *Boku no ongaku musha shugyo*—or "My journey of the way of music," with the word *musha shugyo* invoking the apprenticeship in the way of martial arts— vividly depicts Ozawa's first impressions of Bernstein and the warm support and love with which the American maestro showered him.[21]

The Philharmonic's two weeks in the country were filled with the standard elements of Western tourism in Japan at the time. They enjoyed elaborate Japanese cuisine, were entertained by geisha, saw Mount Fuji, stayed at a traditional inn, and visited a Shinto shrine, Buddhist temple, and Japanese-style garden. They watched a kabuki performance and attended a gagaku (court music and dance) performance in the Imperial Palace. In his report to the board, the Philharmonic's executive director David Keiser conveyed the party's fascination with the exotic culture. He reported that at a press conference "a rather 'fresh' American girl" asked a question but "on being told by the Embassy representative that in Japan men came first, she had to yield to the floor!" After watching a couple of acts of a kabuki performance, the party went backstage to be introduced to the performers. "They are all men," Keiser wrote, "and to see a 'Geisha' with elaborate coiffure and very white complexion changing his muscular torso into another costume is, to say the least, incongruous!"[22]

FIGURE 2.1 Leonard Bernstein with Japanese Imperial Court musicians, 1961. Photo by Don Hunstein. Courtesy of the New York Philharmonic Archives.

FIGURE 2.2 Leonard Bernstein at Kiyomizu-dera Temple, Kyoto, 1961. Courtesy of the New York Philharmonic Archives.

While these commentaries represented typical American perceptions of Japan at a time when it was quickly shifting from a hated wartime enemy to a junior "geisha ally," Bernstein's own encounter with Japan was much more complex and profound.[23] A serious intellectual of the Renaissance type, Bernstein already had some knowledge about Japanese history and culture, but his more personal interest in Japan was awakened by his young protégé. Ozawa taught him some Japanese phrases as well as customs and culture in preparation for the tour, and the maestro immediately fell in love with Japan and its people. He became a fan of kabuki, noh, and gagaku and made a point of going to see performances during all of his subsequent visits. He wrote his wife Felicia about the gardens, rooms in the Japanese inn, temple, castle,

> And oh, the girls . . . crowd around, laughing, attending, bubbling, dressing and undressing you, preparing your kimono, your bath (oh, that wonderful bath of old scoured wood)—and with none of the artificial gaiety of the Geisha (who embarrass the wits out of me) but with a natural spontaneous *joie de vivre* and delight in making you happy.[24]

Bernstein got more than a superficial tourist's view of the country. Composer and music critic Heuwell Tircuit, who wrote for the *Asahi*

Evening News and *Japan Times* and also served as the chief writer for *Gramophone Japan,* showed Bernstein a seedy part of Tokyo filled with drunkards, rats, and bar hostesses accosting foreigners. According to Tircuit, rather than expressing displeasure or disgust, Bernstein showed sincere empathy for those living in difficult circumstances.[25]

Bernstein's genuine interest in the country, efforts to engage the audience, and friendly and charismatic manner captivated his Japanese fans. Bernstein greeted audiences with Japanese sentences that Ozawa had taught him. After an acoustically disappointing and physically exhausting performance at the Tokyo Gymnasium, the staff told him that there were over a thousand people in line for his autograph, and they could not possibly accommodate all of them. Always eager to meet his fans, Bernstein insisted on generously and patiently interacting with the entire crowd.

The musicians and the orchestra staff were impressed with the cultural sophistication and attentiveness of their Japanese audiences. "We learned here that the Japanese audiences sit quiet as mice—might they be emulated by [New York audiences at] our Friday afternoons! At the intermission they applauded enthusiastically but not ecstatically. At the end they really applauded hard and long and simply refused to move until rewarded with an encore," Keiser reported.[26] One of the last concerts of the tour was held in Hitachi, an industrial city seventy miles north of Tokyo.

FIGURE 2.3 New York Philharmonic concert in Tokyo, 1961. Courtesy of the New York Philharmonic Archives.

The Hitachi Company had built a fine concert hall on a hill overlooking the town and the sea in memory of its founder and offered a concert series for its employees. Clearly impressed, Keiser wrote to the board, "This is an example that I hope may be followed in the United States by similar manufacturers!" and again reported the enthusiasm of the audience.[27]

Keiser's reports about the positive responses of the Japanese audience may have been overly rosy, however. Despite all the political and financial investment in the East-West Music Encounter, the Philharmonic did not play to a full house in Tokyo. This may have been partly because of the controversial politics surrounding the tour, or because the final concerts fell on a holiday weekend. It may also have reflected the traditional preference for European conductors and orchestras among Japanese listeners of classical music. But most likely, the issue lay in the programming. The festival concert consisted of Roy Harris's Symphony no. 3, Bartók's *Music for Strings, Percussion and Celesta*, and Ravel's *La Valse*.[28] In addition to this opening concert, the Philharmonic performed two additional concerts, the first consisting of Hindemith, Berg, Chavez, and Mayuzumi; the second featured Ives's *Unanswered Question* and Symphony no. 2 and Stravinsky's *La Sacre du Printemps*. Although such bold programming was chosen in response to the organizers' request that the orchestra perform twentieth-century music, it was perhaps too avant-garde for the audience of the time. According to the recollection of music critic Sekio Tojo, the applause after the performance of Ives was sadly sparse. Even the eagerly awaited *La Sacre du Printemps* was, to Tojo's ears at least, hollow and bland.[29]

* * *

THE LESS THAN impressive attendance and tepid response notwithstanding, there were also some highly enthusiastic listeners in the audience, chief among them Amano.

Upon Bernstein's arrival in Japan, Amano wrote to him at his hotel, apologizing for not having welcomed him at the airport—her domestic responsibilities as a housewife limited her free time—and expressing her great sadness at not being able to attend his first concert. But she had tickets for his concerts in Nagoya and Tokyo and could barely contain her excitement: "I just can't wait to meet you <u>really</u>, to hear and see you conducting! I feel excited, happy, and emotional."[30] Like a classic fan girl, she repeatedly listened to Bernstein's music and sang along to "I Feel Pretty" and "Somewhere" as she anticipated his arrival.[31]

During this visit, Amano presented to Bernstein a music book she had created. She selected Japanese folk tunes she thought Bernstein would like,

FIGURES 2.4A, 2.4B, 2.4C Music book presented by Kazuko Amano to Leonard Bernstein, May 5, 1961.

FIGURES 2.4A, 2.4B, 2.4C Continued

translated the words into English, and wrote the words and melodies in a bound music staff made of handmade paper with woodblock prints.[32] She must have thought of this personalized gift long before Bernstein's arrival and prepared it in stages, finding time while her children were asleep.

To Bernstein's concerts, Amano brought not only her husband but also her four-year-old son and one-year-old daughter, who had listened to classical music since birth. She made sure to train the children so that they would sit through the performance quietly and not bother others in the audience. She never considered leaving them at home, because it was important to her that her children be exposed to Bernstein's music and have him in their lives. Sure enough, both children sat quietly and attentively through the concerts. When the Amanos went to meet the maestro in his dressing room after the performance, her infant daughter clung to Bernstein's neck, while her son wrestled with the maestro, who loved playing with children.[33]

After their first in-person encounter, Amano started to address her letters to "My Dear Lenny." Immediately after the end of the tour, she wrote:

> What a great joy it was for me to meet you <u>in person</u>, and to be able to see you conducting. You were a wonderful artist through records and radio, but the real "Lennys" are more wonderful than I thought, and I was happy and proud to be in love with your marvelous music since 1948. Now that I met the musician of my dream, and know that my musical instinct and conviction were right, I feel so happy and satisfied that even if I will have to die soon, I shall be glad of my life. Thank you, beloved musician, for your beautiful inspiring music you gave us. The memory of your unique marvelous concerts is still living in our hearts and when Reiji and I (sometimes with Shigeo) are enjoying your records, we are brought again in the Concert Hall and the magic effect of your music works on us. . . . .
>
> At the airport, when you disappeared in the plane with Helen [Coates], I felt discouraged and very weak. I felt as if I found suddenly an empty hole in my life. I tried to tell myself, "Don't be too difficult. You met him after a dream of 13 years. They were so kind and affectionate toward you and yours. Isn't it enough?" But this wise philosophy doesn't help. . . .
>
> I had many things to tell you, but now I realize that I forgot almost all of them. Perhaps I was emotional and shy like a little girl in presence of her hero! . . .
>
> After your visit to Japan, Reiji became as enthusiastic as I am for your music. Before, it was mine to put your records on the player and invite him to listen with me, but now he will go by himself to the record cabinet and pick up <u>your</u> records. And what is more for me is that when I am nervous or low-spirited, he will put your record on the player for me without saying a word about it. He knows so well that his wife can be no more low-spirited with your music! You can see that we are both enjoying the beautiful memory of your visit here. Your inspiring art, and your magnanima, warm

personality made me so happy indeed. We love you, Beloved
Musician, thank you, Lenny.[34]

After encountering the real "Lennys"—in plural, indicating that she saw
many facets of his character on and offstage—not only her instinctive admiration for him but also the nature of her love began to change. Meeting
him in person made Bernstein far more real than the figure she had
imagined through correspondence only. She was probably shocked by the
intensity of her own emotions. As if to dampen such feelings and to put
Bernstein in the proper context of her real life, she inserts references to
her husband, who had also become an avid Bernstein fan. Bernstein and
his music now occupy a central place not just in Amano's heart but in her
marriage and family life. Showing admiration for his music became a way
for her husband to express his love for his wife, and sharing her love of
Bernstein with her husband and children strengthened her connection
with her family.

Amano was no longer just a young female fan in a faraway land. She
was a woman with a family and a rich and complex emotional life, of
which Bernstein was a precious part.

3

Growing Pains

ON SEPTEMBER 23, 1962, Bernstein conducted the inaugural concert of the New York Philharmonic at its new home, the Philharmonic Hall in the Lincoln Center for the Performing Arts. Opening with the national anthem, the program consisted of Gloria from Beethoven's *Missa solemnis*; the world premiere of Aaron Copland's *Connotations for Orchestra*, commissioned for the occasion; Vaughan Williams's *Serenade to Music*; and Mahler's Symphony no. 8.[1]

Just as the opening of Tokyo Bunka Kaikan the previous year announced the cultural status of postwar Japan, the modern architecture of the Philharmonic Hall and the grandeur of Lincoln Center symbolized New York of the 1950s and 1960s. The urban blight and ethnic tensions of this neighborhood were the backdrop for Bernstein's most popular work, *West Side Story*, which had opened on Broadway five years earlier. In the show, Bernstein brilliantly expressed the contradictions between the dreams of postwar America and the realities of immigrant life through the voices of Puerto Rican characters. These contradictions were played out in real life in the neighborhood. Just as the show was enjoying unsurpassed popularity, Robert Moses's urban renewal displaced the area's residents like the characters in the show. In their place came a white conglomerate of high art that was to be the home of the Metropolitan Opera House, New York State Theater, Alice Tully Hall, and the Juilliard School as well as the Philharmonic. The construction of Lincoln Center and the glamor and splendor of its opening declared New York City's status as the nation's unrivaled artistic center and proclaimed the United States as the world's the cultural capital.[2]

Bernstein standing on the podium of this inaugural concert also symbolized his place in New York City, the United States, and the world during this decade. In the 1960s, his fame and popularity, particularly as a conductor, was unmatched. In addition to taking the New York Philharmonic to new heights in his capacity as the music director, he made his debut at the Metropolitan Opera House, continued his work with the Israel Philharmonic Orchestra, and began a long working relationship with the Vienna Philharmonic Orchestra and Vienna State Opera. As a master recording artist, he was the king of the LP era. He was dynamic and charming on screen, and his Young People's Concerts that were broadcast as a television series made him an international celebrity.[3]

Yet Bernstein's phenomenal success and popularity during this period masked his growing frustration with the changing dynamics of the American music industry. The turbulent decade was marked by fame and fortune as well as growing pains.

President John F. Kennedy's assassination left an unspeakable sadness in Bernstein. He was a dear friend of the Kennedy family and was one of the artists invited to the inaugural ceremonies in January 1961.[4] The president and the first lady made an explicit commitment to nurture relationships with the nation's artists and intellectuals and frequently hosted them at the White House. Bernstein was an important guest at such events. After the president's death in November 1963, Jacqueline Kennedy asked Bernstein to perform at the funeral ceremony. He chose Mahler's *Resurrection* Symphony for the occasion and also dedicated his Symphony no. 3 *Kaddish*, which he had recently finished, to the president's memory.

Bernstein's attendance at Lyndon B. Johnson's inaugural ceremony in January 1965 signaled his continued commitment to working with the White House in promoting the arts.[5] Not many perceived Johnson, a Texan whose humble educational and cultural background was a clear contrast to that of the president he served and succeeded, as a connoisseur of the arts. Yet in many ways he was instrumental in pushing US cultural policy forward and carrying on Kennedy's legacy in the realm of culture and the arts. During his administration, Johnson laid the foundation for the establishment of the National Council on the Arts and the National Endowment for the Arts, in both of which Bernstein played a prominent role.

Congress voted to name what had been planned as the National Cultural Center for Kennedy as a "living memorial," appropriating $15.5 million to match funds raised by the public.[6] Along with other leading figures in the arts such as violinist Isaac Stern, Bernstein was appointed to the Program Advisory Committee. He remained in close communication with Roger L. Stevens, chairman of the board of the Kennedy Center, and other key figures in the center's planning and contributed his ideas about the mission and operation of the center.[7] The protracted congressional debates in the course of planning and securing appropriations for the center raised many questions about the meaning of "national," "public," and the "performing arts."

Bernstein was ideally suited to addressing these questions, having tackled many of these issues in his own work as a music director, producer, and educator, as well as a composer and performer. Once the serious search for the artistic director for the center began, it did not take long for Bernstein to become a lead candidate. The correspondence with President Johnson reveals unwavering enthusiasm for Bernstein's nomination from all corners. On May 18, 1966, Stevens wrote to the president in no uncertain terms: "Leonard Bernstein is without question the man most eminently qualified for this task. In fact, there really is no one else that remotely approaches his prestige, his talent or his ability to guide the destiny of the Kennedy Center." He assertively wrote what was at stake in this decision, both for Bernstein personally and for the nation:

> I believe it would be a great coup for the Administration and the country if you saw fit to call him and persuade him to take the job. It will mean an immense personal and financial sacrifice for him, especially the enormous and irretrievable loss of time which he now devotes to his own work as a creative artist. But he is an idealistic man of great vision. If you could convince him that he is the best qualified man and that he should do this for the sake of his country and the contribution it would make to future generations, I think he will accept the responsibility.[8]

Harry McPherson, special counsel to Johnson, also strongly urged the president to persuade Bernstein to accept the position. The center needed a "brilliant and aggressive" artistic director in order to prevent it from falling into the control of the cultural elites of New York, McPherson asserted. Although it was ironic to call upon Bernstein, so strongly identified with New York, for this role, "he would become a vigorous advocate for the Center." It was certain "that he would be completely devoted to giving it an independent identity," and that by appointing Bernstein, the center would get "the best-known American musical figure, a dynamo and an undoubted genius" who would strengthen both the center and the administration.[9]

In the end, Bernstein's other commitments kept him from taking the role at the Kennedy Center. He generously gave to the nation's causes, but he was not to be contained within a single national center. Yet the changing dynamics of the American music industry in the 1960s proved that market forces were no less constraining than a government appointment might have been.

For Bernstein, having the Amberson organization was less important for maximizing his profit than for enabling his freedom from business dealings. By enlisting personnel who had deep appreciation for his art as well as practical skill sets for navigating the industry, Bernstein was able to devote his time and attention on his art while leaving his staff in charge of the financial operation and other details of his business.

One such figure was Schuyler Chapin, who produced numerous landmark records with Bernstein during his tenure at Columbia Records. Chapin left Columbia to become vice president for programming at Lincoln Center, but when Bernstein formed Amberson Productions, a branch of Amberson, Inc., in 1969 to make videotapes and films of his performances, Chapin became the executive producer of Bernstein's new company.

In light of the growing scale and complexity of Bernstein's projects, Chapin sought to professionalize and institutionalize the company's operation. Shortly after assuming his post at Amberson, he proposed establishing a consistent chain of command within the company, instructing that all business inquiries and correspondence be directed to him and then forwarded to the appropriate staff for action. He drew an organization chart showing Bernstein presiding over Chapin, who then oversaw Abe Friedman (attorney), Robert Lantz (agent), and Gordon Freeman (accountant), with Helen Coates and Jack Gottlieb (editorial assistant) working directly under the maestro.

While the Amberson staff freed Bernstein from the daily operation of the business, his notes and markings on the organization's documents show that he paid close attention to what went on and remained the captain of his ship. In response to the proposed streamlining of the administrative procedure, Bernstein used a red pencil to underline Chapin's phrase "any professional matter of whatever type [should be first directed to Chapin]" and wrote in the margin, "HC [Helen Coates]?" Where Chapin suggested, "Ideally, this should be the moment for Helen to retire from the daily personal secretarial chores," Bernstein wrote in, "Still my private sec'y."[10] These notes that hint at Bernstein's ambivalence about the businesslike model; his pushback against the recommendation suggests that perhaps the "Bernstein business" was growing at a faster pace than he was ready for.

Bernstein's own hesitation aside, Amberson's corporate structure and professional staff proved crucial in navigating the competing demands of art and commerce. As successful as Bernstein's recordings were, sales suggest that his artistic goals and the interests of the commercial market did not always coincide. Take, for instance, the Columbia account sheet for June 30, 1969. The total balance of the Bernstein account for the period was a highly respectable sum of $427,639 (approximately $2.9 million in 2018). But the itemized sales records show that many of the records did not sell in large quantities, and a great many of the "classical" repertoire—including Bernstein's own compositions—sold little more than one hundred units. The records that sold on the scale of thousands were "popular" works such as the soundtrack to *2001: A Space Odyssey* (the film was released the previous year), *The Joy of Christmas, A Treasury of Christmas, Grand Canyon Suite* (an orchestral suite by Ferde Grofé), and classical works with crossover appeal, such as Rossini's *William Tell Overture*, Tchaikovsky's *The Nutcracker*, Gershwin's *Rhapsody in Blue* and *An American in Paris*, Copland's *Billy the Kid* and *Appalachian Springs*, and Prokofiev's *Peter and the Wolf*. Among the classical works, the high-grossing albums were well-known works of the standard repertoire, such as Beethoven's Symphony no. 5, Beethoven's Piano Concerto no. 5, and Dvorak's Symphony no. 5. Even works that Bernstein had a strong affinity for—such as symphonies of Schumann and Mahler—only sold in the low thousands or even low hundreds.[11]

Considering the major contributions by Jewish musicians in writing and recording Christmas music in America, it may not be surprising that Bernstein made and sold so many Christmas records. In the first half of 1972, his top selling records were *Home for Christmas* (approximately 175,000 units), *The Best Loved Music of Christmas* (60,000), *Great Marches* (22,000), *Bernstein Conducts Fireworks* (22,000), and *Tchaikovsky's Greatest Hits* (22,000).[12] Bernstein's two gold records, meaning 500,000 unit sales, were Gershwin's *Rhapsody in Blue* and *An American in Paris* and *The Joy of Christmas* with the Mormon Tabernacle Choir.[13]

Given these successes, it is no surprise that Columbia tried to steer Bernstein to record more such works. The lifeline of the recording industry clearly came to lie in the rock and pop genres, as the Beatles sold tens of millions of albums. However, the popular leanings of Columbia and the recording industry in general began to raise questions for Bernstein. In the 1960s, he was establishing himself as a conductor of operas in both the United States and Europe, yet Columbia was not planning to consider recording any operatic repertoire beyond some highly popular works such as *Carmen, Rigoletto, La Bohème, Madama Butterfly*, and *Aida*.

In the face of these commercial demands and constraints, it became increasingly important for Bernstein to have an advocate who could effectively represent his musical goals and protect his artistic integrity. Chapin was perfect in this role, as he had an intimate understanding of the recording business. He told a Columbia representative that "it seemed patently unfair to keep [Bernstein] under contract and on the shelf with repertoire that the Company had no basic plans to record, that this was self-limiting and that there ought to be a way of releasing him for operatic projects any way he chooses to do them." In response to the Columbia representative's claim that the company had made a large investment in producing Bernstein's recordings and that the overall balance was barely in the black, Chapin replied—with the indisputable authority of the former director of Columbia Masterworks—that "it is a record company's business to manufacture, package, promote, advertise and sell recordings" and that "it was not an artist's responsibility to be totally responsible for a profit or loss position."[14] A year later, Chapin wrote firmly that while Columbia apparently wished Bernstein to be more involved in pop or contemporary music, "basically, though, Bernstein is a conductor, and as such must look to the classical repertoire, both symphonic and operatic, for his major disk work." Such correspondence expressed Bernstein's growing displeasure with Columbia's apparent lack of investment in serious concert music and its prioritization of commercial gain over artistic integrity.

Amidst mounting frustration with Columbia and the American music industry at large, Bernstein returned to Japan in 1970 on his second tour with the New York Philharmonic, again with Seiji Ozawa.

4

The Return of Two Maestros

Happy Birthday to you, Beloved Lenny
and
Welcome to Japan again!

How sad that we could not be there before you come, and I hope that this little picture will welcome you heartily and give you our warmest affection and devotion.

We will arrive in Osaka on August 28th in the morning, just in time for your rehearsals that I am so happy to be able to attend. I plan to get in touch with you (if you are busy, with Jack Kirkman), soon after my arrival.

I am free during the day of both August 29th and 30th. If you have some plans about shopping or visiting places, I shall be very glad to help you as I did nine years ago.

Beloved Lenny, sayonara until August 28th!

—Kazuko Amano[1]

ON AUGUST 26, 1970, the day after Bernstein's fifty-second birthday, Amano sent this birthday greeting to his hotel in Osaka where he had just arrived for his second tour of Japan. At the time, she and her family were living in the southwestern city of Shimonoseki, several hours' express train ride from Osaka. Unlike her earlier letters, which were written with a fountain pen on carefully chosen stationery with prints or artwork, this one is written in ballpoint pen on a plain white sheet of paper. The letter is relatively brief, compared to some of her earlier letters, and it was accompanied by a family photo taken around their dining table. At one end of the table Kazuko sits smiling, while her husband Reiji, looking more serious, sits to her left. In between them stand their son and daughter. From the two large plates of roasted chicken, bottle of wine, and greeting cards on the table, it appears that it is a festive meal, perhaps one of their birthdays—or could they have been celebrating Bernstein's birthday as a family? Despite her inability to personally welcome Bernstein upon his

FIGURE 4.1 Photograph of the Amano family sent to Leonard Bernstein, August 26, 1970.

arrival, the letter radiates her excitement about seeing him again. It also indicates that Bernstein granted her special treatment by inviting her to rehearsals.

Although their first in-person meeting in 1961 intensified her passion, Amano's letters to Bernstein had become sparse in the subsequent years. After June 1961, there are no extant letters from Amano until her Christmas greeting in 1964. This was a sign of her busy domestic life. Reiji's job as a civil engineer required the family to frequently relocate from one job site to another in different parts of the country. The family moved thirteen times all over the country, from Yamaguchi in the west to Hokkaido in the north. One can imagine the hectic life of raising young children in an itinerant household, creating a home and leaving again, making sure that the children adapted to their new schools and made friends, and trying to find a sense of belonging for herself amidst constant packing and unpacking. This may have been a different life from what she had imagined for herself when she was a young music student. Even in 1960s Japan, where professional opportunities for women were highly limited, her multilingual skills, international experience, and education might have enabled her to have a career if she so chose. Instead, she dedicated her talents, skills, and energies to her family, and did so with pride and love.

But it was not the case that Amano had no time to write at all. During this period she frequently exchanged long letters with Helen Coates, who had been her primary point of contact with Bernstein and who always treated Amano with deep fondness and care. Their shared love for Bernstein bonded the two women. Over the decades, they wrote many long letters to each other, sharing stories not only about Bernstein but also about their own personal lives. Coates addressed her letters to "My Dearest Little Sister, Kazuko."

The infrequency of her letters to Bernstein also reflects her astute calibration of the appropriate distance with Bernstein. She received occasional letters from him, but they were rarely more than a few sentences long. Coates assured her that the absence of replies from Bernstein was not a reflection of his interest in or affection for her. Amano understood his jet-setting life and her place—or lack thereof—in it and refrained from bothering him with her frequent letters. It may also be that after the intense emotional experience of being in Bernstein's physical presence and seeing him as a real person rather than an object of her imagination, she felt the need to curb verbal expression of her love, lest she allow it to be more than what it should be.

But Bernstein always remained central in her heart and mind. She made sure that he was part of her family life, often talking about Bernstein and listening to his music with her husband and children. In turn, she hoped that her family had a small place in Bernstein's life. In her holiday greeting of 1964, Amano attached a photo of her two children, aged eight and five, shot in front of the stadium that hosted the Tokyo Olympics that year.[2] Then there is another four-year gap until the next correspondence, a New Year's greeting in 1969, with another photo of her children, wishing a "Happiest 1969 to our Beloved Musician and his lovely family."[3]

In 1970, not only Amano but also her children eagerly awaited their reunion with their beloved maestro.

* * *

BERNSTEIN AND the New York Philharmonic arrived in a country that had changed considerably since their visit nine years earlier. The nation's gross national product had more than quadrupled, and per capita national income more than tripled. The Tokyo Olympics in 1964 had prompted dramatic growth in the city and the building of new transportation and other infrastructure. That year, the government liberalized international travel, which had been restricted to business purposes, allowing those with financial means to travel abroad for pleasure.

The Philharmonic's 1970 tour was organized partly in conjunction with the Osaka Expo '70, the first world's fair ever held in Asia. The expo was conceived of as a venue for publicizing the high standards of Japanese industry and promoting domestic products for export. Under the theme of "Progress and Harmony for Mankind," the government led the campaign to feature the expo as a celebratory event for the entire nation. The media joined the government and business leaders in making it the symbol of the nation's progress by offering a wide array of television shows and guidebooks promoting the event. Attendance was more than double the estimate—an extraordinary sixty-four million—resulting in intolerably long lines for entry into pavilions and general chaos in the midsummer heat and humidity.[4] If the opening of Tokyo Bunka Kaikan in Ueno had symbolized Japan in 1961, the Osaka Expo represented the nation's mood and status in 1970.

The Expo '70 Classic Series presented a nonstop series of performances by the world's top performers—pianists Alexis Weissenberg and Sviatoslav Richter; the Paris Orchestra, Berlin Philharmonic Orchestra, Cleveland Orchestra, Leningrad Philharmonic Orchestra, and English Chamber Orchestra; the National Ballet of Canada; and the Bolshoi Opera Moscow—along with performances by Japanese orchestras and opera companies. The New York Philharmonic's tour was organized by Chubu Nippon Broadcasting in Nagoya, which hosted a number of international classical music organizations during this period, including the Royal Concertgebouw of the Netherlands, the Vienna Philharmonic Orchestra, the London Philharmonic Orchestra, and the Czech Philharmonic Orchestra.[5] Bringing these top orchestras to perform was a way for Japan to assert its status on the global stage.

The audience base for classical music in Japan had grown in the decade since the Philharmonic's last tour, in part due to the development of music-related industries. Nippon Victor released Japan's first LP stereo recordings in 1958, and in 1969 recording companies began selling classical recordings for a relatively affordable 1,000 yen (the average starting monthly salary of a college graduate was approximately 34,000 yen). The availability of records led to the rapid spread of the stereo system in middle-class households and the growth of classical music fans among youth, including middle school, high school, and university students. The print media further promoted this trend. The *Record Geijutsu* (The art of recordings), a magazine founded in 1952 specializing in classical music recordings, came to play an important role in Japan's musical culture. Along with other classical music magazines that flourished during this period, some of which dated back to the Meiji era and others founded more recently, the *Record Geijutsu* nourished fans' appetite for the latest news of the classical music world as well as encyclopedic knowledge about various performers and recordings.

Classical music fans were also cultivated by Rō-on, an association of classical music listeners that originated in Osaka and had considerable influence from its founding in 1949 through the 1960s. Its members—typically men and women in their twenties, many recruited through networks of labor and trade unions—would attend regular concerts that the organization sponsored through membership fees. Nourishing a vibrant community of young music lovers, including students and both white- and blue-collar workers, Rō-on expanded into a nationwide coalition of local chapters.[6]

Also behind the growth of Japan's classical music fan base was corporate power, especially that of Sony. The company was co-founded in 1946 by engineers Masaru Ibuka and Akio Morita. Beginning with manufacturing telecommunication devices, the two men quickly achieved success developing a magnetic tape and a tape recorder. Their company entered the international market with the development of transistors when it acquired the technical license from Western Electric in the United States in 1955. Sony's remarkable success with transistor radio manufacturing was an exemplary case of international technological transfer, innovation, and trade that formed the basis of Japan's economic recovery and rise in the postwar era.[7]

In 1958, the company—originally called Tokyo Tsūshin Kōgyō (Tokyo Telecommunications Engineering)—changed its name to simply Sony to appeal to the global market.[8] In 1960 it established Sony Corporation of America, making it the first Japanese electronics company to enter the US market without American middlemen and the first Japanese corporation to sell stock in the United States. In 1962 Sony's showroom, located at Fifth Avenue and Forty-Seventh Street in New York City, opened to the public and displayed the Japanese flag in the city for the first time since before the war.

Key to Sony's rise in the global market was Norio Ohga. Trained as an opera singer at the Tokyo National University of Fine Arts and Music and continuing his studies in Munich and Berlin, Ohga had extensive knowledge of engineering and was given an unusual appointment to work for the company while still a music student. Ohga's unique combination of musical training, technical knowledge, and business savvy helped Sony distinguish itself by simultaneously building audio equipment and musical recordings. In 1968, the company claimed its place in the recording industry by entering a 50–50 venture with CBS to set up CBS/Sony and named Ohga, then age forty, as its president. He drew on his acute understanding of consumers' musical tastes and directed much of the company's resources to cultivating popular "idols" in the domestic market, most notably singer and actor Momoe Yamaguchi, the icon of 1970s Japan, as well as releasing hit American albums such as Simon and Garfunkel's soundtrack to *The Graduate*. Within ten years of its founding, CBS/Sony became the leader in record sales in the Japanese market.

Bernstein's exclusive contract with Columbia Records, part of CBS, was ideal for Sony in securing its place in the classical music market. For the 1970 New York Philharmonic tour of Japan, CBS/Sony launched an aggressive promotional campaign: it issued Bernstein records at the rate of twelve a month and had over fifty titles in the stores by the time of his arrival.[9] Schuyler Chapin offered high praise to Ohga: "May I say once again that I have never seen such a strong and effective promotional campaign as the one you organized for the tour. What a marvelous company!"[10] Toward the end of the tour, Akio Morita, then chairman of the board and executive vice president, hosted an official dinner for Bernstein and staff at his house in the posh Aobadai neighborhood of Tokyo. Bernstein also attended a reception for record dealers hosted by CBS/Sony at the Imperial Hotel.[11] This was the beginning of a long partnership between Bernstein and Sony. Having already built a close relationship with Herbert von Karajan, with Bernstein on its roster CBS/Sony established its indisputable place as the world's foremost recording company for symphonic music.

Bernstein's popularity and critical acclaim had grown exponentially since his last tour. The *West Side Story* film was released in Japan in December 1961, months after his first Japan tour with the Philharmonic, and it became the only work in Japanese film history to run for more than a year. A stage version by an American company toured in Japan in 1964, making it the first live Broadway production there, and the Takarazuka Theatre, an all-female musical theater company, performed the show in 1968. Bernstein was thus popular not only as a symphonic musician but also as the composer for *West Side Story*.

In Tokyo and Osaka, the Philharmonic's concert tickets sold out after only three hours. Photographs of the audiences showcase Japanese fans' "Bernstein fever." The crowd has rushed up to the stage and is applauding rapturously, gazing adoringly at the maestro. In one image, the audience members at the front of the hall are leaning into the stage and reaching out, trying to get Bernstein to shake their hands, much like fans at rock concerts, while the orchestra musicians observe the scene with amusement.[12] Most of these fans are young men in short-sleeved white shirts and ties, quite a few of them wearing black-framed glasses—probably college-educated men in the early stages of their careers.

FIGURE 4.2 Leonard Bernstein during the Japan tour, 1970. Courtesy of the New York Philharmonic Archives.

FIGURE 4.3 Japanese fans of Leonard Bernstein during the 1970 tour. Courtesy of the New York Philharmonic Archives.

Again accompanying Bernstein on this tour was Seiji Ozawa, but his role was completely different than the 1961 visit. As Carlos Moseley, the Philharmonic's managing director, wrote to the representative of Chubu Nippon Broadcasting, Ozawa was not coming to Japan "as an 'assistant,' for he [was] now a conductor of international reputation."[13] Indeed, during the intervening decade, Ozawa had become a star, regularly conducting the New York Philharmonic and other major American and European orchestras while serving as the music director for the Toronto Symphony and the Chicago Symphony's Ravinia Festival. Hailed by the Japanese public as "Ozawa of the world"—the program notes for the Osaka concerts introduce him as "a bright star among Japanese musicians and a hero to his admirers"—he was making regular trips home to conduct the Japan Philharmonic and other orchestras.[14] The program book lists Ozawa's name alongside Bernstein's, allots the same amount of space for their biographies, and features an interview with Ozawa. The photographs of the baseball game that the musicians played in Tokyo capture the camaraderie and friendship between the two maestros.

FIGURE 4.4 Seiji Ozawa and Leonard Bernstein at a baseball game during the 1970 tour. Courtesy of the New York Philharmonic Archives.

Ozawa's performance of Toru Takemitsu's *November Steps* was one of the most artistically significant parts of the tour. This piece was originally commissioned by the New York Philharmonic in 1967 for its 125th anniversary season based on Ozawa's recommendation.[15] Takemitsu began studying and composing music while working for the US Armed Forces during the postwar occupation, and Igor Stravinsky's interest in his *Requiem* launched his international reputation. Moved by the intense power of gidayū (singing of a dramatic or narrative style accompanying instruments during bunraku or kabuki plays) while watching a performance of bunraku (puppet theater that flourished especially during the seventeenth and eighteenth centuries) and influenced by John Cage, Takemitsu became interested in creating pieces using traditional Japanese music and instruments. He composed *Eclipse* for biwa (a lute with a shallow, pear-shaped body and neck that has been played in Japan since at least the eighth century, often in the performance of oral narrative and Buddhist ritual texts) and shakuhachi (end-blown notched flute) in 1966 and numerous soundtracks for films such as *Kwaidan*. Ozawa heard *Eclipse* and brought a recording to Bernstein, which led to the New York Philharmonic commission.

Like *Eclipse*, *November Steps* juxtaposes the sounds of the Japanese against Western instruments, the plucking of the biwa echoed by percussive effects on the strings and the shakuhachi's breath effects resonating in the clusters and glissandi in the strings and harps.[16] While working on the piece with the biwa performer Kinshi Tsuruta and shakuhachi player Katsuya Yokoyama at Takemitsu's cottage in the mountains of Nagano in September 1967, Ozawa became convinced that the piece would captivate Western audiences.

Yet when the musicians arrived in New York in November, their initial reception by the New York Philharmonic was far from cordial. On the first day of the rehearsal, as Tsuruta and Yokoyama appeared in formal kimono and expressed their respect to the orchestra musicians by bowing deeply at the end of the stage, half the musicians began giggling; one musician even jumped down from the stage and ran into the hall, laughing hysterically. Ozawa, who had already experienced the Philharmonic's unenthusiastic attitude toward contemporary music as well as Americans' general lack of respect for non-Western cultures, was unperturbed—he had even warned the soloists and the composer that "anything could happen" at the rehearsal—and spoke passionately to the orchestra about the meaning of Takemitsu's music. Yet the musicians kept behaving disrespectfully.

Takemitsu was so upset that he declared he would relinquish the commission and abandon the performance. Ozawa appeased him and spoke with the musicians in his unpretentious manner. He had the two soloists turn toward the orchestra to play the long cadenza, an intense dialogue between the two instruments painting the universe through colorful sonorities and dramatic temporalities. The restless orchestra was soon entranced and went completely silent. At the end of the cadenza, they burst into applause and shouts of bravo. The premiere of the piece was received with a loud standing ovation. Bernstein was moved to tears by the intense music that he felt embodied humanity and life.[17]

November Steps became one of the most critically acclaimed works by a Japanese composer. Its New York premiere symbolized Ozawa's pioneering role in carving out new artistic ground through the bridging of Western and Asian music. Now, Ozawa was bringing this work of the preeminent Japanese composer back to Japan, conducting Japanese soloists and America's top orchestra for a Japanese audience.

* * *

IN 1970, AMANO'S children were mature and musically educated enough to form their own opinions about Bernstein's concerts. Kazuko's daughter, Kikuko, then a ten-year-old studying piano and violin and developing her own musical sensibility, was stunned by the performance of Beethoven's Fifth Symphony in Osaka, never having heard such a "thickly human" rendition of the canonical piece. For young Kikuko, Bernstein was becoming not simply Uncle Lenny but an artistic hero.

After attending the rehearsals and concerts in Osaka, the Amanos joined Bernstein in Fukuoka, the tour's next destination. The concert there was held in a large sports center with no air conditioning. Between the heat and humidity and the torrential rain pounding the roof, the concert could not have taken place under worse physical conditions. Ozawa tried to salvage the performance by carrying blocks of ice to the podium in between the movements to cool down the maestro, whose expanding sweat marks on the back of his suit were visible to the audience. Amano was nonetheless transported by the sheer force of Bernstein's spirit conveyed through Beethoven's Fourth Symphony and Berlioz's *Symphonie fantastique*.

Bernstein invited the Amanos to a private dinner at a famous high-end Japanese restaurant after the concert. Asked to ride in Bernstein's limousine and escorted into the restaurant by the maestro himself, Kazuko reveled in having his personal attention and affection and sharing that moment with her husband and children.

Yet her joy did not last. Only a few minutes after the first appetizer and local sake were served, Reiji quietly announced that he had a business meeting the following morning and that the family had to catch the last train home. Stunned by the announcement, Bernstein offered them a car ride home so they could stay for the rest of the evening, but Reiji was determined to catch the train. The restaurant staff also showed some signs of panic, as the Amanos were the only Japanese guests in the party and the restaurant had no English-speaking staff to communicate with the famous guest and his company. Kazuko tried to argue with Reiji but quickly saw that resistance was futile. She tore herself and family away from the joyful gathering, assuring the waitresses that Ozawa would be joining the party later and would be able to translate.

The next morning, she woke before sunrise, prepared breakfast for the family, left a note, and went to the airport in Fukuoka to see Bernstein off.[18] After this parting, Amano wrote to Bernstein on stationery printed with Hokusai's *Thirty-six Views of Mount Fuji*.

Instead of the words of goodbye or gratitude for the time they spent together, she begins the letter in a way that indicates her acceptance of who Bernstein was: a great maestro and a married man.

> Beloved Musician,
>
> First of all, I want to congratulate you on your wedding anniversary! I wish you many, many happiness and hope that you found something "marvelous" for your most beautiful wife.

She then quickly shifts to express her intense emotions facing the day of his departure from Japan.

> I've intended to give you a call, because I want so much to hear your dear voice again, but I shall be so emotional and sad at the thought you are going so far, that perhaps I could hardly speak. So I have decided to write.
>
> Beloved Lenny, thank you so much for your affection and thoughtfulness, and for all the beautiful and inspiring music that you gave us through your concerts. We enjoyed your concerts, and my children "felt something" from their first and wonderful experience.

(a)

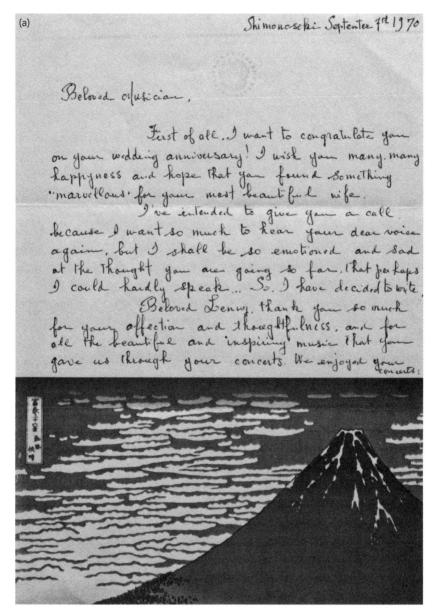

Shimonoseki September 7th 1970

Beloved Musician,

First of all, I want to congratulate you on your wedding anniversary! I wish you many, many happyness and hope that you found something "marvellous" for your most beautiful wife.

I've intended to give you a call because I want so much to hear your dear voice again, but I shall be so emotioned and sad at the thought you are going so far, that perhaps I could hardly speak... So, I have decided to write.

Beloved Lenny, thank you so much for your affection and thoughtfulness, and for all the beautiful and inspiring music that you gave us through your concerts. We enjoyed your concerts.

FIGURES 4.5A & 4.5B Letter from Kazuko Amano to Leonard Bernstein, September 7, 1970.

This summer is just twenty years from the first time I heard your conducting by the WVTR Radio, read your article "The Essence of Music Study" in the "Etude" (I know it by heart . . .), felt in love with your music and wrote you my first letter. Twenty years! I am proud

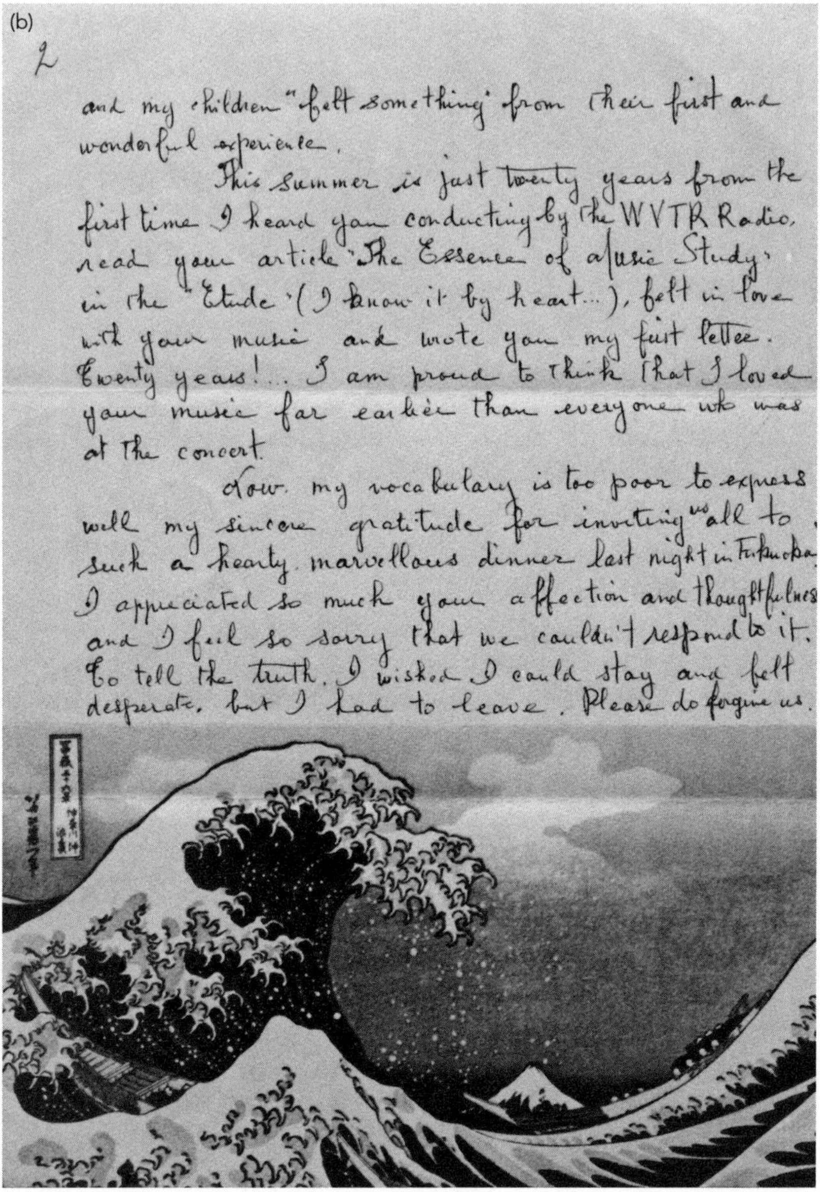

(b)

2

and my children "felt something" from their first and
wonderful experience.

This summer is just twenty years from the
first time I heard you conducting by the WVTR Radio,
read your article "The Essence of Music Study"
in the "Etude" (I know it by heart...), fell in love
with your music and wrote you my first letter.
Twenty years!... I am proud to think that I loved
your music far earlier than everyone who was
at the concert.

Now, my vocabulary is too poor to express
well my sincere gratitude for inviting us "all to
such a hearty, marvellous dinner last night in Fukuoka.
I appreciated so much your affection and thoughtfulness
and I feel so sorry that we couldn't respond to it.
To tell the truth, I wished I could stay and felt
desperate, but I had to leave. Please do forgive us.

FIGURES. 4.5A & 4.5B Continued

to think that I have loved your music far earlier than everyone who
was at the concert.

Now, my vocabulary is too poor to express well my sincere gratitude
for inviting us all to such a hearty, marvelous dinner last night in
Fukuoka. I appreciated so much your affection and thoughtfulness

and I feel so sorry that we couldn't respond to it. To tell the truth, I wished I could stay and felt desperate, but I had to leave. Please do forgive us. Reiji too did appreciate your kindness and didn't mean to hurt you. He loves you too but he is very "Japanese" and was unable to express himself.

She often resorted to French when expressing her most personal feelings for Bernstein. In the rest of the letter, she mixes expressions of her personal affection with those of her family's admiration for Bernstein.

After those days filled by your music, the days are empty and sad. Vous avez emporté mon cœurs avec vous. But I have such nice memories and we are all enjoying again your music through records that you gave us. I love all of them, but particularly your Mahler which sings straight to my soul. We will treasure your hearty presents. Thank you indeed.

I hope that you will have good days in Tokyo. The Hall there is far better than the poor one in Fukuoka (what a hall!). I wish I could fly again to Tokyo as I remember your concerts and rehearsals of nine years ago.

I will write to Helen and tell her how nice and wonderful you and your music were. Thank you very much. And I would like to say you good-bye in French because it means "we will meet again."

Your Kazuko and family will be in your heart at the airport. Au Revoir Bien-Amie Musician et Bon Voyage.

Please give my warm greetings to all the gentlemen who were with you at the dinner.

Affectionately and devotedly yours,
Kazuko Amano[19]

She appears to have reconciled her conflicting emotions by making her family into a Bernstein admiration society of sorts. She speaks both for herself and her family when showering Bernstein with affection and admiration.

She did not speak to Reiji for an entire week after this. Then, believing that running a pleasant household was her responsibility as a housewife, she resumed her regular domestic life.[20]

5

The Maestro Pivots

AN EXCEPTIONALLY BRIGHT, eminently competent, and warmly compassionate man by the name of Harry Kraut arrived at Amberson in 1971 to replace Schuyler Chapin in leading Bernstein's business. That year—the same year that Bernstein's *Mass* premiered at the John F. Kennedy Center for the Performing Arts to wide critical acclaim—Chapin had been hired away by the Metropolitan Opera. Chapin maintained close ties to Bernstein and continued to serve on the boards of various Bernstein-related organizations, but he stepped down from his command position at Amberson. Kraut proved to be an ideal manager for Bernstein in terms of both pedigree and skill sets: a graduate of Harvard and a music lover, he had worked for the Boston Symphony Orchestra for thirteen years, most recently as a manager of Tanglewood, to which Bernstein had a special affinity. He had deep musical knowledge, intelligence and eloquence, shrewd business sense, and the people skills needed to deal with outsized artistic personalities such as Bernstein and many of his collaborators.[1]

With Kraut at the helm, Amberson developed into a complex set of organizations that ran Bernstein's business via individual companies, each of which handled different aspects of the maestro's work. As a corporation, the umbrella organization Amberson Enterprises elected officers, established written bylaws, held regular meetings of the board of directors, retained legal counsels, sold shares of its common stock, and recorded its financial transactions and had them audited.[2] The directors of Amberson and leaders of affiliate organizations reported to each other on the status of various projects, discussed future plans, and made decisions and recommendations for Bernstein. Kraut's exceptional competence and the corporate infrastructure supporting Bernstein's work left the maestro free to focus on his art and served as the engine behind Bernstein's success for the rest of his life and beyond.

One of the most critical parts of managing Bernstein's business had to do with *West Side Story*. Ironically, this most American of Bernstein's works played a major role in causing him to gradually pivot away from the American music industry.

West Side Story was big business. Even though the earnings from the work were divided evenly among Bernstein, director and choreographer Jerome Robbins, author Arthur Laurents, and lyricist Stephen Sondheim, Bernstein's combined earnings from performances, motion picture, record sales, broadcasting, sheet music, and other miscellany related to the work far surpassed his income from all of his other compositions combined throughout his career.[3] The scale of this income made the stakeholders all the more invested in the work, giving rise to some highly contentious disputes.

G. Schirmer, which had exclusively published Bernstein's works since the 1950s, including *West Side Story*, began to cause concern for Amberson in the early 1970s. G. Schirmer's lack of transparent accounting and erratic payments of royalties led Amberson to request an audit and make a formal complaint against the company.[4] With the situation unsatisfactorily resolved, in 1972 Amberson began negotiating with the British publisher Boosey & Hawkes as a possible alternative.[5] In the subsequent years, Boosey & Hawkes gradually acquired rights to Bernstein's music, starting with *Dybbuk Variations*.[6] In the meantime, in 1979 Amberson established another company, Jalni Publications, Inc., to handle some of Bernstein's compositions. Jalni signed an agreement with Boosey & Hawkes, which now served as the sole and exclusive publisher to print, sell, and license those compositions.[7]

The financial dispute surrounding *West Side Story* took place not only in publishing but also in recording. The accounting for the film soundtrack album caused disagreements with Columbia Records, which eventually resulted in a $900,000 settlement and growing tension between Bernstein and the company.[8] This dispute, combined with mounting concerns with what appeared to be the dim future of classical music at Columbia, led Amberson staff to begin exploring possible alternatives as the expiration of Bernstein's exclusive contract in 1979 approached.

As early as 1969, Chapin had inquired with Deutsche Grammophon about the possibility of recording works in which Columbia was not interested.[9] Hanover-based Deutsche Grammophon was a highly respected

German recording label with a long history of specializing in classical music and an impressive roster of the world's top conductors such as Herbert von Karajan, Claudio Abbado, and Christoph Eschenbach. Reflective of the shifting configuration of media corporations, in 1971 Deutsche Grammophon group became part of PolyGram International, a Netherlands-based conglomerate seeking to expand its share in the American market by buying out several labels, including MGM, Verve, and Decca.[10]

Deutsche Grammophon's artistic visions markedly contrasted with Columbia Records'. The company's representative stressed that they were committed to supporting Bernstein's "way as a composer and conductor in a professional and successful manner." He emphasized the importance of building an image of unity between the conductor, the composer, and the orchestra. Underlining the need for a coherent artistic vision, the company envisioned recordings in terms of cycles rather than single performances. The company staff provided a detailed assessment of the repertoire and orchestras that Bernstein might consider recording. The company's understanding of Bernstein's musical goals was evident in statements such as this: "Dear Maestro, we know how much you are devoted to Schumann's Symphonies and though just having recorded them for the third time in stereo and being aware of their rather limited sales potential, we would consider it a lack of respect for you and your art not to include them in an exclusive offer to you. The Vienna Philharmonic . . . would certainly be an ideal partner for you."[11]

Deutsche Grammophon's approach also differed from Columbia's in terms of promotional strategy. Columbia had featured the maestro's "cross-over" image to appeal to the American audience, designating February "Leonard Bernstein Month" and celebrating his role in "remov[ing] the 'STUFFED-SHIRT' idea that many people have entertained about classical music."[12] Deutsche Grammophon, in contrast, tried to promote Bernstein with a "new European image." The company's representative consulted with Bernstein's promotion coordinator about a campaign focused on Bernstein's activities "as pedagogue, lecturer for the youth, founder of youth orchestras, composer, university professor, president of the English Bach-Festival and his 30 years conducting in Israel, etc. etc."[13] The company thus tried to foreground Bernstein's image as an artist, intellectual, pedagogue, and scholar with a long-standing connection to Europe.

Both Bernstein, who was seeking a recording company that was committed to classical music and embraced his artistic vision, and

Deutsche Grammophon, which was trying to secure a foothold in the American market, had much to gain from forming a relationship. As Columbia did not express any interest in recording operas, in 1972 Deutsche Grammophon recorded *Carmen* with Bernstein conducting the Metropolitan Opera. Despite the staggering production cost of $275,000, the recording became the company's best-selling opera, with more than 100,000 copies sold within the first few years.[14] In 1976, Bernstein had scheduled almost one hundred recordings for the next five years: forty-six with Columbia, most of which were with the New York Philharmonic, forty-six with Deutsche Grammophon, many of which were with the Vienna Philharmonic, and four with the British record label EMI.[15] This was a sign of his gradual shift toward working more closely with European orchestras and recording companies.

Bernstein's turn to Europe was also propelled by the growing importance of the visual media. Amberson was proactive in producing films and videos of Bernstein's performances since the early 1970s. Given the popular success of *Young People's Concerts* in which Bernstein masterfully and engagingly demonstrated the wonders of classical music to a mass audience, it made sense to further explore the possibilities of the visual media for classical music. Especially with regard to operas, Bernstein felt that it was frustrating and even wasteful to spend weeks preparing for a few performances with limited audiences, so he wanted such productions to be recorded for audio and video. Yet the American film industry was not interested in classical music programs that did not quickly generate profit. Bernstein's agent, Robert Lantz, was frustrated that the leaders of the American film and entertainment industry simply "don't have the imagination or the means to finance something that doesn't open at the Music Hall soon after the completion of production and returns its cost and profit fast."[16]

Bernstein thus turned to a European company instead, just like he did for publishing and recording. In 1971 Amberson entered into a six-year agreement with the German company Unitel to co-produce a series of audio-visual recordings.[17] Under the agreement, the two companies produced a series of videos of Bernstein's performances of Mahler, Brahms, and Haydn symphonies. As the end of the contractual period approached, Kraut reported to the Amberson Executive Committee that "the Company's overriding concerns in this area [videotaping of Bernstein's performances] were its commitment to the building of 'shelf product,' whether or not the product was commercially viable on an immediate basis, and its obligation to preserve artistic control in the hands of Mr. Bernstein."[18] Unitel was committed to the continued production of Bernstein's videos and offered a five-year contract renewal in 1977, almost tripling the fee paid to Bernstein and Amberson for roughly the same amount of music recorded under the 1971 contract.[19]

Although European companies were more supportive of all major areas of Bernstein's artistic vision and business than US ones, the decision to work with these companies was not an uncomplicated one. Although he had been conducting in Germany and Austria for many years, he felt a moral conundrum as a Jew when he signed contracts with German companies.[20] While Bernstein was contemplating the contract with Unitel, his agent Robert Lantz cautioned him:

> We have always been aware of the interest of the Germans now working in close association with Sony, but I do believe a great deal of hard thinking has to go into tying you prominently and permanently to the Germans, Japanese and other foreign interests. We would most certainly have to have a complete record of having tried to bring it all about in this country. One must never lose sight of the immense public interest in your doings, and the last thing we want is to make your work in this country in any way uncomfortable for you.[21]

At a politically turbulent time for the country, it was risky for Bernstein, a bona fide American musical icon, to be perceived as turning his back on the US industry and market and choosing foreign companies instead. The Amberson staff discussed the issue further as he contemplated a contract with Deutsche Grammophon. The board of directors discussed "whether, in light of current political developments, Mr. Bernstein's signing exclusively with a subsidiary of a foreign company might prove to be a future public relations liability."[22]

These debates illustrated the entanglement of Bernstein's artistic goals, political commitments, and commercial interests. The changes in the American music industry in the 1970s made it increasingly challenging even for Bernstein—the country's foremost classical musician, with a corporate infrastructure to support his endeavors—to conduct business in a way that was true to his artistic goals, economically sustainable, and culturally meaningful to a wide audience.

Europe beckoned. But so did Japan.

6

Japan Beckons

AMANO'S NEXT LETTER was written a full year after Bernstein's tour:

> It is already a year since your last visit to Japan, but I still remember
> it so vividly with the living memory of your wonderful music still
> vibrating in our heart and soul, and along with the sweet memory
> of your affection and thoughtfulness for me and my family. How
> I wish I could welcome you again! Last year you arrived in Osaka on
> the happy day of your birthday.[1]

For his birthday on August 25, 1971, instead of using a card, she penned
four pages on stationery with bamboo prints. It appears she put great care
into each word. After a birthday greeting and recollections of the previous
year, she quickly shifts to her report about watching Bernstein's video
of Verdi's *Requiem*. The recording at St. Paul's Cathedral was Schuyler
Chapin's first project upon the establishment of Amberson Productions
in 1969. In Japan, it was broadcast on NHK, Japan's public television network, on August 15, 1971, the anniversary of the end of the war.

> Requiem was most beautiful, by all means, and I am sure that all
> the audience in the Cathedral prayed with you, consciously or not.
> And I do not doubt that every Japanese who enjoyed the prayer
> prayed in their heart. I prayed with you, too, and I had to try hard
> not to show tears before my children. Your message before the con-
> cert was beautiful and warm and I liked it very much. You are not
> only a great artist but also a warm hearted great man, Lenny.

As she explains, by being broadcast in Japan on the anniversary of the
end of the war, Bernstein's prayers delivered meanings that transcended

religion, culture, and history. She expresses her hope that he can "find plenty of time to concentrate on" the composition of *Mass*, which she had heard about from Coates. As a Catholic, she must have been especially interested in this work.

Amano then gives updates on her family. Reiji had recently gone through some health issues and spent time in the hospital but had recovered and gone back to work. Her son, Shigeo, was busy preparing for the competitive high school entrance exam. Her daughter, Kikuko, now eleven, was studying piano and violin, and the mother and daughter were practicing Handel's violin sonatas together. She also reports that Bernstein's *Trouble in Tahiti* was performed in Japan, and enclosed a copy of the musical magazine that reviewed it. She did not attend the performance, but the critics were enthusiastic about both the composition and the performance, she says.

She closes the letter with a statement she had never made before: "Please give my sincere greetings to your dearest Felicia whom I want to be able to meet some day." Perhaps after the intense conflict she had felt the year before, torn between her wish to stay with Bernstein and her loyalty to her family, she felt it necessary to keep her emotions in check by focusing much of her letter on updates on her family and also more forthrightly acknowledging Felicia's presence in Bernstein's life.

Amano's only letters in the next two years are holiday greeting cards sent in 1972 and 1973. Both are cards with the prints of Mount Fuji—one a well-known woodblock print by Katsushika Hokusai and the other a modern painting—which Amano probably chose for Bernstein as the iconic image of Japan.

The card sent in December 1972 is presented as a family greeting rather than her personal message to Bernstein: she addresses the printed portion of the card "to our Beloved Lenny and his most beautiful Family" and writes the names of each of her family members. Next to her children's names in Chinese characters, she writes them in the English alphabet and puts their ages, sixteen and thirteen, in parentheses, to remind Bernstein of their growth. In the upper blank portion of the card, she writes:

> Just a week ago we had a splendid surprise. We saw the video-tape of "Bernstein in Vienna," "Beethoven's Birthday Celebration in Vienna." It was just wonderful and we enjoyed it very, very much. I always like your beautiful "singing" piano and it was the first time that I saw you playing the piano. Your speech and many

directions were so interesting, living and warm, too. In a word it was splendid! I felt as if we were really with you like two years ago in Japan. . . . I am really glad of your success in Europe and I hope that you could work as you like, as you want. Although I wish too, that you will be able to take a good rest and enjoy a peaceful family life during the holidays. Lenny dear we wish you a great success but don't work too hard, please. I liked your words in the interview (one with ASCAP that Helen gave me): "Everything is hard work. There is nothing that's easy if it's any good." This will be my motto for the coming year.[2]

She signs her own name at the bottom of this message, distinguishing it from the other half of the card.

The video she refers to is the documentary about Beethoven's two hundredth birthday celebration held in Vienna in the spring of 1970, during which Bernstein performed Beethoven's Piano Concerto no. 1 and the Ninth Symphony with the Vienna Philharmonic and his opera *Fidelio* with the Vienna State Opera.[3] The video mixes Bernstein's insightful narration about Beethoven's tortured life and sublime art with performances of his music, and the camera takes the viewers through Viennese scenes, archival materials, and clips from rehearsals and performances. The viewer sees him giving directions during rehearsals and performing onstage, hears his commentaries about the meaning of the works, and sees him in the car traveling to the concert hall, in the pit, and backstage. As Amano writes, the viewer feels the immediacy of the experience and closeness to both Bernstein and the music.

She instinctively knew that Bernstein was at a point in his life when he wanted to work in a way that best realized his goals without feeling the need to fulfill others'—including the industry's—demands and preferences. Her expression "Lenny dear" reveals the intimacy she has developed with him, and her request that he takes a good rest and not work too hard shows her care for him as a beloved friend. At the same time, her resolve to make his words about hard work her motto for the coming year is reminiscent of her younger self, who had looked up to him for inspiration.

Having read about Bernstein's upcoming Japan tour, Amano sent a holiday greeting card in December 1973 and pasted a family photo taken in what appears to be their family back yard. Similarly to the previous year, she addressed the card "to Our Beloved Musician and his lovely

Family" and signed the names of all four family members. Next to the children's names, she again put their ages and added parenthetical comments: "Shigeo 17 (bigger and taller than his father) and Kikuko 14 (bigger and more glamorous than her mother. Ah . . . !)." Under the photo, she wrote a brief personal message:

> We came back to Tokyo and feel happy of it for the children's education. I read in a music magazine that you are coming again to Japan in September. How I wish it could be true! . . .
>
> With my hearty wishes for your happiness and success.
>
> Devotedly,
Kazuko[4]

The brief message does not convey much about her life, but the photo and her parenthetical comments show her pride in her children's growth. After many years of being unable to put down roots as the family moved from city to city, dutifully performing the role of wife and mother, and living a life that must have been distant from the musical aspirations of her youth, she must have been relieved to be back in Tokyo, not only for her children's education but also for her own sense of belonging and stability. With the most intensive period of childrearing behind her and her husband moving into upper management, perhaps she was hoping for a more settled life in which she could carve out more time for her own interests and pursuits in the nation's cultural center.

When Bernstein arrived in Tokyo at the end of August 1974, he found a card and flowers from Amano waiting for him at the Imperial Hotel. He must have written to her prior to his arrival, letting her know of his schedule and that he would be bringing his son, Alexander. The front of the card features an image of Mount Fuji in black ink painting. Strikingly, Amano's message in this card is written entirely in French, which reads in translation:

> Welcome to Japan, dear Lenny, and I did not forget to pray for you on your birthday. What a feeling to think that it has been almost 25 years since the first letter I sent you.
>
> I wish you a grand success and I have no doubt it will be one. You are very much loved here, and we have been waiting for you impatiently.

To use a banal expression, I am entirely at your disposal during your stay in Tokyo and will be happy to do anything I can for you and Alexander. Therefore when you need me, please do not hesitate to let me know. (my tel: 461-8606)

Since words of welcome are inadequate, I offer these flowers along with my heart; they can surely express better than I can my joy at seeing and hearing you once again.[5]

Bernstein, who had a strong command of multiple European languages, would have had no difficulty reading the message. Yet the content of this message does not appear to convey anything so personal that could not be said in English or more personal than what she had not written in her other letters.

Why did she write in French, when she had been writing him in English all these years? Perhaps it was a way for Amano to communicate with Bernstein in a way that she could claim only for herself. Her husband Reiji, whose mother had been raised in the United States, was fluent in English; whenever they met, Reiji and Bernstein would have a lively discussion of Japanese society and economy. Her children, now college and high school aged, also were studying English. Sharing love and admiration for Bernstein with her family had been her way of juggling her emotions for him with her role as a wife and mother; perhaps she wanted to communicate with Bernstein just for herself, like she did during the first years of her correspondence, and resorting to French was one way to do so.

In September, Bernstein and music director Pierre Boulez conducted the New York Philharmonic in Tokyo, Nagoya, Toyama, and Osaka after touring New Zealand and Australia. The two maestros conducted alternating concerts, Bernstein performing a program of Mozart's Piano Concerto no. 25, K. 503, as soloist-conductor and Mahler's Symphony no. 5, and another with Beethoven's Symphony no. 3, his brand new *Dybbuk Variations*, and Stravinsky's *Firebird*.

CBS/Sony used the tour as an opportunity to ramp up its promotion of Bernstein recordings. The company released three new recordings by the two maestros and also promoted Bernstein's already-released and soon-to-be-released records, including *Trouble in Tahiti* and *Dybbuk*. The company also packaged and promoted three-album sets, six for Bernstein and two for Boulez.[6] By this time, Sony's Akio Morita and Norio Ohga both had close relationships with Bernstein and his staff. Prior to the tour, Bernstein sent

Morita personal invitations to the Philharmonic concerts, along with a series of videotapes of his Norton lectures delivered at Harvard University the year before.[7] During the visit, Morita invited Bernstein, Boulez, and staff to dinner after a reception hosted by the US ambassador, whose guest list was a veritable who's who of Japan's culture and arts.[8] Ohga's personal thank you letter to the maestro after the tour indicated that he and his wife spent private time with Bernstein and his son.[9]

Despite Japanese classical music listeners' traditional preference for what they perceived as the orthodoxy and authenticity of European traditions and inclination toward European performers rather than Americans, in the early 1970s the Japanese media, critics, and fans increasingly paid serious attention to Bernstein. The magazine *Record Geijutsu* frequently ran detailed articles on Bernstein. As was the case with American and European media, the Japanese press also frequently compared Bernstein and Herbert von Karajan, sometimes exaggerating the rivalry between the two titanic twentieth-century conductors. Publications fed the emerging culture of hardcore classical fans, a tribe comprised mostly of highly educated men with a penchant for snobbish pride in specialized knowledge—such as comparative assessment of different recordings of a particular symphonic work. The conditions were ripe for the Japanese to welcome Bernstein even more enthusiastically than on his previous tour.

As much as his fondness for Japanese culture and people, it was the steadily growing fan base, corporate endeavors, and professional networks that beckoned Bernstein to Japan. The nation was no longer an emerging market for classical music but a society with sophisticated consumers and a mature industry.

There are no extant letters from Amano written during this tour, so what she did during Bernstein's visit is unknown. Now living in Tokyo, she would have found it easier to go to his concerts, and it is likely that she, and possibly her family, attended both performances there. Having long wished to see Bernstein play the piano, she must have been thrilled to see him conduct and perform solo in Mozart's piano concerto as well as a Mahler symphony to which he felt special affinity. Attending the Japan premiere of his *Dybbuk* must have equally brought joy and pride.

The Amano family's evolving relationship with Bernstein is conveyed in the next correspondence, more than two years later. The holiday greeting sent in December 1976—with the red print of bamboo symbolizing virtue, sincerity, grace, humility, eternity—is now divided in two.[10] On the right side is Kazuko's personal message:

Happiest 1977 to you, Beloved Lenny!

Of course you know that your Age of Anxiety was performed here last year? I enjoyed it so much and remembered vividly the happy time I had copying its full score that I found at CIE Library where Ernest worked when I was then in my late teens! . . .

Devotedly,
Kazuko

Unlike the greeting cards sent in the previous years, in which she separated her personal message from family greetings, here she simply takes up the space to express her own feelings of connection to Bernstein. Although she still signs the names of her husband and son at the bottom, she does not bother to represent them in her message. Her son was in college, and she probably felt that he would send his own greetings if he so wished.

On the left side of the card is a separate message from Kikuko, who was studying violin at Toho Gakuen, the prestigious music conservatory where Seiji Ozawa once studied:

Dear Mr. Leonard Bernstein!

Please come to Japan as early as possible!

I want to meet you in person, because, now, I began to study conducting, and, you will certainly inspire me.

love,
Kikuko

She dots the "i" in her name with a heart and draws a cute illustration of a violin and a conductor with a top hat with his left hand high in the air and his right hand holding a baton. As she was raised and educated entirely in Japan, Kikuko's English writing does not have the same proficiency as her mother's. But her direct message and the use of the word "love"—which would be culturally foreign for most Japanese—reveal the closeness she feels toward Bernstein, having first met him in 1961 as a one-year-old and having had her mother reinforce this throughout her life. Her connection to Bernstein must have had no small role in her decision to study music seriously. Now that she was studying conducting, her personal affection for Bernstein was growing into an artistic and intellectual interest in his work as a conductor.

Kazuko's mission of raising a loving family that shared the love of music and admiration for Bernstein was bearing fruit.

7

Unions and Reunion

JUST AS THE Amanos were settled comfortably in Tokyo and the children were growing into thoughtful music lovers, Bernstein was going through the most tumultuous period of his family life.

Felicia Montealegre, a Chilean actress who had studied piano with Claudio Arrau and was introduced to Bernstein by him, was aware of Bernstein's attraction to men while they were dating. She still loved him profoundly, and the couple married in 1951. Shortly thereafter, knowing Bernstein's feelings of guilt and agony over his sexuality, she wrote him a letter that revealed her true embrace of who he was. "You are a homosexual and may never change," she wrote and declared, "I am willing to accept you as you are, without being a martyr or sacrificing myself on the LB. altar. (I happen to love you very much—this may be a disease and if it is what better cure?) . . . Let's try and see what happens if you are free to do as you like, but without guilt and confession, please! . . . Our marriage is not based on passion but on tenderness and mutual respect. Why not have them?"[1]

Leonard and Felicia had maintained a loving and happy family life with their children, Jamie, Alexander, and Nina. Felicia continued acting onstage and television—she narrated the New York Philharmonic concerts, including a performance of Bernstein's *Kaddish* Symphony, among other performances—but spent much of her married life focused on her family as well as antiwar and civil rights activism. Bernstein had agreed to be discreet about his attraction to men and not put her in humiliating situations. This arrangement had mostly worked, and Bernstein had many liaisons with men while keeping the marriage intact. Felicia was a loyal wife, Bernstein was a loving husband, and they were best friends who understood each other.

Yet Bernstein found it harder to restrain his behavior as he became increasingly concerned about his mortality, which intensified his wish to live as he liked. He became more public about his homosexual attractions, particularly his relationship with his lover Tom Cothran. In 1976, he made the decision to leave Felicia to live with Cothran, infuriating her and agonizing the children. Bernstein's behavior during this period was often erratic and tactless, and at times outright hurtful to Felicia. Most damaging and humiliating was Bernstein telling people that Cothran was his "best friend," since Felicia had always been the one who truly understood him—the man and his music—and in his heart he knew that as well. He was deeply torn between his sexuality and his love for his family, as he confessed to his close friends. The media reported the news of the Bernsteins' separation, adding to the family's pain.

Spending the winter together in California proved that Bernstein and Cothran were incompatible as living partners. Despite their affection for each other, they were too different in lifestyle and proclivities to share a home. Bernstein missed the joy and comfort of family life. He moved back to New York to make an awkward and gradual reconciliation with the still angry and reluctant Felicia.

Soon after Bernstein moved back in with Felicia, she was diagnosed with inoperable lung cancer. Bernstein was devastated, believing that he had caused her illness. He made arrangements for the best care possible as he continued his performances.[2] By early 1978, she was in the final stages of cancer. Bernstein was scheduled to return to Japan with the New York Philharmonic that summer but announced the cancellation of all concert engagements, leaving the tour to Erich Leinsdorf.

Although the reason for Bernstein's withdrawal was not widely publicized in Japan, Helen Coates notified Amano of his decision in May. Amano then wrote one of her most heartfelt letters yet. Unlike the previous greeting cards with images of Mount Fuji, this one is on a blank card with a print of irises. Her message takes up the entire spread of the card and shows immense care and thought.

Dearest Lenny,

What a disappointment it was for me to learn from Helen's letter that you are not coming to Japan, but it was a greater shock and sorrow to know about your beloved Felicia's serious illness. Poor Lenny, how anxious and depressed you must be! I wish I could do something for you, but there is nothing except prayers and these I won't neglect. I am praying for her, praying for you, please be sure of it.

It was wonderful of you to give up your concert tours in order to be with your wife and take care and comfort her. Being myself a middle-aged wife, I can easily imagine how she feels and I am glad to think that you are with her. Your affection and tender attention are more than everything for her now.

A man really worthy of the name and especially artists love their work more than everything, and I understand the meaning and weight of such a decision and sacrifice. But you did it. It is wonderful and heart warming! It is your warm, sincere and beautiful personality that ordered such an act, and I believe that it is this rare personality along with your genius that made your music so beautiful and appealing.

Beloved Lenny, we are all praying and praying with our whole hearts. Please be courageous, please don't be desperate. And please be good to yourself. Please don't forget that we are all with you. With much and many prayers, devotedly yours,

Kazuko Amano[3]

This is the first time Amano expresses her identification with Felicia as a wife and her admiration for Bernstein's dedication as a husband. Bernstein was no longer just a great maestro but also a fellow spouse.

Felicia passed away exactly a month later. Bernstein was inconsolable. Despite his recent hurtful behavior, he had loved her profoundly. In many ways, he never fully recovered from her death.

That summer, Amano went to the New York Philharmonic concerts in Tokyo—conducted by Erich Leinsdorf and featuring Martha Argerich as a soloist on Prokofiev's Piano Concerto no. 3—despite Bernstein not being at the podium. On his sixtieth birthday, she sent him a card, again with a black-and-white print of Mount Fuji.

Happy Birthday Beloved Lenny!

It is unbelievable that you are now sixty and that I will be fifty on my next birthday! At heart I have not changed at all, and still remain the same excited young girl that I was when I sent my first birthday greetings more than thirty years ago.

I wish this greeting to be a very special one, for I know that you are terribly lonely. I do wish you the best of everything and I pray for you.

I have something very important to tell you: everyone who came to the N.Y. Philharmonics' concerts missed you very much. I heard voices here and there whispering: "Wonderful orchestra, but how I wish it could be Leonard Bernstein." You are so loved here. . . . And I must tell you that it was almost unbearable for me to listen to it, because the orchestra sounded so different without you, and my heart ached when I thought of your great sorrow and unhappiness.

Beloved Lenny, my best prayers are yours on this very special day. Please be happy and good to yourself.

> Devotedly yours,
> Kazuko Amano[4]

Speaking not only of her own longing for him and his music but that of the whole Japanese audience's, this message was of an entirely different sort than her earlier birthday greetings.

That year, her daughter Kikuko sent him a separate birthday missive, written on stationery with a colorful print of the back of a woman in kimono. Inserting her illustrations of musical notes and staves, she wrote:

Dear Mr. Leonard Bernstein

Happy birthday to you!

I wish I could meet you in person and congratulate you.

I still remember vividly your last concert in Japan. I missed you very much when the N.Y. Philharmonic came to Japan. But I understand how unhappy you were. . . .

I am looking forward to your next visit to Japan. I wish, along with all my friends at Toho Gakuen, that this time will come soon.

> Yours sincerely
> Kikuko Amano[5]

Her handwriting appears a little more assured and comfortable than in her last holiday message, and her decision to send her own letter indicates her growing independence. Her last sentence, representing her wishes along with those of her friends at the conservatory, shows that she is writing not only as a family friend but also as a musician who respects and admires his work.

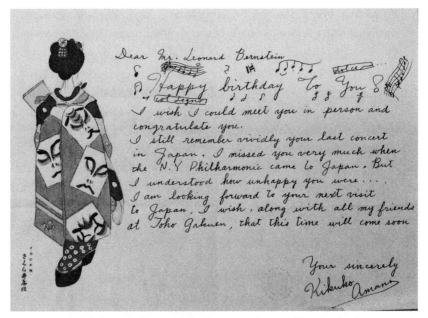

FIGURE 7.1 Birthday card from Kikuko Amano to Leonard Bernstein, August 1978.

To fulfill the wishes of his fans who sorely missed him in 1978, Bernstein's tour with the New York Philharmonic was rescheduled for a year later. But Kazuko had not written to him since her last birthday greeting. She had not sent letters expressing her excitement about his impending visit as she had always done in the past.

That spring her husband Reiji had been diagnosed with pancreatic cancer. She had not told Bernstein. Coates had advised her not to use the words "cancer" or "Felicia" in her communications with Bernstein, who was still in deep grief a year later. Kazuko had faithfully kept her promise.

* * *

BERNSTEIN ARRIVED IN Japan in the summer of 1979. This time he came to the country as a widower. He was accompanied by his younger daughter Nina, who had grown closer to him and protective of him as the only family member living at home with him.

By the time of Bernstein's arrival in Tokyo, Reiji had only days remaining in his life. Kazuko was spending nights by his side at the hospital. She had not sent a letter upon Bernstein's arrival at the hotel as she had done on his previous visits. She was not planning to attend his concerts, the first time she would have missed his performances.

It was Kikuko who urged her mother to go meet Bernstein and brought a change of clothes to the hospital so that she could attend the concert. Some may have frowned at a woman dressing up and leaving her dying husband in order to attend a concert, let alone meet another man at his hotel. But Kikuko knew that precisely at this moment it was important for her mother to see Bernstein and listen to his music.

On July 1, the day of Bernstein's arrival in Tokyo, Kazuko went to see him at the Hotel Okura. She knew the approximate time of his arrival, and, with a bouquet of roses in hand, she waited for him at the lobby. Unlike the glitzy décor of Tokyo's other luxury hotels, the Okura's lobby had a classic and dignified but also tranquil and intimate ambiance created by its subdued lighting with shoji screens and lantern-shaped fixtures and a simple, open floor plan. It was the sort of space that naturally makes one speak in a low, calm voice.

When Bernstein and his company walked in, Kazuko almost did not recognize him. He looked much older, grayer, and paler than she had remembered. Clearly delighted to see her but a little surprised she was there without her family, he asked, "The family is well?"

When she told him about Reiji's condition, he took her in his arms and cried loudly and uncontrollably. Everyone in the quiet lobby turned to look and stood in silence.[6]

The next day, she went to Bernstein's first concert at Tokyo Bunka Kaikan and heard Schumann's Symphony no. 1 and Shostakovich's Symphony no. 5. In light of Bernstein's physical and emotional frailty, few were allowed access to the maestro during this tour. But Kraut had arranged for Kazuko to spend time in the green room with Bernstein after the performance and press conference. She went to see him again the next morning at his hotel, and the two spent brief but deep, intimate moments together.

Reiji passed away two weeks later. Kazuko was a dutiful, caring wife and mother who loved and served her husband until the end of his life.

Bonded by their shared grief, Bernstein and Amano entered a new phase of their special friendship. But Bernstein's fourth trip to Japan in 1979 was not just the occasion for an emotional reunion with his most loyal fan and understanding family friend. It also brought the beginning of another relationship that was no less special, with a young man he met on his last day in Japan.

8

The Maestro's Place in
a Changing World

WHEN BERNSTEIN ARRIVED in Japan in 1979, the global landscape of classical music was undergoing significant transformations. The New York Philharmonic itself was showing signs of change. Whereas during the 1961 tour the entire orchestra consisted of male musicians, in 1979 the Philharmonic had several female players, including violinist Yoko Takebe, one of the first Japanese women to have a classical musical career in America. It was the beginning of a wave of East Asian musicians who would come to occupy a sizable proportion of orchestras around the United States.

The Philharmonic's itinerary also reflected the changing geography of classical music. On this tour, the Philharmonic gave nine concerts in five cities in Japan, sandwiching in two performances in Seoul, South Korea.[1] At this time music lessons had become a common pursuit among South Korea's urban middle class, and the nation's Young Chang and Samick companies joined Japan's Yamaha and Kawai in the ranks of the world's largest piano manufacturers. The members of the Chung family—cellist Myung-Wha Chung, violinist Kyung-Wha Chung, and conductor and pianist Myung-Whung Chung—were establishing themselves as international musical figures during this period. The inclusion of Seoul in the Philharmonic's itinerary was a sign of South Korea's rise as an industrial nation and its growing importance in the world of classical music.[2]

The Japan that welcomed Bernstein in 1979 held a different status in the world than the nation that hosted his earlier visits. Whereas in 1961 the currency exchange rate was 360 yen to one US dollar, in 1979 a dollar was worth approximately 215 yen, indicating the growing strength of the yen and the Japanese economy overall. That year Harvard scholar Ezra Vogel published a book explaining how Japan had become the world's most competitive industrial power and a model for productivity and efficiency. Entitled *Japan as Number One: Lessons for America,* the book became an international bestseller at a time when the United States was suffering from deep national malaise.[3]

As if to mark Japan's seemingly invincible technological and industrial power, on July 1, only weeks before Bernstein's arrival, Sony released the product that made the company's name a household word: the Walkman. The product embodied the combination of Sony's technological innovation, design savvy, and creative marketing. To commemorate the company's thirty-third anniversary, the Walkman was priced at 33,000 yen (approximately $125 at the time, $430 in 2018). Every facet of the Walkman campaign was carefully orchestrated: from the press conference held outdoors in Yoyogi Park—located in a fashionable neighborhood that draws many young people—where Sony staffers and models demonstrated how to enjoy listening to the device while on roller skates or skateboards, to print ads aimed at the young and active, the Walkman's marketing emphasized lightness, speed, mobility, and stylishness. It became an instant hit worldwide: 30,000 units were sold by mid-September, and production had to be doubled and tripled each month thereafter. Highlighting the relationship between Bernstein and the company, Sony presented the Walkman units as gifts to the musicians of the New York Philharmonic.[4] Immediately following the tour, Kraut wrote to Ohga: "The 'Walkman' cassette players have been all the rage of our friends in New York. They may even help reduce the noise pollution from the thousands of disco players being carried on the streets!"[5]

The importance of CBS/Sony in Bernstein's business was evident in the company's central involvement in the 1979 tour, during which it produced a live audio and video recording of Schumann's Symphony no. 1 and Shostakovich's Symphony no. 5 for the CBS Masterworks series. To commemorate the tour, the company launched the campaign "Maestro 1800," selling Bernstein's select LPs, including the recordings of the pieces performed on the tour, at 1,800 yen per record.[6]

While CBS/Sony brought many resources and much positive publicity to the tour, this corporate involvement added new dimensions to the tour planning. For instance, the company wanted to arrange a public conversation between Bernstein and a prominent Japanese cultural figure—novelist/journalist Ken Kaikō, painter/sculptor Taro Okamoto, and filmmaker Akira Kurosawa were suggested—and to carry an article in Japan's *Playboy* magazine (the invitation was declined).[7] To celebrate the tenth anniversary of CBS/Sony, the company wanted to host a competition for Japanese composers, to be judged by Bernstein. (Kraut responded that this would be difficult to schedule but suggested Lukas Foss and/or Aaron Copland as judges instead.)[8]

In addition to Sony, one of the important players in the 1979 tour was the nonprofit organization Amnesty International Japan. Felicia had been a dedicated supporter of Amnesty International; Bernstein had performed a charity concert for the organization in Munich in 1977 and was eager to support its Japanese chapter. Despite Bernstein's enthusiasm, the missions of the nonprofit and commercial enterprises involved in the planning did not mesh well. Ohga made it clear that Sony could not openly support the organization, because it could negatively influence its business in Asian countries, many of which Amnesty International had criticized for human rights violations. The Japanese representative of the organization complained that this attitude was typical of Japanese businessmen's positions on humanitarian causes and that, even though CBS/Sony was willing to offer records for publicity, Ohga "refused to give even one per cent of the record sale's production to [Amnesty]."[9] As a compromise arrangement, the company agreed to host Bernstein's charity autographing session for Amnesty at the Sony Building in Ginza, which generated much attention in the Japanese media.[10]

Whereas the 1961 and 1970 tours were arranged with clear governmental involvement, the commercial interests driving later tours created different dynamics in the political economy of classical music.

* * *

BY THIS TIME, Bernstein was much more than an individual artist; he was a larger-than-life figure throughout the world. Supported by the Amberson corporate infrastructure, Bernstein's work had developed into an industry in and of itself.

The scope of the maestro's work in the late 1970s can be glimpsed from Amberson's new organizational and staff chart, created by Harry Kraut. Under Bernstein as president—with direct oversight over his secretaries, housekeeper, musical assistant, and promotion director— was Kraut, the executive vice president. Kraut supervised key units and personnel—the production company, promotion and sales director, assistant for production and promotion, and assistant for business and legal matters—in addition to overseeing his own assistant and the controller. Beyond these in-house units, Amberson worked closely with other important professionals and services, such as press relations, sound consultant, legal counsel, foreign counsel, and tax and investment counsel.[11] The Springate Corporation was set up to make grants to institutions "in the areas of Jewish affairs, music, education and civil liberties," by pursuing the "opportunity to turn to profit some of the writings and compositions given to [the corporation] by Mr. Bernstein."[12]

The complexity of Bernstein's work is also evident in the job descriptions of key Amberson personnel. For instance, among the responsibilities of editorial associate Jack Gottlieb were assisting Bernstein's composition by preparing materials, acquiring rights clearances, communicating with and overseeing copyists and publishers, helping with copying and orchestration, assisting in his conducting by preparing score and parts, setting up rehearsal schedules with artists, managing auditions, researching and writing program and jacket notes, and serving as a publishing liaison by editing and reviewing arrangements, ordering reprints, and overseeing television script publication.[13] No less revealing of the maestro's professional and personal life were the tasks of Bernstein's personal assistant, which were divided into "When in New York" and "When on Tour." In both settings, he was to "1. Assist at rehearsals and concerts (15%), 2. Pack, unpack (3 times each) (5%), 3. Tend to office functions (10–6) (15%) (telephone, mail, supplies, errands, library maintenance, typing and filing, travel arrangements), and 4. Household duties (misc. times) (15%) (clothing, cars, substitute cook & cleaner, kitchen supplies, bartending)."[14]

From the early days of the company, Amberson had allocated considerable resources to marketing and public relations. Seventy percent of Amberson's public affairs coordinator John Epstein's elaborate set of responsibilities involved coordinating promotion activities, handling press inquiries and developing features, and developing and maintaining photo materials and monitoring clipping services.[15] Epstein also worked with the public relations firm of Margaret Carson, whose responsibilities included writing and distributing a newsletter, coordinating press inquiries and developing features, conducting special promotions, coordinating record companies' promotional efforts, and assisting and coordinating promotional efforts for concerts, publications, and videos.[16] Bernstein's image was thus carefully packaged, disseminated, and guarded by professional staff dedicated solely to him.

With accelerating globalization of the industry in the late 1970s, the foreign market became an increasingly important part of Bernstein's business.[17] Reflecting his growing power in the European market, Amberson had staff focused specifically on German and Italian matters.[18] Amberson's sales director was responsible for conducting video sales campaigns in "Latin America, Canada, and the Far East" in addition to domestic markets.[19] Amberson's business structure thus propelled Bernstein's reach far beyond the United States.

All was not rosy on the business front, however. Deutsche Grammophon's commitment to Bernstein's art and his "European" identity notwithstanding, industry changes brought new challenges for Bernstein. When he began recording for Deutsche Grammophon, its parent conglomerate PolyGram's seven classical labels accounted for 50 percent of the US classical market. However, when PolyGram took over Decca Records in 1980, the reorganized corporation instituted a new policy of coordinated repertoire among the companies under its control. This meant that Bernstein faced competition from other artists on Deutsche Grammophon's roster in negotiating future repertoire.[20] As a result, much to Bernstein's and Amberson's frustration, some of the recordings that Bernstein had great artistic investment in—including Mahler, Schumann, and Tchaikovsky—were postponed, recorded by another conductor, or canceled.[21]

Thus, even for a musician of Bernstein's caliber, artistic endeavors were increasingly steered by the interests of global media conglomerates.[22] While Bernstein's shift in his business to Europe likely softened the effects of declining share of classical music in the American market, it only went so far in resisting the forces of globalization in the music industry.

Bernstein's increasing turn to the foreign market also took place as the recording technology was changing from LP records to cassette tapes and then to compact discs. Both Japanese and German manufacturers and media corporations were pioneers of these new technologies, and Bernstein was quick to ride the wave. The industry trends with regard to new media worked in Bernstein's favor. The dominant media conglomerates were often technologically innovative but artistically conservative, preferring to make long-term contracts with high-profile stars rather than cultivating new talent.[23] In this environment, what Michael

Jackson and Madonna were to popular music Bernstein was to classical music. Along with Herbert von Karajan—who took an obsessive interest in new recording technologies and became a cornerstone of Sony's transition to digital media—Bernstein's international stardom smoothed over the recording company's transition to new media.

It was amidst this shifting geography of the classical music industry as well as changes in media and technology that Bernstein reached an ever more global audience, especially in Europe and Japan. This was the backdrop against which Bernstein toured Japan in the summer of 1979.

PART II

From Dear to Dearest

Dear Lenny,

. . . After you left Japan, my mind became vacant, because the one night and afternoon that we had were like a beautiful dream for me. And after the awakening, I noticed that the dream had gone and I was sad to see that it was a dream. But in spite of my lonely heart, the sunset that I looked at from the bus to Tokyo from the airport was the most beautiful and fantastic that I had ever seen. Around the sun, beautiful white clouds were whirling and streamed like they were dancing with happiness and joyfulness. It was like a great symphony. And the sun was very beautiful red with mystery, fantasy, tenderness, and love. I believed that you arranged and conducted the great, fantastic, symphonic view. And in that view at that moment, I felt our future with happiness.

Now, I am writing this letter in my room after coming back from the sea. I did not enjoy myself today. At the sea, I sailed for a long, long distance, but all I saw was that America did not appear. The ocean was too large and cold to me. Every moment I was thinking about you. Nothing is joyful or happy for me without you. If I play sports, go to the movie or theater, have a delicious dinner, and wear nice clothes, I still cannot enjoy myself without you. I am waiting for tomorrow to come. Because I must work tomorrow and being busy may help to take you off my mind. But I think about you—in New York, your busy life is waiting for you, and I am afraid that it will erase me from your mind. I know this is inconsistent—I would like to forget you, but I am afraid that you forget me. However, this is my true mind.

I am lovesick about you. It is quite serious and painful. But I know I have to endure it alone, because I am not able to talk with my friends. I am able to guess their answer—"It is stupid! That is only one night love affair. Mr. Bernstein has a lot of lovers, and you are a minor presence for him. So you had better forget him soon."

But I love you so much. I can never forget you, Lenny. I remember you told me that you were afraid to fall in love with somebody because it makes your life change.

I know I have to give up, but you were so kind and lovely that I cannot give up.

Would you not be burdened in your mind by my love to you, please!! Because I would like to keep our relationship, even if it is friendship, not love. I am sorry that I am writing you such an urgent, worried letter. Next time I should write a more joyful letter to you. And I am also sorry. It was very kind of you to invite me, but I cannot come to Europe to have a vacation with you. Because I have no money after my trip to Europe in May (I went to Paris in May). And although you offered me the ticket as a present I am not able to take up on your kindness. It is too expensive. And besides I think it may be difficult for me to take vacation days. Will you please understand? I want to see you again as soon as possible, and I want to have every minute with you. I love you so much, Lenny. I will write to you again.[1]

THIS IS THE first of the many letters from Kunihiko Hashimoto to Bernstein. Hashimoto's words exude every emotion of a young man who has fallen deeply in love: yearning for the moments that have passed, sadness after parting, beauty of the world seen through the eyes of love, dreams of the next encounter, and a passionate declaration of endless love.

The letter was written on July 8, 1979, the day after Bernstein left Japan upon the completion of the New York Philharmonic tour. Although it is clear that the two men spent Bernstein's last night together and that Hashimoto saw him off at the airport, the letter provides no clues about the specific circumstances of their initial encounter. But it says much about the sort of man Hashimoto was and hints at the contours of his life. His references to the natural world in connection with his feelings for Bernstein reflect the Japanese literary tradition and cultural sensibilities in which nature and seasons play a central role. His comparison of the sunset—and the world—to a symphony shows his artistic propensity, familiarity with classical music, and sensitivity to life and emotions. Going sailing suggests his comfortable upper-middle-class lifestyle and pastimes. His return address on the envelope is a single-family house in an established middle-class neighborhood outside central Tokyo likely owned by his parents, an index of his family background. The fact that he pondered what his friends might say about his "one night love affair" with Bernstein suggests that he had a circle of friends who knew about his sexuality and were also familiar with Bernstein's stature.

Yet it is also clear that Hashimoto was far from free to live an independent life unconstrained by social conventions. His reference to his work life and his suggestion that it would be difficult for him to take a vacation indicate his status as a Japanese salaryman working in a conventional corporate environment and living in a culture of conformity and social hierarchy. The combination of elements mentioned in the letter—that he does not have to stay in the office until late at night every day, that he can relax on weekends, that he has limited control over his own vacation days—suggests that Hashimoto was probably not fresh out of college but had not spent too many years rising up the corporate ladder.

The letter also intimates the sort of relationship that blossomed between the two men. Hashimoto opens the letter with a standard salutation "Dear" but calls him "Lenny." That nickname was commonly used by Bernstein's friends, colleagues, and students, but Japan's seniority-based social hierarchy and protocol would likely have kept Hashimoto from expressing such familiarity in the absence of an intimate personal relationship. Hashimoto must have called him "Lenny" both in person and in the letters because Bernstein told him to do so. His use of the nickname "Kuny"—sometimes spelled "Kuni"—also hints at their agreed-upon terms of endearment: Lenny and Kuny. Furthermore, Hashimoto sent this letter—and all subsequent ones—to Bernstein's home at the Dakota apartment building on Manhattan's Upper West Side, rather than to his business address, and marked the envelope "Personal." Bernstein must have given him this address and taken care to ensure that his letters did not get mixed up with business correspondence and were not read by others.

The content and tone of Hashimoto's writing also reveal the interaction and connection between the two men during their night together—one that was intense and passionate but also tender and frank. The fact that Hashimoto writes about his emotions and thoughts so openly and expressively, especially to a man of Bernstein's stature, illustrates the earnestness and purity of his feelings as well as his confidence that he would be understood, accepted, and loved in return.

It is clear that he was right. The letter indicates that he was well aware of the unevenness of the relationship and its outward appearance. Indeed, many may have seen a young unknown Japanese man's encounter with one of the world's most prominent artists as little more than a dalliance. Yet the letter shows signs that this was not merely a one-sided infatuation of a young man under the spell of an artist with magnetic charm and charisma. The letter reveals that Bernstein shared some intimate emotions and thoughts with Hashimoto during their short time together. Moreover, he apparently offered to fly Hashimoto to Europe to visit him. The price of a plane ticket would have meant little to Bernstein, of course; Hashimoto's concerns about the expense and his declining the offer are all the more heartbreaking as they underscore the vast difference in the worlds they inhabited. Yet Bernstein's invitation was a sign that he too wanted to see Hashimoto again.

Despite the odds against a long-term relationship, Hashimoto declares his passionate, selfless, and lasting love. He wrote to Bernstein almost daily, pages and pages at a time. His English is comprehensible but also contains many grammatical errors and usage quirks common to Japanese; it is clear that, unlike Amano, he was raised and educated in Japan. His prose and handwriting convey both a sense of urgency and careful thought. He writes like someone who is accustomed to writing letters, moving freely between his seasonal greetings and descriptions of the weather and natural surroundings (common features in Japanese correspondence), factual updates on his life, his observations of the world, and his expressions of love. He often uses English words that are not commonly taught in Japanese schools. He likely picked them up by watching English-language films, listening to the radio, or reading English books and magazines. Perhaps he remembered the expressions that Bernstein used in their conversation. Sometimes he must have used a Japanese-English dictionary. For anyone to write about personal and intimate feelings, especially in a language that bears no resemblance to one's own, involves deliberate effort. Writing these long, thoughtful letters must have taken Hashimoto a great deal of time and labor. The intensity with which he kept writing to Bernstein shows the irrepressible passion that drove him—passion for Bernstein and for life that was ignited by his encounter with him.

* * *

AS HASHIMOTO'S NUMEROUS letters reveal, his and Bernstein's relationship was distinctly defined by its epistolary form. Unlike Kazuko's early letters, which were sent by sea, Hashimoto's letters were sent by air, so they would have taken at most a week or two, rather than months, to be delivered. Yet a week or two is a long time in the mind of a young man in love. Furthermore, Bernstein was traveling so frequently that it could have taken much longer for Hashimoto's letters to be read. The lag between the time when a letter is written and when it is read is an inevitable part of the act of letter writing and the writer's state of mind. Hashimoto's letters convey his longing and frustration as he knew that his words would not reach Bernstein immediately. He often wrote knowing that Bernstein had not yet read the previous letter—or letters—he had just sent. Less than a week after sending his first letter, Hashimoto writes,

> I spread out the map of New York City and I checked your address—facing Central Park, near New York Philharmonic Hall, Lincoln Center, Metropolitan Opera House, Peak [*sic*] Royal Hotel, etc. . . . I imagine you and your life in New York, and when you read my letter. But it will be ten days later that this letter reaches you. And I think that you haven't received even my first letter yet.—Oh, I have to talk to you in the future, don't I? But in the future, my mind will surely be the same.[2]

His phrase, "I have to talk to you in the future," is awkward yet accurate and articulate. The epistolary relationship collapsed a sense of time, merging the past that they spent together, the present when Hashimoto was writing to Bernstein, the future when Bernstein would read the letters, and the unforeseen future in which they would be reunited.

Hashimoto's second letter, written the day after the first, opens with a sense of impatience: "I write to you again, just after mailing my first letter to you, because I would like to talk to you about a lot of things. But to my regret, I cannot now except in my letters." After asking him to send his itinerary so that he can follow and imagine Bernstein's life, he writes: "I said I had a lot of things to talk to you about. However, they are all about only one thing. It is that I love you. When shall we see each other again? Where can we meet? I am looking forward to that day. And I cannot live without the promise to see you again."[3]

Absence and distance magnified his yearning within a matter of days. The following day, he writes,

> A letter, what a slow and heavy thing it is! It is like talking to a mirror—no sound, no expression, and no answer. (I am afraid that you will not receive and read my letter, because I am sure that you receive so many letters.)
>
> In Japan, I promised to you that I would write to you once a week. But now, I am doing so every day. For, this is the only way for me to contact you. (Telephone is difficult. For I don't know your daily schedule, and also because between New York and Tokyo, time is different.)
>
> Are my letters standing out in your home or office? Or does it disturb you for me to write so often? However, I would like to write you

in my free time. During busy times, my love sickness is comforted, but when I have free time, even for one moment, I am always thinking about you. So I write. But I think I had better write once a week, not every day. Because I must, I need to, endure this sickness. I hope that every day keeps me very busy for 24 hours.[4]

He could not keep his resolution to write only once a week, however. Writing his fourth letter in four days, he sheepishly admits: "I write again. Am I persistent? Do I bother you? But you have to endure, because I cannot hear your answer now. Besides, I want to write before the weekend when the post office closes."[5]

Within four weeks of their initial encounter, Hashimoto sent twenty letters to Bernstein. He continued to write with similar frequency throughout the next year.

Sometimes he included photos of himself. One is a childhood photo of him playing violin onstage with several other children. Others are more recent photos, taken in a park under blossoming cherry trees or in front of a bare tree in wintertime. There are also photos taken at an iris garden in Kyoto where he went for a friend's wedding. In one of the photos taken at the beach, he is holding a surfboard with one arm and a young bikini-clad woman with the other. In another, he stands with several men and women all in bathing suits. There is also a photo of him in kimono, standing in front of his house decorated for the New Year. All of the photos confirm that Hashimoto is a handsome, stylish man in his mid- to late twenties, with a thoughtful expression, perhaps a little shy but strong willed, living in an environment that is distinctively Japanese both physically and so-cially, while also inhabiting a cultural world that is open to life far beyond his immediate surroundings.

* * *

KNOWING FULL WELL the busy life Bernstein led, Hashimoto did not ex-pect him to reply to all, or even any, of his letters. But he knew that he would read all of them. In one letter, he writes: "While writing to you, I am very happy. I can imagine you reading my letter, and I thank you for this moment when you read this, and I thank that you make time for me in spite of your busy life. So I continue to write."[6] He was overjoyed when he received occasional letters or phone calls from Bernstein. Having received a letter at the end of the month, he writes:

Today, I have received the tenderest letter from you. I read it over and over again. And how can I express the great thanks for you? Until now,

I felt like I was talking to myself on these papers. So I was looking forward to the letter from you. I knew that you were very busy, and your schedule was quite hard. However now you gave the letter to me. It relieved me and I get confidence. And it made me happy.[7]

Hashimoto's letters were neither one side of a conversation nor a monologue; they were more akin to confessions to a greater being that he knew was listening and would endow him with power and bless him.

Within a week of their encounter, Hashimoto is reminiscing about every moment they had together, as if a year has passed since: "One week has gone by since you left Japan. I never forget the time we met, the time we spent together, the conversations we had, with each other." Then he recalls,

At first, you told me that I looked lonely. I think that I might have been lonely because I had no lover, no friend to talk with about my true mind, and I had not done so with my sister. However, after you left, I am more lonely than one week ago. And I am living with the memories of you.

This weekend, I did not go to the sea because it was raining. So I have to kill time in my room. This is a pain. Without the sun, when I close my eyes, I can see your face. And even when I open my eyes. . . .

One week ago, I could not talk to my sister about myself. But now I am able to tell her that I love you. Because this is my pride.[8]

These words suggest that upon falling in love with Bernstein, Hashimoto confided in his sister about his sexuality and his love for Bernstein. Rather than hiding his identity, he now took pride in who he was and whom he loved. Falling in love with someone distant made him even lonelier, but that love made him embrace his true self and take comfort and pride in his solitude.

In a letter several days later, he reflects:

When I think about what you think about me, I get to think about myself.—At my office, my friends say that I am always cheerful without suffering any worries and that I am an optimist. And my girlfriend tells me that I am a man who can live alone and that I can do everything by myself without her help and that I am always cool, not passionate. And my sister has the same opinion.

I know, I have grown up without difficulties, wrapped by much love of my family, and I got everything that I hoped for (but I was never spoiled) and I don't know poverty. My parents gave me the many chances for education—a private teacher, violin lessons, and so on. And I passed examinations without effort. My life was satisfactory. But since I have known about my taste and when I thought about it, I got lonely. So, I had to hide myself behind my smile and cheer, and I got to know how to live and get over difficulties, alone, and I got a cool mind. But I got there easy, without toil, because I have much adaptability. I am not pessimistic. I am an optimist, because I did not know difficulties, and I take everything easy without effort. But I have always envied and respected the man who gets over the difficulties. And I know that I will encounter some difficulties some day, and I must get over it. And about my not being passionate . . . I am cool always, but I envy a passionate man.

And now, I find that my behavior to you is not cool. I think maybe my letters make that clear. You may laugh at my letter, but it is my sincere mind. I would like to become cool to you. However, even when I get cool, my mind will not change—I love you.[9]

Hashimoto's self-reflexivity, both social and emotional, is evident in this letter. He is aware of the blessings of his loving family and his comfortable and cultured middle-class life. He indicates that he successfully navigated Japan's competitive education system in which admissions to high schools and universities are determined strictly by the applicants' scores on a one-shot entrance examination. Although he never elaborates, his intellectual and artistic bent and his employment at a major insurance company suggest that he attended a respectable university in Tokyo. Such self-reflection is also directed at his own psychological and emotional life. He realizes that his seeming "coolness" was not due to the lack of emotions but rather because he had not found the object of his passion until he met Bernstein.

Coming to grips with his own sexuality was a significant part of this self-discovery. His mention of his "girlfriend" in his love letter to Bernstein is striking but not anomalous for a man who identifies as gay, especially given his social status. In the Japanese corporate environment, particularly in the conservative insurance industry, getting married and having a family was not only an expected course of life but was also considered a sign of being a mature, responsible man. He would not have been open about his sexuality, especially at work. But his letters make clear that he had been aware of his own sexual orientation—the word "taste" is a translation of the Japanese word *shikō*, meaning "preference"—for some time. His mention of his social circle also makes it plausible that he had some connection to the growing community and networks of gay men in Tokyo. Japan's first commercial magazine catering to gay men was launched in 1971, and by the end of the decade there were over 170 gay bars in Tokyo's Shinjuku Ni-chōme neighborhood where homosexuals could explore their identities and find each other outside the parameters of their everyday lives.[10] Yet his letters also indicate that his sexual orientation did not define who he was. Whereas there are countless references to concerts, recordings, films, plays, and exhibitions in his letters, there is no mention of a visit to a gay bar or reading a gay magazine.

What mattered to Hashimoto was that meeting Bernstein—to whom he could unwaveringly proclaim "I love you"—made him embrace who he truly was.

* * *

THE BURNING, ALMOST desperate emotions building in Hashimoto are most evident in a heartbreaking letter dated July 21, two weeks after the two men met. It opens with the description of the weather as a form of greeting, combined with Hashimoto's characteristic self-reflection:

> We have a rainy day in Japan again. It brings calm, quiet, purity, and the green in the garden are refreshed, dust on the road is washed away and get clean. And in my room I gaze at myself.
>
> I remember how people talk about love—that love changes like rivers, and that love is treacherous. I am sure this is how they talk, and I know facts like this. Especially today, in big cities, people have cold mind, egotistic, more and more, and the moral is down in the name of freedom. And some people think that honest love does not exist. However, I believe in conscience, and I believe that I can find honest, true love, and I can keep it forever.
>
> Do you think that I am an old type man? Some people are looking for a man to make love for one night, and they change the man every time. But I am not like them. I know that I need a settled life with somebody whom I love. For a long time I have hoped for a settled life and I am looking forward to it.
>
> I remember that you told me that next year, you will stop your concert work, and you will devote yourself to writing books. And I never forget that you asked me where we should live. Your question was where "we" should live, wasn't it? Did you ask me that as the "unanswered question"? I think that you did so with half [a] mind, while thinking about our circumstance.

But, I hope to do it. I would like to live with you.

Even as a maid (but I am not good at cooking and sewing).

Even as a secretary (but I cannot type quickly).

Even as like a doll (but I have a mind).

—I hope to live with you. If you want me to be a maid, I will learn cooking, and if you want me to be a secretary, I will go to a typing school.

I would like to be useful for you. I would like to help you. The rest of my life, I shall be with you. (Because I was born to meet you and to be with you.)

These are what I have been thinking for two weeks since you left Japan.

I know there are a lot of problems to do it, for you, and for me, too. And I know it takes a big decision to do it. But I can overcome problems. I have confidence to do it.

Because, I love you, and I need you.

I would like to hear your answer. Will you write to me.[11]

As if to make sure that Bernstein understands his seriousness, he adds a postscript dated the following day directly below on the same stationery:

P.S. I think I offered it to you suddenly. But if it will be realized, I would like to do it as soon as possible and decide our mind soon. And I have to prepare to live with you.

I must work until this December, and I have to talk to my section boss about next year. If you would like to decide after seeing me again, I can take holidays. (I have 25 days for holiday vacation until December. In spite of it, my boss does not want me to take it. This is a strange custom in Japan.)

And of course I hope to see you again, soon.

I wonder if this is my own hasty conclusion. Because in spite of the fact that I have received no letter from you, I am writing like this.

In two weeks' time, not only did Hashimoto determine that he wanted to live with Bernstein and spend the rest of his life with him, but he began to consider the practical issues involved in doing so. Hashimoto's sincerity and urgency is evident in the declaration of his resolve to change his life entirely to live with Bernstein mixed in with the mundane issues of his work life.

Is this simply a typical state of mind for a young man in love? Perhaps. Yet Hashimoto's yearning is compounded by the particular dynamics of the relationship. The roles he imagines for himself—subservient, typically female roles—reveal his awareness of the all too obvious difference in status between the two men: even if Bernstein were to agree to be in a relationship, it would not be one of equals.

But Hashimoto did not see his place in the relationship as one of blind subservience. After offering to be "like a doll" for Bernstein—implying the role of Bernstein's "boy toy"—Hashimoto makes a point of stating in parentheses "but I have a mind," as if to remind Bernstein that he is, after all, an individual with his own free will.

In fact, all his letters eloquently demonstrate that Hashimoto's love for Bernstein was far more than romantic love and sexual attraction: it was admiration, awe, and worship for what he saw as a truly great power. While Hashimoto wished to be useful to Bernstein—and felt frustrated that all he could do was write and wait—he also felt joy in knowing a great man in whose presence he could simply be himself. In the letter of August 1, he writes: "I keep reading the letter from you over and over again. It is full of your tenderness, and your tenderness is deep, unfathomable. My mind is purified by it. In front of you, I worry about nothing, I am honest and obedient like a child. I thank you so much, and I love you. My love to you is eternal."[12]

* * *

THE EMOTIONAL INTIMACY between the two men grew as Hashimoto kept writing to Bernstein. Beginning with the letter dated August 2, 1979, Hashimoto begins to open his letters with "Dearest Lenny" rather than "Dear Lenny," reflecting the increased familiarity he has come to feel. Over the next decade, Hashimoto would begin all of his letters this way.

Shortly thereafter, Hashimoto received an invitation to join Bernstein in Europe for a week. The urgency and sincerity of Hashimoto's feelings clearly touched Bernstein, who was in the middle of negotiations with Deutsche Grammophon and strengthening his ties to European orchestras. Although Hashimoto had previously declined his invitation, he changed his mind upon receiving Bernstein's letter. He sent information about his bank account to which the money for the airfare could be deposited. Kraut instead arranged Hashimoto's travel. When Hashimoto went to the Lufthansa office per Kraut's instruction, he found a first-class ticket for a flight that would arrive in Munich on August 25, 1979, Bernstein's sixty-first birthday.

10

Faith and Resolution

UPON ARRIVAL IN Munich, Hashimoto checked into the hotel, took a shower, changed his clothes, and immediately went to the concert where Bernstein was performing Prokofiev's Symphony no. 5 with the Israel Philharmonic Orchestra. He reunited with the maestro at the stage door after the concert and accompanied him to his birthday party, hosted by the orchestra.

The week that followed was a whirlwind of events that reflected Bernstein's expanding activities in Europe. Hashimoto traveled to Hamburg with Bernstein for the recording of "Big Stuff" from *Fancy Free*. He watched him give a television interview in fluent German. They attended Deutsche Grammophon's anniversary party and met conductor and pianist Christoph Eschenbach. During one of the few quiet moments, the two went sailing. A photo Hashimoto took of Bernstein, smiling in his striped sailor's shirt and a red scarf around his neck, shows the tenderness and connection between the photographer and the subject.

The two then flew to Naples on a private jet owned by Deutsche Grammophon. From there they were driven by limousine to the cliff-side village of Positano to spend time at filmmaker and opera director Franco Zeffirelli's summer home. The five days in Positano allowed the two men to spend private time away from the maestro's busy work. Zeffirelli's villa consisted of a main house surrounded by small guest villas. Bernstein and Hashimoto took the villa that had just been vacated by Elizabeth Taylor. Among the other guests staying in the compound were conductor Carlos Kleiber and the wife and daughter of the late filmmaker Vittorio De Sica. During the days in Positano, the two men spent their leisure time swimming, sailing, cooking, and socializing with other guests. When they sailed to Capri one day, they enjoyed a chance encounter with Harold Prince, who had produced *West Side Story* on Broadway, and his wife, who were staying on the island. In the evening, the guests gathered at the living room of Zeffirelli's main house. While watching the video of *La Bohème* that Zeffirelli directed at La Scala, Bernstein wept at the final scene of heroine Mimi's death, remembering Felicia's passing.

While it must have been an extraordinary experience for a young Japanese salaryman to spend a luxurious week with Bernstein and his European social set, Hashimoto's letters after the trip convey a sense of exaltation that is much more spiritual. In fact, these letters are somewhat different in tone from the first two months of correspondence. His love and admiration for Bernstein and his desire to be with him are just as strong or even more intense, yet he seems to have gained a clearer sense of his own emotions and his relationship to Bernstein. In the letter dated September 2, written just after his return, he writes: "I love seeing you when you give somebody a good talk. At Positano, when I saw you talking to Carlos, and two young men on a rock, I thought like this: 'You are like Jesus. Jesus is sermonizing to his disciples.'" Aware of Bernstein's strong Jewish identity, he puts in parentheses, "I am afraid that this is not a good metaphor for you. But then this is what I thought surely." He was referring to seeing Kleiber talking intensely with Bernstein day after day, seeking the maestro's advice as he was struggling with his complicated relationship with his father, Erich, a world famous maestro. Hashimoto watched Bernstein listen to him like a father and talk to him like a spiritual guide.

> Just as many people loved Jesus talking, we who are around you love your talking. And just as Jesus loved everybody, you love everybody. Your broad, tender mind is deep and unlimited. We who are listening to your talking and teaching are like disciples of Jesus. And I am one of your twelve disciples. And I wonder if my character is like John in twelve disciples.

> I never forget when you taught me about Italian and German language and the table at Franco's villa, and when you talked to me about Visconti, Israel Phil., and [the Jewish] new moon in the airplane to Hamburg. . . . I was excited for joy that I could listen to you talking. I love so much your good talking, teaching. I am not a musician, so I am not to be your musical student. But I would like to learn every kind of knowledge from you. I would like to learn all of you. Because you are great and you have a great spirit. You remember that you asked me in Positano why I loved you so much?

Then I answered, "Because of your passion." But I understand now.—I love you because of your great spirit.[1]

"Great spirit" is probably the translation of the Japanese phrase *idai na seishin*, better translated as "great mind" or "noble aspirations" than in a religious way. Yet Hashimoto also seems to refer to a sort of spirituality that he feels in Bernstein's presence. His comparison of Bernstein to Jesus and himself to Jesus's disciple speaks eloquently of the nature of his love, one that was not unlike religious faith and worship. Although, unlike Amano, Hashimoto never specifically mentioned his faith and was probably not Christian, his general familiarity with Christianity is evident in many of his letters.

Seeing Hashimoto's love as akin to religious faith helps to explain his relationship to Bernstein. The words he uses later in the letter resonate with the earlier one in which he offered to be Bernstein's maid, secretary, or doll, yet the tone is somewhat different:

I never forget the night when we talked about ourselves. I will be your servant with my pleasure. When I did something for you during that week, I was very happy. I will give you my whole life with my heart. You thought about my being the "servant of your life." But I would like to say that you should not be bothered by it. A man can live everywhere, in any way, just like St. Francesco. The happiness of a man is not about money, fame, or looks. So I can manage myself.

Here, the word "servant" does not connote subservience to Bernstein but serving a greater being and purpose than oneself, not as an act of blind submission but a willful choice. He describes a conversation he overheard, in which Zeffirelli told Bernstein to let go of Hashimoto: "You caught a fish from the sea, but once you have looked at the fish in your hands, you have to let him go back to sea." Hashimoto was aware that in the eyes of many he was only one of maestro's "catches." Yet he objects to this perception. He spends several pages describing his sense of how animals fit into the order of the world:

You remember when we tried to make Franco's dog sit down. Then Franco asked us why we wanted dogs to sit down before we give them food. And I answered with a joke that it was [to teach] the

dog's [good] manner, and of course he made fun of my answer.—
He was right. Animals are to live free, naturally, and fish are to live
in the sea or in the river. However, I am not a fish. I am not a bird or
a dog, either. I am a man!! I have a will. I have a spirit. . . . And for
you, I am never a fish. I am a man. I have a will and a spirit! . . . But,
I wish that I could be a flying bird and I hope to fly to you, and
I would like to say, "I love you so much, Lenny."

In these letters he repeatedly avows his own choice to love Bernstein
and to serve him however he can. In numerous other letters, Hashimoto
makes religious references in describing his feelings, indicating his sense
of awe and worship of Bernstein.

Ten days later, Hashimoto writes:

And I never forget you said that you love me like music. You said it
on the bed, our last night in Hamburg. Is it true, in spite of talking
on the bed? I remember everything that you said as far as I could
understand English. And every time I am honest and obedient to
you, even if it is on a bed.

I love you, and I know that you love me. I am not living by bread.
I am living by your love to me.[2]

His combination of the word "obedient" with "honest" suggests that what
he is trying to convey is less subordination than openness and sincerity
to Bernstein, who became a source of sustenance of his humanity. Such a
spiritual nature—in both the Japanese and Western senses of the word—
of Hashimoto's admiration for Bernstein is not surprising, especially if
the maestro told him that he loved him "like music." It is difficult to imagine that for Bernstein there was any form of love more profound.

Hashimoto's particularly moving letter of September 30, an eleven-
page missive in small, meticulous handwriting, crystallizes this spiritual nature of his love for Bernstein. Referring back to Mishima's story
"Hanjo," which he wrote about in a prior letter, he writes:

I have different points from Hanako. It is that I love real you, not a
vision. And I don't go mad. But it is a fact that I love you passionately and crazily. When I looked at "luna" with the memory of what
you said about the Jewish new moon, I was afraid that I would be lunatic, mad. But I know one way not to be lunatic. It is "Resolution."

When I resolve on something once, I must obey it. And I resolved
to endure. But it takes believing to resolve on it. It is necessary to
believe that I will see you again. And until we will see each other,
I must wait and endure. So, I resolved on it with belief. This is like
a process of faith. "Faith is a belief in things which are not seen, and
to endure." And I believe that I will see you again, and I endure. But
I don't know when, where and how we will see each other—like you
told me on the day when I left Hamburg. I am only waiting for the
answer and the day.[3]

He then recalls Bernstein telling him that the frequency of their face-
to-face encounters—whether they see each other once a year or five times
a year, or every day, or once every two years—was irrelevant as long as they
loved each other. He writes: "Thank you for your tenderness. But at the
same time, when I imagined the external meaning [of what you said]—I
can see you only once a year or once every two years—I, who hope to be
with you every moment, get deep sorrow. It made my uplift and tension
of spirit kept by resolution waver. . . . Do you know how much I love you?
I am alive while loving you moment by moment. It is like my whole life is
for you." Many pages later, he writes:

I remember one of the things that I told you in Positano—"If I live
with you, I would like to do it as soon as possible, because we do
not have so much time." There is not much time, for you and for
me. I am afraid that I get old. I hope to learn many things from you,
and experience with you, while young—when I have keen senses.

Even though Bernstein was old enough to be his father and was often ill,
Hashimoto's statement about them not having much time was a reference
to his own age. Hashimoto is worried more about the time left for himself,
because he wanted to absorb all he could from the man he admired and
respected. He closes the letter by saying,

Do not be sickened by this letter, please. It is only that the fixed
tone of uplift and tension which are maintained by writing—one-
way speech, is moved by conversation—the letter from you. And
the Resolution that I have to endure wavers, and I hope to see you
soon, now—that's all. But I know myself—this stir and heavy sickness will become well in one week. And I will recover the resolution

again. But then, I don't want to decide to "give up." I love you so much. Please, don't feel a heavy burden of my love.

For Hashimoto, his commitment to his love for Bernstein was an act of faith—in Bernstein as the object of love as well as in the possibility of being together—and of resolution to live by that faith.

Hashimoto's faith in Bernstein is expressed in the letter of April 28, 1980:

Thank you for the letter—If I had a wing, I would fly to you as soon as possible. I would like to come to you. I would like to do something to help you. I will help you to the best of my ability. When you are sleepless, I will sing a lullaby and talk some story to help you sleep. And when you are sleepy, I will become a pillow and I will keep sitting besides you and watch you while you sleep. When you are tired, I will massage you. When you feel that your arms are at a distance, I will become your arms.—I know that I can do it, everything for you. Because, my life is for you. I was born for you, I am living for you.

When I was with you for one week in Europe last year, I knew it. It was like a miracle for me. Because, then my spirit pointed toward you, I concentrated on you, every moment—even while sleeping. (I remember that I felt your eyes during my sleep and woke up, the last night in Hamburg.) I had never had such a full life. I was really vivid. I felt the power of life. It was one miracle for me. Then I knew that I can give my everything to you.[4]

Whereas his declaration that he would do anything to help Bernstein may be no different from the sentiments of a man in love, his time in Europe clearly gave his love a more spiritual shape beyond romantic yearning. It is no accident that he uses words like "miracle," "spirit," and "power of life" in describing what he found during their time together. He realized that Bernstein gave new meaning to his life.

* * *

HASHIMOTO'S REPEATED REQUESTS to Bernstein not to be burdened by his love also reveal the unselfish quality of his love. Although he loved Bernstein deeply, he never sought an exclusive relationship with him and was fully aware that Bernstein had much love—and many lovers—in his life. Bernstein told Hashimoto about his other lovers, some of whom Hashimoto met. The fact that Bernstein was so full of love was precisely what drew Hashimoto to him, rather than a cause of jealousy or resentment. In the same letter, he writes: "I envy you, because you live with many loves—of your family, Bobby [likely Robert Lee Kirkland III, a journalist for *Newsweek* with whom Bernstein was close with at the time], and many other people, and music. And I envy that you have men with whom you talk about me. Harry, Bobby . . ." He thus envies Bernstein for the love that fills his life as well as for the other men with whom he can share his love of Hashimoto.

The letters also indicate that Bernstein told Hashimoto to seek and find other love, not because he wanted to push him away but because he wished Hashimoto to have love in his life. Several pages later, he continues, asserting that he is envious "without jealousy":

> I envy Bobby—without jealousy—who has much free time. And I regret that I could not take a holiday longer than one week. One week was very short. (But there are so many memories in my heart, and I feel like it was one year.) Although a memory is only a thing of the past, it makes an experience, and experiences build up life. When I said that I had the happiest time in all my life, on the last night in Hamburg, you taught me that I had to encounter many happier somethings in my future. And then I told you about the last scene of "The Turning Point."—Deedee (Shirley Maclaine) told Emma (Anne Bancroft) about her daughter if she had better get the knowledge which they get through experiences—what she had to stop ballet some day. Emma answered that she did not need to know about it and prepare for it.—That's right. For me, I did not need to know that some happier things would come to me in the future. I just enjoyed one week when I had with you, as the happiest week in all my life. Now I think that there may be many happy things in my long life, and I will encounter happier something than that one week, and you have many happy memories, experiences, and life. I would like to ask one question of you.—when happier things than that one week will come to me.

Bernstein must have told Hashimoto multiple times to seek love, both in person and in letters, perhaps because he knew that he was not in the position to offer him a lasting living arrangement and did not want Hashimoto to spend the rest of his life waiting for something unlikely to materialize. In the letter of December 20, 1980, in response to a letter from Bernstein (in which he invited Hashimoto to join him in Egypt), Hashimoto writes:

> You wrote that I looked happy and busy. Indeed, I am busy. But I try not to think about happiness, and busy times make me forget whether I'm "happy or unhappy."
>
> I have never had busier times than the one week that we had in Europe. I am busy now—but only "busy." When I had one week with you, it was busy—and "<u>vivid</u>." I have never had a happier time than <u>that time</u>. It was my happiest time that we had in Europe. You wrote me to "seek love." But who is better than you?
>
> —I am happy. Because I love you.[5]

* * *

A YEAR AND a half after his first trip to see Bernstein, Hashimoto flew to Munich to spend another week with him. Earlier that year, after a remarkable thirty-year relationship with Columbia Records, Bernstein signed an exclusive contract with Deutsche Grammophon. The agreement allowed Bernstein to record works with other companies that Deutsche Grammophon declined to produce. Thus, in the 1980s he also made some recordings with British label EMI and the Dutch-British group Philips.

During this stay in Munich, Bernstein was recording Wagner's *Tristan and Isolde*, which he saw as "the central work of all music history, the hub of the wheel," with the Bavarian Radio Orchestra. The opera was performed in concert form with live telecasts, one act at a time at three different times of the year, so that singers did not tire and compromise the music. Hashimoto attended the performance of act 1, in which the Breton nobleman Tristan, who has killed the Irish princess Isolde's fiancé, is delivering her to be betrothed to his uncle King Marke. As the ship approaches Cornwall, Isolde, determined to avenge her fiancé's death, offers Tristan a drink and takes some herself to poison them both. But her maid Brangäne had switched the poison with a love potion, and Tristan and Isolde fall into each other's arms, in love instead of death. It is the beginning of a tragic, forbidden love. With Peter Hofmann as Tristan and Hildegard Behrens as Isolde, this became one of the most acclaimed performances of the opera, and when the project was completed, Bernstein exclaimed, "My life is complete. I don't care what happens after this. It is the finest thing I've ever done."[6] The fact that Bernstein invited Hashimoto to join him on this trip shows that he wanted him to share in this deeply important artistic experience.

Hashimoto wrote a couple of weeks after returning to Tokyo:

> You told me in Munich that you fell in love with me over again. So do I. I fall in love with you over and over again in every moment.
>
> I never forget that you told me about your fist visit to Munich— you met Margot and a young beautiful sportsman, and your first concert in Munich with many troubles but great impression, and when you went to Israel, your secret but romantic love, and you played the piano with him.—And you told me, even if you were to die tomorrow, you would be happy, because you had a good marriage and wonderful children and you had fantastic loves.—And me, even if I die tomorrow, I am happy. Because, I know love. I fell in love with you and I love you.—When I listened to you talking about your life and experience, tears fell down, for I was affected by your special and wonderful experience. And I know that I have not many experiences like yours. I don't know wars, I haven't yet gotten married. I have no children or many loves like you. Your life is wonderful, your experience is wonderful, and I have not even one percent of yours. But I am happy enough. Because I love you so much. I was born to meet you, to love you. Do you think that Isolde was not happy? Isolde did not get married to Tristan. And they did not have any children. The most strong and serious love of Isolde was for only Tristan. She did not have many loves. But I think that they were happy. Because they loved each other with all their hearts.
>
> You told me that Bobby left you, so now I had a chance to get you.— (I am sorry that I forget your exact words, but I think you meant it.) But I am not Bobby. I am not Tommy, either. I am me, Kuny. I don't mind that Bobby loved you, and also Tommy. Because you are great, wonderful and attractive. Everybody loves you and of course your music. You gave me the names of your beloved men—Bobby, Tommy, and the man in Vienna (I forget his name). . . . Then, honestly, it did <u>not</u> make me comfortable. I know that you had many loves and I should not worry about it. But, please understand. I am not Bobby or any other man. I am myself. In the story of "Tristan and Isolde" by Bedier, Tristan got married to the same named but

a different girl: <u>Isolde with white hands</u>, while leaving true Isolde. But he found that Isolde with white hands was not Isolde. And even after marriage, he did not touch Isolde with white hands. I am not Isolde with white hands, I am Isolde. I am not a replacement for somebody. And it is impossible to find anybody instead of you. Because you are Isolde for me. I love you with all my heart, and I am happy.[7]

Hashimoto's use of the noun "love" in a plural form reflects his renewed admiration for Bernstein's love-filled life. At the same time, his own love for Bernstein, which he compares to Isolde's love for Tristan, is singular and all-encompassing. His declaration of complete and eternal love, combined with his insistence—with a new, almost defiant tone like Wagner's chords—that he is no replacement for any of Bernstein's other lovers, expresses both his unconditional love and his desire to be loved by Bernstein for who he is.

He brings up Bernstein's other lovers in another letter several months later:

How have you been? I always think of you. I wonder why you don't write me. I know one reason—you are very busy. And I think about another reason, and I wonder if you met new beloved person or Tommy came back to you. . . . Anyhow, I would like to know what you are doing now. If you found a new friend, although it will make me sad a little bit, I should not mind, and I don't care.[8]

He goes on to write about the play *Same Time, Next Year*, which he had seen recently, and compares their relationship to the story. He says that he is thankful that he can keep writing to Bernstein before he sees him "same time, next year." His tone is far more relaxed than in his earlier letters. One senses that he is moving forward in exploring and carving out his own life even as he continues to have a strong connection to and love for Bernstein.

* * *

THROUGH HIS TWO trips to Munich, Hashimoto's love for Bernstein seems to have evolved into a new phase. It is as pure, passionate, and all-encompassing as it was in the early phase of the relationship. Yet, compared to his initial, almost desperate desire and yearning, his feelings appear to have developed into something more spiritual. Just like a disciple following a preacher's teaching understands that his relationship is not exclusive and that the preacher's greatness lies in his love of all beings, Hashimoto began to see that in loving Bernstein he was drawn to a spirit much bigger than the object of his personal love. He began to explore his own way of following the path, realizing his love for Bernstein while living his own life.

New Beginnings

Beloved Lenny,

Thank you so much for your card and here are the warmest wishes of all the family except my poor Reiji's. . . . I know that you do not celebrate Christmas, but I wanted to show you the little card on which I worked—layout, choice of lettering and color, etc. After my husband's death I am working as a member of the editorial staff at this children's books publisher and I am enjoying my new work. "The Smallest Christmas Tree" from which this picture was taken will be published in England, France, and Germany in July '80. Now I am very busy corresponding with these overseas publishers, making the contract and giving orders to our printer through the films and layouts that were sent to us from foreign publishers. I was unable to go to Frankfurt this autumn to attend the Book Fair, because I had (and still have) a lot of things to do with the inheritance procedure which requires time and papers after papers! . . . And as you said, even if you think you are prepared, it is not the same thing! It is absolutely not.[1]

SEVERAL MONTHS AFTER her sorrowful reunion with Bernstein and her husband's passing in 1979, Amano sent this holiday card. Unlike her greeting cards from the previous years depicting Mount Fuji, this one had an illustration of a donkey and a little bird against a light blue background.

Although she begins and ends with references to her husband's death and the challenges of its aftermath, rather than dwelling on her sorrows, much of her message is devoted to describing her new life with specificity and detail. An educated, multilingual woman who had spent more than twenty years as a full-time housewife, she must have felt excited to have new professional responsibilities and an outlet for her creative energy and her international background. The card was material proof of her new life and labor that she wanted to share with Bernstein.

In October 1980, after a business trip to London and Frankfurt, Amano visited Bernstein in New York for the first time. Writing from London in anticipation of her visit, she confirms Bernstein's success and visibility in Europe:

the same thing and found myself the weakest
and most tearful woman in the world...
But I have to be brave. Shigeo and Kiku
are well and help me in their ways.
Your wonderful music is such a nice
and warm consolation to me. I do hope
that you too Beloved Lenny are well
and not too sad. I pray for you
and wish you the happiest 1980
to come. May be I shall go to
Frankfurt next year, and I will not
forget to write.
                    devotedly yours,
                         Kazuko Amano

"The Smallest Christmas Tree" by Masahiro Kasuya

FIGURE 11.1 Holiday greeting card from Kazuko Amano to Leonard Bernstein, December 1979.

It is unbelievable that I am really going to New York! I am eager to see you there although I know that you are quite busy.

Too many things have happened since I saw you last in Tokyo. . . . It was so encouraging to think that you were with me in my sadness. Now I am almost happy having an interesting work.

I am here in London before going to the Frankfurt Book Fair! I have met a lot of interesting people here, most of them editors of children's books.

There is a library, the Swiss Cottage Library, near my hotel, and there I found scores of your "Fancy Free," "On the Town," "Chichester Psalms," and the book "The Joy of Music." In fact, here it is no wonder to find them because you are so well known and loved, but please do imagine my joy when I found them! Sometimes when I feel exhausted after a hard day of work, I go here for a while and have a restful and lovely time with your music, although it sounds only in my heart.

Beloved Lenny, I wish you the best of everything.

Devotedly yours,
Kazuko Amano[2]

Over thirty years after reading his essay at the CIE library in Tokyo, Amano was again spending time with Bernstein's writing in a library. Both excited about a new career that was taking her physically and socially far from her prior domestic life and exhausted by the demands of her job, she was finding solace and healing in Bernstein's music and writing.

Visiting Bernstein in his New York home brought Amano's love to a new phase, much like Hashimoto's love evolved into a new stage after spending time with Bernstein in Europe. She wrote after her return:

Beloved Lenny,

Many thanks indeed for your thoughtfulness [for] me during my short stay in New York. It was just more than thrilling to be invited to your studio where I was lucky to be the very first one to appreciate the manuscript of your "Touches," dedicated to the keyboard, your first love, and to listen to your very beautiful "Divertissement" [*Divertimento*] by following the score. It really was the nicest experience I ever had in my life! And the delicious drinks and "finger foods" that you have prepared for me, the concert that I enjoyed with you seated beside [me], and finally the dinner at La Scala . . . thank you very much, thank you again. I am unable to find suitable words for expressing my feelings but I should tell you that I felt very warm inside, quite happy and encouraged. How kind and thoughtful of you it was, since you are more than busy! I enjoyed also meeting Jamie and Alexander and I missed a little your pretty Nina. I was relieved to see how happy you were being with your children. My beloved Lenny, I wish you could be very very happy. Do you know that I prayed and offered a special little white candle for you at the St. Patrick's Cathedral? I stopped there for a short but peaceful time while taking a walk alone, looking after the bookstores in order to find some interesting children's picture books. I am enjoying my work, but I have to study hard. I am rather new in this field. Please find enclosed my "official" name card, just to let you know what I am. . . . As I have a telex right in front of my desk, please do use it in case you need my help for some urgent information. I will be so happy to do something for you.

Beloved Lenny, thank you again for your warm thoughtfulness [for] me. The children send you their love, and of course I give you mine along with many prayers.[3]

During their decades of friendship, every in-person meeting had taken place in Japan, and Amano's husband and children were almost always present. This was the first time that she was meeting Bernstein in his home and was brought into his family life. How special it must have been for her to be in the studio where he composed and to be the first to look at the manuscript of works he had just written.

Touches is a solo piano piece written for the Sixth Van Cliburn International Piano Competition, to take place the following year. In the manuscript, which Amano may have seen, he explained the various meanings of the title:

Touches = (French) the keys of a keyboard

= different "feels" of the fingers, hands and arms: deep, light, percussive, gliding, fleeting, prolonged, caressing . . .

= small bits (cf. "a touch of garlic"); each variation is a soupçon, lasting from 20 to 100 seconds a piece.

= varied emotions: brief musical manifestations of being "touched," or moved.

= gestures of love, especially between composer and performer, performer and listener [4]

The piece begins with a chorale taken from "Virgo Blues," a short tune Bernstein wrote for his daughter Jamie's twenty-sixth birthday in 1978, followed by eight variations and a coda.[5] The chorale, to be played "with blues feel," is meditative, solitary, and searching. The variations cover a wide range of moods and styles, from playful and jazzy to dark and meditative. The coda is a climactic restatement of the chorale followed by a soft echo of the opening tune, disappearing without resolution. Bernstein dedicated the piece to "my first love, the keyboard." The encounter with the piano was his entry into a life in music, his aunt having given him a piano when he was ten years old. While the piece has many of the Bernsteinesque musical gestures in melody, harmony, and rhythm, it is also disarmingly bare, vulnerable, and introspective. It is as if Bernstein, still in deep pain and sorrow over Felicia's death and also aware of his own mortality, removed his celebrity persona and exposed his lonely soul.[6] Bernstein probably played the piece as he showed the score to Amano, who must have felt and understood his every "touch."

Divertimento, an orchestral suite written for the centennial celebration of the Boston Symphony Orchestra, had just been premiered under Ozawa's baton a few weeks before Amano's arrival in New York. It was probably a recording from the premiere that Bernstein played for her as she followed the score. The mood is a striking contrast to *Touches*. The bursting fanfare is followed by a series of dances, blues, and marches with varying tone colors, rhythms, and tempi, all in a spirit of joy and fun. Amano was probably relieved and delighted to see and hear the bright side of Bernstein's spirit in this freshly composed music.

Amano seems proud to have a new professional identity, symbolized by her business card and her own desk with a telex machine, and eager to share it with Bernstein. Perhaps she hoped that, as a working woman, she could be useful to him beyond personal friendship. Her work became an increasingly important part of her identity. Her holiday greeting at the end of the year is again written on a card published by her company. Amano opens her message with a mixture of amusement and pride: "How do you like this little girl?" explaining that the girl on the front of the card, "Stephanie," will appear in a French children's book.[7]

Entering the workforce in her fifties, Amano quickly became an independent professional woman traveling regularly to Europe. In the following years, she sent Bernstein postcards and letters from London, Vienna, Gravenbruch (Germany), and New York, and wrote about her trips to cities such as Bologna. Her international travels indicated not only her increasing responsibilities in the company but also the expanding career opportunities for educated Japanese women and Japan's growing economic and cultural presence in the world.

It was fortuitous that this was also the period when Bernstein's musical activities were gradually shifting to Europe. In October 1981 she met Bernstein in Frankfurt, where she was attending a book fair and Bernstein was performing.[8] She flew from there to New York and spent time with Helen Coates. On the eve of her return to Japan, she writes to Bernstein:

Beloved Lenny,

Before leaving this big city for Japan after a very short but nice stay with Helen, I would like to say how very happy and enchanted I was to meet you and listen to you in Frankfurt! It still seems like a miracle or a dream to me indeed. . . . You always play or conduct in a marvelous way, but truly it was more than that this time, and I was so happy, probably more than you can imagine, and also because I knew that you were satisfied with the result. I would like to thank you also for bringing me to the party at the beautiful castle. Everything that night was so nice and warm and I will treasure its souvenir. I feel very sorry that I did not see you off the next day, but I was unable to leave my stand at the Book Fair. . . . The last day is more hectic than ever.

Here in New York, besides enjoying meeting Helen every day, I had a chance to visit the Metropolitan Museum (but only a part of it), the Donnell Public Library and the Morgan's. They were inspiring. Thank you very much Lenny, thank you again.

With much love and many prayers for your happiness,

Kazuko[9]

Attending Bernstein's concert in a European city during her business trip was surely quite a different experience from going to his performances in Japan with her husband and children. Bernstein had always treated her as a special guest and included her in private dinners, but being invited, on her own, to a party in a German castle must have felt like a fairy tale. But she was not only the maestro's special friend but now a globetrotting professional woman. Being unable to see him off because of her own work responsibilities must have felt entirely different than not doing so due to family obligations.

Her season's greeting card sent two months later reminisces about the time in Frankfurt. She writes: "I do know that you had the hardest schedule in the world afterward, and hope and pray that you are not too tired, and are now able to enjoy being with your children in your homeland, having some quiet time as a 'composer.'" The quotation marks emphasizing the word "composer" suggest that Bernstein shared his frustration about not having enough time for composing—which had troubled him since his appointment as the music director of the New York Philharmonic in 1957—and his desire for quiet time to focus. Having sat in his studio and seen the manuscripts of his music must have also strengthened Amano's appreciation for Bernstein's identity as a composer. Having her own work life also seems to have given her a new understanding of what it means to have the time to nourish one's mind and soul. She closes by reporting on her own life, with red dots under the last sentence for emphasis: "As for myself I am more than busy with my work, but I like it, although I wish I could find time, during the New Year holidays, to enjoy again listening to your Norton lectures and your other beautiful readings! I need to be refreshed inside." On the opposite side of the card, she gives updates on her children: Shigeo, now twenty-five, was working at a technical publishing firm, and Kikuko, twenty-two, was about to graduate from the conservatory and start teaching at a music school while preparing for study abroad. While these messages and updates are written in black ink, she signs her own name in red, putting a question mark instead of her age in parenthesis, followed by "with much prayers and everlasting love."[10]

As Amano was enjoying her new life and work, her daughter Kikuko was beginning her professional life as a musician. In the fall of 1982, Amano sent Bernstein a belated birthday greeting from Germany where she was attending a book fair, not far from where she spent time with Bernstein the previous year. Half of her message expresses her concern for his health—Coates had written her about the pneumonia he had suffered from—and reminisces about the time in Frankfurt. In the remaining half, she proudly reports on the recital Kikuko gave in September, enclosing materials—probably a flyer and a program—from it:

> I had been very busy too with my work at home and at the publishers. Besides, as you will see from the materials you will find enclosed, I had so many things to take care of for Kiku's <u>first</u> Duo Recital she

gave with her friend this September 16. This was decided all in a sudden, after the advice of Akira Miyoshi, composer and head of Toho, and Toshiya Eto, violinist and pupil of Zimbalist at the Curtis Institute. . . . So we have decided to do it after all; it was a big burden but also a good experience by all means. The concert was more successful than expected, with the small auditorium (400 seats) completely filled up. Kiku was able to play with ease, forgetting almost completely the audience, and she told me that she felt that she "loved" the piece and nothing more, even on the stage. Of course Kiku is not a genius nor a student of the top [caliber], but she loves her violin and I hope that she will find her own way. At any rate, life is hard and it is better to do something we could devote ourselves. We had a manager of course, for this was an "official" concert with tickets sold at the play guide, but nevertheless I had to be her private manager![11]

Even as she describes Kikuko's abilities as modest—probably a mixture of Japanese propriety, by which parents should not brag about their children, and a realistic assessment of her daughter's talent and prospects—and writes about the time and labor she devoted to helping with the concert, Amano is clearly proud of her daughter's achievements. Most importantly, she was delighted that she had grown to be a musician who performed out of pure love and that she was able to report to Bernstein about it.

She was certainly not the young woman that she was when their friendship began, but she displayed the same independence and audacity by quickly standing on her own and soaring into the world far beyond what had been her life as a housewife. Her new sense of self gave her a new understanding of and appreciation for Bernstein as an artist and a human being, and their friendship too entered a new phase.

* * *

JUST AS AMANO was carving a new life for herself, Hashimoto was also taking a decisive step in his life and career.

It is evident from frequent references in his letters to the plays he saw, concerts he went to, and films he watched that Hashimoto was a cultured man deeply interested in the arts, particularly the performing arts. He was clearly raised in a household where culture and the arts were part of everyday life and educated in an environment where artistic interests were encouraged. He studied violin as a child, and he was also involved in theater during his student years, at a time when Japan had a vibrant modern theater scene.

At the early stage of their relationship, however, theater did not appear to be much more than Hashimoto's beloved avocation, one that also gave him a sense of connection to Bernstein. There was little sense, at least as expressed in his letters, that he harbored more serious aspirations. In the letter of November 29, 1979, he had mentioned that he was assisting a friend in producing, directing, and selecting music for a play for children: "I know that your concentration is marvelous, and it is very important to concentrate on something. And when I help producing the play, I forget the time. And besides that, I concentrate on my love to you."[12] Here, even as he writes about his involvement in theater and the concentration required by creative labor, the main point of the message was to declare his love for Bernstein.

Then, a year and a half later, Hashimoto took what appears to be a sudden, decisive step in his life. In May 1981, he writes to Bernstein:

> The insurance business does not become me in spite that I can do it well and get high salary. So I made up my mind to work for a drama as a director, an actor, and a writer. I had wished it for a long time but I could not decide upon it, because the business like this was very risky.—But now, I have gone to the drama school of a theatre company on Sundays and helped directing for another dramatic company on Thursday evenings, since this April. And I keep working for the insurance company on weekdays.—I did not write you about this decision. Because I was afraid of failure—I am a careful man about everything, even love. But I am running to my decision now. I have very busy days but I live a full life.[13]

None of his letters had explained how he had come to work in the insurance business in the first place. Perhaps the two had already talked about it in person, or perhaps he felt that explanation was unnecessary. For a college graduate in Tokyo in the 1970s, a career in a major insurance company ensured high income, stability, and prestige. Hashimoto's writing shows that he was an intelligent, articulate, savvy man, and he must have been a highly competent employee who would have steadily risen in the company. Although he was outwardly successful, perhaps he began to feel increasingly that the nature of work was too distant from his true interests and talents. In addition, major Japanese financial institutions such as banks and insurance companies typically transfer their employees on the management track from one office to another in a different city every few years, for the purposes of training them in diverse environments and preventing corruption. Hashimoto was reaching the stage of his career when transfer was imminent. For a man deeply immersed in the artistic offerings of Tokyo, the prospect of living in a smaller city might have been less than desirable. Furthermore, the conservative culture of an insurance company where men were expected to marry and have children might have become increasingly uncomfortable for him. His relationship with Bernstein perhaps ignited his desire to pursue his true passion.

Despite this major decision, Hashimoto does not dwell on his thinking, and his tone is rather matter of fact as he describes his decision. Clearly Bernstein approved and encouraged his choice. Hashimoto wrote six weeks later:

> Thank you very much for the letter. Especially I thank you for continuing to read my letters, and for encouraging my decision. Your strong and dignified pen not only gives me courage, but it reflects you like a mirror, it lets me see you—writing to me in the room in Rome in the beautiful dawn, and conducting your music, wrapping in full screaming audience with Bravo!! and changing cities so often. How busy you are!! It is superhuman energy. But I am anxious about your health.[14]

He then informs Bernstein of the new schedule that came with his change of career: having been among thirty out of 2,700 applicants to pass a competitive audition, he was going to attend a private drama school run by a famous television director in the fall and would possibly get the chance to work with the drama company. He had decided to leave the insurance company at the end of the year. At around age thirty, he was giving up job security throwing himself into a career in the arts.

Curiously, when he writes to Bernstein while attending drama school, he makes only a few references to his experiences there. He includes a flyer for the play that he directed, underlining his name to show that he is prominently featured, but he does not describe the play or say much about the performance.[15] In January 1982, he writes briefly that he is performing in a short black comedy by a famous Japanese writer, but again, he says little.[16] Shortly after the performance, he reports that it went well and also that he was invited to join the theater company in April, but for some reason left unexplained, he did not feel comfortable with the company. He was searching for an agent.[17] Three months later, he still had not found one, but he simply says, "I know that it is hard to work in show business. But I can endure because I love it and trust my talent. Anyhow except [for the fact that I have not yet found an agent], my life is working well—also except I think of you so often."[18]

For a man who just made a major career change into a field where one's livelihood and future are highly uncertain, he sounds unusually confident and clear-headed. His deep familiarity with the world of the arts—both the contents of the arts and the nature of careers in the field—that he had cultivated even as a layperson must have prepared him for the challenge. The letters convey his stoic determination: he never mentions anything about the concrete elements of his training, such as his instructors, his peers, or even the works he was learning. Instead he writes only about his determination in the pursuit. This contrasts with the letters written during his days at the insurance company, in which he would make references to his section boss, the business cycle, and other practical matters. Having entered the world of the arts, Hashimoto appears to have risen above the mundane travails of everyday life and gained a larger vision for himself and his life.

Not until November 1982, three years after their initial encounter and a year and a half after he set foot in the world of professional theater, did Hashimoto write about his new work with any specificity. Explaining that there were few open auditions in Japan because of the entrenched system of theater companies, he reports that he passed the audition for the Shiki Theatre Company. The company was established in 1952 mainly to produce French plays such as those of Jean Racine and Jean Giraudoux and had become known as the nation's best company for musical theater. It had a license to perform not only Bernstein's *West Side Story* but also works such as *A Chorus Line, Jesus Christ Superstar, Evita, A Little Night Music*, and *Cats*. Hashimoto became one of ten out of a thousand applicants to qualify for membership in the company. Stating that he passed the audition based on his singing and acting and that he still had to learn to dance, he writes: "Although I have been learning ballet since this January, I am very afraid that this is too late. But I want to try!"[19] A few months later, he reports on his progress:

> You know that my life changed, and I am learning ballet and jazz dance. It is very hard work, more than I thought. I have two hours

of ballet lessons and two hours of jazz dance lesson in the morning (from 8 o'clock) and it continues from Monday to Saturday. I am a member of the theatre company, so I don't need to pay for these lessons and this is only one good point for me now.—Because it is quite hard.—But I know that all of this will become good for me at last.

I am writing this letter with muscle ache. However, only when I think of you, it cures this ache, and gives me comfort and courage. Now I have no time to play, to go to drink. Because I can't manage myself—except dancing, sleeping, seeing movies, plays, listening to music, and thinking of you.[20]

Hashimoto's life had clearly taken a decisive turn in a more creative direction. As he wrote to Bernstein in the spring, in addition to acting, he had cofounded an editing company and was writing for a magazine.[21] While his musical and theatrical talents had gotten him into the nation's most prestigious musical theater company, that he had enough interest and skills in writing and editing to derive income from them explains his articulate, thoughtful, sensitive letters to him.

By October, he had landed a good role in a musical that toured all over Japan for two months. He explained to Bernstein that he had not been able to write recently because he was busy with rehearsals.[22] While on tour, he sent many postcards to Bernstein, writing, for example, "Trip is good sometimes, but a long tour of one month is hard—makes me feel loneliness, a little bit. . . . But only one good point at least is that I can send you the card to you from different places."[23] Until recently, Hashimoto had received Bernstein's letters from various cities in the world; now he was himself a touring performer sending postcards from different cities to Bernstein. Being on the performer's side of the stage undoubtedly gave him a deepened appreciation for Bernstein's work and a connection to his life.

Even after Hashimoto entered the world of performing arts, he never once used his intimate relationship with Bernstein to his own advantage, in either his personal or professional life. According to his letters, he only told a handful of people—his sister, parents, best friend, and, interestingly, his girlfriend—about his trips to Europe, and he kept his relationship with Bernstein a precious secret. He probably did not want to tarnish his relationship with Bernstein by using it for his own gain. He must have understood that if he talked about it, many would misunderstand the nature of their relationship or misconstrue Hashimoto's intentions in mentioning it. As if to ensure the distance between his professional life and Bernstein, Hashimoto wrote to him about his involvement in theater only after the fact; he never sought any advice or help from him in making this significant career change.

Hashimoto's life now consisted of writing articles for magazines by day and rehearsing in the evenings for *Never on Sunday*. Yet as he updates Bernstein about his work, he writes less with excitement than with serious awareness of what lies ahead: "However, Lenny, I don't content myself with my life. I want to do more creative things. But now, I am getting good experience. I could not get it through underwriting desk work in an insurance company. I am going up the stairs and I hope to get one step higher."[24] Clearly he was no longer just a young man infatuated with Bernstein. Here his tone is assertive, sure of what he wants in life and how he is going to achieve it. He himself sounds like a man with "passion" and a "great mind," the qualities he so admired in Bernstein.

12

A Quiet Place

WHILE AMANO AND HASHIMOTO were beginning new chapters in their lives, Bernstein too was undertaking a serious new endeavor: composition of an "American Opera."

In many of their letters, both Amano and Hashimoto asked about how Bernstein was doing with his composing. Although Bernstein thought of himself first and foremost as a composer and had written many important symphonic and other works from the 1940s through the early 1960s, his growing fame as a conductor and numerous other projects kept him from having the uninterrupted time and solitude required for writing major works. He must have talked with his two Japanese friends about his on-going struggle to carve out time for composition.

Bernstein had long wanted to write a major opera. He always had great affinity for the theatrical form: his early works included the musicals *On the Town* and *Wonderful Town* and a one-act opera, *Trouble in Tahiti*; he achieved superstardom with *West Side Story*; and he chose to use the dramatic form in *Mass*. However, he had yet to realize his artistic goals in composing a full opera. The operetta *Candide* was not critically or commercially successful at its premiere in 1956 despite the work's musical brilliance and philosophical wit; *1600 Pennsylvania Avenue*, written with Alan Jay Lerner for the nation's bicentennial in 1976, was an outright failure. Bernstein's desire to write a serious opera intensified as he aged.

Finally in the early 1980s he got the chance to realize this goal. His new opera was to be premiered in Houston. The production was a joint commission of the Houston Grand Opera (HGO), the John F. Kennedy Center for the Performing Arts, and Teatro alla Scala in Milan, making it the first triple trans-Atlantic commission in operatic history.[1] Between the Houston and Washington performances, the US premiere easily cost well over a million dollars, quite a lavish amount for a new opera.[2] New American operas were rarely premiered in New York; the Metropolitan Opera tended to shy away from American works, and the New York City Opera premiered only a handful of works in the 1970s. The fact that Bernstein's work would open in Houston had a great deal to do with the creative and entrepreneurial vision of HGO's general director, David Gockley. Under Gockley's leadership, the HGO's budget grew from $420,000 to nearly $9 million; the number of performances increased from 30 to over 250, and the company rose to become one of the country's top five opera companies. Gockley took on a number of bold initiatives, especially the production of major works by American composers.[3] He had approached Bernstein in 1977 about a commission and waited patiently for him to find a suitable librettist. It was the appearance of Stephen Wadsworth—a writer, editor, singer, director, opera critic, and friend of Bernstein's daughter Jamie—in Bernstein's life in October 1980 that set the path for the realization of the opera he dreamed of.[4]

* * *

We wanted to write an opera in the American language—the American language as it is spoken by Americans to express their American selves. Unless we create operas that are about Americans and deal with American problems, opera will not be an unavoidable or necessary art for Americans—only something borrowed from Vienna or Milan. We need more American operas—our culture is rich, our communities are little worlds, and now that we are coming of age with the disillusionment of Vietnam, Watergate and the backlash of conservatism, our pain is great.[5]

As Wadsworth later reflected, *A Quiet Place* was Bernstein's audacious attempt to create an "American opera." By this, Bernstein did not simply mean using vernacular musical elements, which he had already done in many other compositions. Rather, he wanted to take on real-life issues of the contemporary United States and express them in a distinctly American language.

This vision of an "American opera" is evident in both Bernstein's initial conception and the work's evolution. From the outset, he conceived of the new opera as a sequel to *Trouble in Tahiti*, which premiered in 1952. *Tahiti* had dealt with the unhappy marriage and spiritual emptiness of the characters Sam and Dinah. It caricatured the happy façade of white, suburban American domesticity through a vocal trio singing catchy, syncopated jazz tunes interspersed with the scenes of marital tension. Sam and Dinah's son Junior was mentioned in their dialogue but was never seen or heard onstage.

The new opera was set three decades later. Bernstein insisted in his notes that the new work be performed as a double bill with the original. At the same time, he stressed the crucial differences between *Tahiti* and the new opera. He described the libretto as "heavy . . . strong, sad, even depressing, and deeply investigatory of interpersonal pain." He specified that both the libretto and the music stay away from "obvious rhyme" and "sequential forms, as in pop music" but subtly play with vernacular elements.[6]

Bernstein's insistence notwithstanding, the double-bill production proved ineffective, and the work was later rewritten to insert flashbacks from *Tahiti* into the new opera. Yet Bernstein's desire to put the two works together illustrates his wish to stress both the continuities and contrasts between the two stories and their settings.

In his preliminary sketch, Bernstein had already conceived of Junior as the protagonist. Having just finished his junior year at Princeton, Junior rebels against his father by "consort[ing] with negroes" and "maybe smok[ing] reefers." He is a "social justice type" who wants to expose the prejudices exemplified by his parents, but he "has no real talent." The story would begin as the parents are packing to leave for a summer in Vermont. Newcomers—including "certain undesirables"—were moving into their suburban neighborhood, and the parents are thinking of moving away. Junior refuses to go with them, ostensibly to be socially "useful" but really because of a girl, possibly a "negress." Bernstein's one-page note ends with "Has to give her up. Why?"[7]

This scenario, which resonates with the ill-fated romantic narrative of *West Side Story*, would likely have been more accessible to the general audience than what *A Quiet Place* turned out to be. In *A Quiet Place*, Junior is still the protagonist but is a completely different character: he is a homosexual with a mental illness that causes him to speak in rhyme when in distress and who has not been back to his hometown in twenty years. Matching the disturbing sonic opening, the story begins with Dinah found dead in an alcohol-induced car accident. Friends gather for her funeral; Junior, his younger sister, Dede, and her husband, François, arrive from Quebec. The opera traces the emotional turmoil of these four characters over the course of twenty-four hours.

Beginning with Dinah's death, the opera shatters the ideal of hetero-sexual marriage and the nuclear family from almost every possible angle. It is evident that Dinah was profoundly unhappy in her marriage. Dede's husband François was Junior's lover. Dede and Francois are estranged from their father and have difficulty communicating even in the moments when they become closer.

The opera is not just a sexual and family drama but a specifically American one. Viewers learn that Junior moved to Canada to dodge the draft, making him not only a sexual but a political outsider. The characters' dialogue stresses François' foreignness by characterizing him as "sort of French." Dede makes references to the bucolic landscapes of Vermont, Robert Frost, the farms and the cows, and abruptly belts out, "It's like Hello America!" "It's like God bless it, I mean America!" The melody, harmony, and meter of the music bring back *Tahiti* to hint at the falseness of it all.

The tension that drives the opera is most evidently expressed in the contrasting voices of Sam and Junior. When Junior makes a raucous entry, Sam responds with the aria "You're Late," a lengthy rant about his wounded masculinity, disappointment in life and self, and feelings of victimization, anger, and confusion at his children and the world at large.[8] Sam's discom-fort with suburban domesticity and the life of a company man was central to the narrative of *Tahiti*; in post-Vietnam America thirty years later, his words carry greater anger, directed at himself and his family as well as at American society, which he perceives as threatening the patriarchal au-thority of white, middle-class men like himself. Whereas Sam's wounded masculinity and failed authority are loudly vocalized, expressions of sexual agony are more tortured. In one scene, in the midst of a psychotic break, Junior provokes François by rambling about his father having found him having sex with his sister. But his voice is overlaid, almost overwhelmed, not only by François's lament about Junior's pain and illness sung in long melodic lines—as if refusing to be drawn into Junior's narrative—but even more by the melody of Dinah's garden theme. The confused suggestion of incest is overwhelmed by voices of idealized heterosexual domesticity.

In the final scene, Sam abruptly warms up to François and shows his acceptance. Yet even when the characters happily begin planning to spend the coming days together, one hears the *Tahiti* trio in the background, hinting at the falseness and emptiness of the surface harmony. Sure enough, the mundane conversation quickly descends into chaos. As the characters slowly pull themselves back together, Junior sings a beautiful aria in which he seeks his father's acceptance and love, yet he struggles to keep himself from breaking down. Both in words and music, the finale sung by Sam is saturated with hope as well as ambiguity. As the music slowly fades, there is no sense of resolution.

Bernstein thus completely dropped the interracial, heterosexual romance and reconceived the scenario around the turmoil over gender, sexuality, and family.

He insisted on putting sexuality at the center of the narrative rather than treating it as an incidental element. During the writing and rehearsal process, he acknowledged the validity of many of the critiques and suggestions by Gockley—whose intervention ensured that HGO served as an artistic collaborator rather than merely providing its hall as a venue—and tried to address them through instructions to the singers and suggestions for some restaging. But he adamantly refused Gockley's suggestion to call less attention to the characters' homosexuality:

> After all the wierd [sic] relationships dramatized through Scene 2, I found myself taking offense at the Mrs. Doc love declaration (admission) to the dead Dinah. It's as if the libretto is frantically making an effort to cover all the combinations of love relationships in one hour and fifty minutes. When the Mrs. Doc thing comes up, it really <u>calls attention to itself</u>, suddenly makes the piece one about gayness, be it overt or repressed, and ultimately dilutes the universality of its "message." Can't Mrs. Doc just be missing Dinah as a friend?[9]

Next to this comment, Bernstein underlined and emphatically wrote: "<u>No</u>." He was clearly invested in the portrayal of homosexuality and bisexuality as the central theme of the opera.

* * *

WHY DID BERNSTEIN make such a drastic change in themes and narrative from his initial sketch?

The rewrite demonstrated Bernstein's astute grasp of the nation's political, social, moral state in the early 1980s. Debates and backlash over gender, sexuality, and family were precisely what drove American politics during this period. The social movements of the 1960s brought about a series of advances in terms of legal rights and institutional protections for racial minorities, women, and sexual minorities; yet with the consolidation of the New Right culminating in the election of President Reagan, the struggle for equal rights was usurped by the defense of "family values." When less than one-third of all families in the United States were heterosexual couples with male breadwinners and children, the idealized notion of the nuclear family was turned into a political ideology. Along with communism and civil rights, "family" became a major battleground on which conservative politicians, ministers, and activists waged war against liberalism. The individuals and groups perceived to threaten the lynchpin of the nuclear family, the male breadwinner—feminists, single mothers, gays and lesbians, nonconformists of all kind—became targets of moral, social, and political attack in all facets of life, ranging from taxes, welfare, and housing policies to anti-obscenity laws and reproductive rights.

The AIDS epidemic further fueled the battle over "family values." Public discourse on the disease was shaped by the fact that 75 percent of AIDS patients in the United States during the 1980s were gay men. New Right politicians and religious leaders saw AIDS as not just a medical but a moral crisis and used the epidemic to discredit the gay rights movement and the liberal worldview in general.[10]

In 1982, Kathy Whitmire became the first mayor to openly support gay rights in Houston, one of the most liberal places in the conservative state of Texas. In the subsequent years, the city showed slow but steady progress in legislating basic civil rights for its gay residents. Yet the intensification of the AIDS epidemic against the backdrop of the rise of the New Right nationwide fueled a backlash.

Once the opera's premiere was announced, an undated, unsigned flyer with the hyperbolic title "Warning: Leonard Bernstein's Operas Spread Herpes" was circulated around the city:

> Houston has been chosen as the site for the premiere of Leonard Bernstein's new opera "A Quiet Place." It is being promoted as an opera about the "common" folk, in "common" dress, using "common" vernacular. One wonders what "common" strains will be spread by this new "opera"?
>
> What suckers we have become! It used to be that we did our dirty laundry—germs and all—in private. Now it is put on stage and called "popular culture" (or perhaps "popular cultures"). Next we will be told that Leonard Bernstein is preparing a follow-up opera about a man suffering the woes of those nasty sores (how appropriate for

Houston, the herpes capitol of the southwest). Maybe he will call it "Troubles in my Pee-Pee."

The fawning critics, those cosmopolitan sophisticates, tell the suckers, (in a pseudo-British accent) "Remember, this opera is in the truly American vernacular." Perhaps Bernstein's new opera should premiere in the Bronx Zoo—grunts and groans, snorts and moans—isn't that fast becoming the "new American vernacular"?

How quickly we forget. A mere sixty years ago, operas of the anti-semite Richard Wagner created the cultural pessimism which brought Hitler to power. Today punk rock, jazz and so-called modern art and music, such as that of Bernstein, are perverting the minds of this country, generating the same cultural pessimism as that of Weimar Germany. While you may suffer only mental clap by being a "patron of the arts" and suffering through a performance of Bernstein's opera, the cultural pessimism this kind of "art" breeds is giving your kids the real thing.

Mayor Whitmire recently issued a call to change the image of the city of Houston. Let us begin by cancelling this opera, proving that Houstonians are not dumb suckers who will bankroll the trash produced by the "sophisticates."

Let us make Houston "A Quiet Place."[11]

The text is an extraordinary example of the politics and rhetoric of the New Right.[12] It fuels cultural paranoia by characterizing all forms of "popular culture" as leading to fascism and places Bernstein's work among them. It derides the opera's use of the "common" and the "vernacular" and puts quotation marks around the word "opera," suggesting that the piece cannot possibly be a serious work of art. It also drives a wedge between the readers and "cosmopolitan sophisticates," code for East Coast urban intellectuals and artists, and urges the readers to assert control over their local culture. In making these points, the flyer likens the opera to a plague. With the mocking "Troubles in my Pee-Pee," the text attributes "germs" and "nasty sores" to homosexual men without ever using the word "gay," "homosexual," or "AIDS."

Shortly before Bernstein's arrival in the city, the HGO office received phone calls asking whether there was any homosexual sex onstage. The staff responded to the queries by linking the themes of *A Quiet Place* to an iconic scene from an opera classic: "No explicit sex of any kind. A passionate love scene between soprano & tenor which ends in an embrace similar to last act of Traviata."[13]

Against this far from quiet backdrop, Houston officially welcomed Bernstein with great fanfare when he arrived for rehearsals. On May 26, 1983, welcoming ceremonies were held at the South Plaza First City Tower downtown, including speeches by Mayor Whitmire and James A. Elkins, Jr., the senior chairman of First City Bancorporation of Texas, whose $150,000 grant made the Houston production possible.[14] In honor of the occasion, Whitmire proclaimed May 26 "Leonard Bernstein Day" in the city.[15]

Things did not go entirely as planned, however. At the press conference, a heckler commented: "Classical music in the Renaissance and throughout history has always served to up-lift people. It seems to me what you are doing with an opera of this sort is not to up-lift people at all, but to mire people in the muck of a very rotten situation that many people find themselves in." Another asked whether Bernstein was aware that the families funding the opera were financing terrorists in Europe. Bernstein responded with gracious humor, and Gockley quickly brought the press conference to a close.[16] These incidents exposed the disquiet mood in which the opera was about to open.

Just before the premiere, Bernstein sent an impassioned, eloquent message to an AIDS benefit event he could not attend. He was deeply concerned about the epidemic and outraged about government inaction on the crisis. He read widely and collected information from a variety of sources about the crisis. He astutely understood the urgency of the situation and was furious about the devastating effect of the politicization of the issue.

> I wish I could be with you tonight, but the podium is a strict taskmaster. If I could have come, I would no doubt be haranguing you, however briefly, about our country's Number One health hazard, and beseeching you to double your efforts to fight AIDS or, if you already have, then to redouble them. AIDS is not, repeat not, the Gay Plague it is so often made out to be; it is part of the human condition, and must be universally researched and annihilated. But it is a drastically urgent problem for communities like yours, owing to the politicization of the disease, which has become the new lethal weapon against the sexual liberation for which you have

struggled so long. It is <u>that</u> threat which you must now combat, with all your strength, dignity, and passion. I wish you every success and Godspeed.[17]

As indicated by his use of the second person in referring to the gay community, he did not base his advocacy for AIDS research and activism on his own sexual identity. Whereas on countless occasions Bernstein wrote, spoke, and acted as a musician, as a Jew, as an American, or as a liberal, he did not publicly do so as a gay man. While he was supportive of the gay liberation movement, he did not explicitly place himself in the movement. Rather, he lived a life of which sexual, emotional, and social relationships with men were an integral part, without feeling compelled to publicly announce his sexuality or to make it a political issue. He let his opera express the understanding and acceptance he hoped the audience would share.

On June 17, the world premiere of *A Quiet Place*, conducted by John DeMain, was performed in Houston. The premiere was followed by a midnight gala supper underwritten by Texas Eastern Corporation, the Four Seasons, and Houston Center.[18] The owners of the Houston Astros invited the visiting guests of the opera to dinner and drinks in a private box at the Astros/Braves game.[19]

A Quiet Place generated media attention well beyond the local community. The media outlets that sent reporters to the premiere included the *New York Times, Washington Post, New Yorker, New York Magazine, Newsweek, Time, House and Garden, Christian Science Monitor, Village Voice,* and *Vanity Fair,* as well as *Süddeutsche Zeitung* (the largest-circulation German newspaper) and ORF (Austrian Broadcasting).[20]

The reviews of *A Quiet Place* ranged from tepid to hostile. The *Newsweek* review did not mince words: "Four hopelessly uninteresting people slog through a dreary psychological quagmire toward the unenlightening reconciliation that any watcher of soap opera could have predicted at curtain's rise." The review concluded with a damning note: "Americans are admirably indulgent toward their aging wunderkinder, no matter how depressing their later careers. But the spectacle of a prodigious talent in decline, or at least in eclipse, is never a heartening one."[21]

Despite multiple revisions by Bernstein and Wadsworth, this "American opera" was rarely produced since the premiere. Only twenty years after Bernstein's death did the opera earn critical acclaim, when it was performed by the New York City Opera in 2010.

* * *

The opening of *A Quiet Place* was reported worldwide, including Japan. Hashimoto wrote on July 14, 1983:

> Congratulations to the birth of your new opera!! At last I have found your news in music magazines.—Your new opera "Calm Place" (the magazine didn't say exact English title) was performed in Houston in the middle of June. Japanese music magazine did not write their own article, they showed a few lines of terrible Newsweek criticism. I was not surprised at the criticism. I had prepared my mind to hear it. Because you already wrote to me about the new opera that nobody would love except us. I wonder that your great opera was born too early. My friends said that great artistic things are too difficult to be recognized under the Reagan politics. And I agree with this opinion. The story of your opera is surely Reagan's unfavorite one.
>
> Anyhow I am very glad to hear the birth of your new opera. I was waiting for it for a long time. I am excited with joy at the news. I know that your baby will become popular when he grows up.
>
> —Congratulations! [22]

The letter provides insight into Bernstein's own understanding of the opera during the writing process and his knowledge that it would fail to be appreciated in its own time. But the letter also shows that Bernstein knew that Hashimoto would understand, even without seeing the opera.

13

A Peaceful Place

ON MARCH 23, 1983, a few months before the opening of *A Quiet Place*, President Reagan announced the Strategic Defense Initiative (SDI), the so-called Star Wars program, to create a massive space-based shield against intercontinental ballistic missile attack. If realized, the SDI would empower the United States to launch a first strike against the Soviet Union. Many feared that it would further intensify the nuclear arms race and jeopardize the balance that had been precariously maintained between the Cold War superpowers.

A longstanding advocate for nuclear disarmament, Bernstein was greatly alarmed by news of the SDI. He was an early supporter of the National Committee for a SANE Nuclear Policy (SANE), which conducted grassroots organizing through college campuses and the mass media, gained visibility through large events, and secured the support of influential public figures. Even when his heavy performance schedule prevented him from attending its events, he took SANE's calls for action very seriously.[1] In the wake of Nikita Khrushchev's announcement that the Soviet Union would resume testing nuclear weapons in the fall of 1961, Bernstein wired a message to President Kennedy, National Security Advisor McGeorge Bundy, and US Ambassador to the UN Adlai Stevenson, urging a postponement of any US nuclear testing until the United Nations met on the issue.[2] He officially became a national sponsor of SANE in December 1961 and sent signed letters on SANE letterhead to his friends seeking support and donations to the organization.[3] The conflict over US policies in Vietnam between the liberal democratic and militant radical groups within the organization resulted in the collective resignation of a number of leaders and supporters, including Bernstein, in 1967.[4] Although there is no record of Bernstein formally rejoining SANE after it reorganized under new leadership, his commitment to nuclear disarmament never waned. In 1982, he endorsed the Congressional Nuclear Freeze Resolution, sponsored by Edward Kennedy and Mark Hatfield.[5] A year later, he would write to Harvard University President Derek Bok that he was discontinuing his donations to the university in opposition to a study by a team of Harvard professors who claimed that universal disarmament was never a certainty and that the United States should remain armed.[6]

The growing antinuclear movement provided a platform for Bernstein's advocacy. With the end of the Vietnam War in 1975, opposition to nuclear weapons became a top issue among pacifists, and many organizations staged numerous protests and demonstrations. The Nuclear Weapons Freeze Campaign, launched by Randall Forsberg in 1979 to call for US-Soviet agreement to stop the testing, production, and deployment of nuclear weapons, caught fire among peace activists in the 1980s. In addition to grassroots activism, professionals in diverse fields also mobilized for nuclear disarmament, forming numerous organizations such as the Union of Concerned Scientists, Physicians for Social Responsibility, Lawyers Alliance for Nuclear Arms Control, and Educators for Social Responsibility.[7] Performing artists also helped raise awareness and mobilize action. Performers and Artists for Nuclear Disarmament (PAND) was founded in 1982, and Bernstein pledged strong support and a desire to participate in its actions.

After the opening of *A Quiet Place*, Bernstein turned his attention back to the antinuclear movement. Amberson arranged for a special campaign in honor of his sixty-fifth birthday. In lieu of parties and performances, Bernstein and his friends decided to commemorate his birthday by wearing sky-blue armbands to show support for a nuclear weapons freeze. On behalf of the Leonard Bernstein 65th Birthday Committee, Harry Kraut sent a letter to musicians and music lovers around the world:

> We invite friends and admirers of Leonard Bernstein—especially his fellow musicians, but also music-lovers from every nation and walk of life—to join with us on August 25, 1983 in a demonstration of support for a mutual and verifiable nuclear weapons freeze. We ask that you distribute the enclosed sky-blue arm bands to musicians and any others who wish to wear them while playing concerts (symphonic, rock, chamber, recital or cocktail), taking tickets, selling records, or even while at the beach

on Thursday, August 25, to show their individual support for a mutual and verifiable nuclear weapons freeze. If you can't, please pass this letter on.[8]

Attached was a list of names of approximately three hundred committee members, including Bernstein's family members, Amberson staff, and musicians and artists ranging from Claudio Abbado, Aaron Copland, and Mischa Maisky to Mia Farrow, Paul Newman, and Elizabeth Taylor. As one of three Japanese individuals on the list (along with the philanthropist and artist manager Kazuko Hillyer and Kazuya Sakuma from Chubu Nippon Broadcasting, who had worked on the New York Philharmonic's Japan tours), Hashimoto sent blue ribbons to many Japanese organizations and individuals with whom Bernstein had worked.

On August 25, the maestro's many friends and colleagues around the world proudly displayed their blue ribbons. In Japan, conductor Akeo Watanabe wore the ribbon during his chorus rehearsals. Bernstein himself spent the day at the inauguration of the Leonard Bernstein Outdoor Theater in Lawrence, Massachusetts, where he dedicated his entire speech to a call to end the nuclear arms race. He pleaded in his deep, throaty voice:

> It seems so simple, but it isn't, as long as we passively accept the power-madness in which we are caught up. We must make ourselves heard, against the cancerous tumorous proliferation of nuclearity, and for an immediate stop to it. This thought that our combined voices could possibly make a difference; this sight of you all gathered to make this statement; this outpouring of joy and affection and belief—these have already given me the happiest of birthdays, for which I am eternally grateful.[9]

He closed his speech by introducing a young Japanese conductor to the audience. Bernstein's choice to feature his protégé—who began studying with him when Seiji Ozawa brought him to Tanglewood in 1978—on this occasion was itself a strong message to the world. The exuberant young man who stepped onto the podium to perform Copland's *A Lincoln Portrait* was Eiji Oue, born and raised in Hiroshima.

Exactly three months after Bernstein's birthday, Hashimoto was in Hiroshima on tour with the musical theater company. He sent a postcard to Bernstein:

I am in HIROSHIMA—The city itself is pretty, and new beautiful streets make us forget Atomic Bomb. But I can feel some hard feeling at the corner of old streets. [10]

On the other side of the postcard is a haunting image of the city's Atomic Bomb Dome at dawn. Hashimoto's use of all capitals shows that the proper noun had come to mean far more than a mid-sized Japanese city that was a wartime military-industrial center. Especially with the international circulation of John Hersey's 1946 reportage, "Hiroshima" became a universal signifier of atomic bombing, the suffering of its victims, and aspirations for peace and a nuclear-free world.[11] Hashimoto knew that Hiroshima residents' "hard feelings"—against the follies of humanity, the politics of the Cold War, and their own government's treatment of the victims—would resonate with Bernstein.

Little did he know that just a year later he would be involved in bringing Bernstein to the city.

14

Representing Lenny

COMPARED TO THE frequency of Hashimoto's letters in the first few years of their relationship, his correspondence with Bernstein became much more sparse after he joined the Shiki Theatre Company in 1982. Over the next two years, he sent a number of greeting cards and postcards from different cities he was touring, and while his messages were just as heartfelt as his earlier letters, they were much shorter. This was the time when Hashimoto was juggling acting, running a company, and working as a writer and editor, and one senses in his correspondence his busy but stimulating life and new sense of self.

And yet during this period, Hashimoto's name begins to appear not just in Bernstein's personal correspondence but also in Amberson's business papers. On August 6, 1984, Nicholas Davies at Amberson Enterprises sent a letter to Hashimoto, letting him know that Kraut was arriving in Tokyo the following month and wanted to see him. The letter then says: "Also, as he will need an interpreter/guide while he is in Tokyo, Mr. Kraut was wondering if you might know of someone, at once pleasant and knowledgeable, who might be available at that time."[1] Kraut himself followed up on telex a couple of weeks later:

Dear Kunihiko:

My plans have changed slightly. I arrive in Tokyo on September 10 at 1435 on PA801 and depart on JAL717 on September 19 at 1255. I will stay at the Hotel Okura while in Tokyo, but must go to Hiroshima for several days during my stay. I hope that you have been able to find someone to translate for me and help generally, as Ned Davies wrote to you some weeks ago. How about you? How's your English these days?

My trip is in connection with Lenny's trips to Japan next year about which we wrote to you last spring. He will be with the European Community Youth Orchestra in Hiroshima on August 6 and 7, 1985 and then in Tokyo, Osaka, and Nagoya with the Israel Philharmonic from September 1 to 15, 1985.

I look forward very much to seeing you again. All best wishes,

Harry Kraut[2]

Davies's letter had asked for Hashimoto's recommendation for a suitable assistant, so the idea of hiring Hashimoto himself must have occurred to Kraut later. This was not the first time that Kraut communicated with Hashimoto independently of Bernstein. He had arranged for Hashimoto's travels to Europe, and Hashimoto had written him thanking him for the wonderful time and all his help. On one of Kraut's prior business trips to Japan, Hashimoto had accompanied him to a meeting with the representatives of Deutsche Grammophon's Tokyo office to assist in the negotiations. Kraut thus had gotten to know Hashimoto and clearly liked and trusted him.

But it had been over twenty years since Bernstein's first trip to Japan, and he and the Amberson staff had a wide network of professional contacts in the country, including executives at arts management companies, television networks, and Sony. It would have been easy for Kraut to find an assistant, someone with professional experience in the industry, through any of these contacts. Plus, Hashimoto's English was decent but nowhere near that of a bilingual speaker. There would have been plenty of professionals with better English-language skills who were "at once pleasant and knowledgeable." Why, then, did Kraut ask for Hashimoto's help, especially on major projects like the Hiroshima Peace Concert and the Israel Philharmonic tour?

No documents exist that answer these questions. But all sources indicate that Kraut was an exceptionally savvy businessman and a good judge of character. From his interactions with and observations of Hashimoto during their time in Europe, he must have sensed that Hashimoto was much more than an adoring follower of Bernstein. The maestro probably told Kraut about Hashimoto's intelligence and sensitivity. Hashimoto often wrote detailed and insightful accounts of reviews of Bernstein's compositions, recordings, and performances in the Japanese media, which must also have added to Bernstein and Kraut's esteem for him. Kraut may also have liked the fact that Hashimoto was not himself a classical musician or a member of the industry with self-interest in handling Bernstein's business.

Whatever Kraut's reasoning might have been, his suggestion that Hashimoto work as Kraut's translator and assistant must have come as an extremely flattering surprise for Hashimoto. Shortly after receiving Kraut's telex, he wrote to Bernstein, the first multi-page letter in four months.

Dearest Lenny,

At last you will come to Japan!!

How long have I waited for this news? How many times have I imagined of you in Japan?

Now my mind flies to August and September of next year. I forget that it is 1984. I feel impatient of only one year difference.

I don't know what I shall do until next August.—Maybe just survive carefully, quiet my excitement, get cool, and just wait. But now I can't stop this excited feeling.

I was in bed with high fever with a swollen tonsil this week. In bed, I had nothing to do except thinking about next year. When I came back from a tour at the end of June, I caught a cold also from the hard tour. And July I was too busy, because daytime I went to the editing office and every evening I was on stage. This month is all right. I go to the pool every morning and I go to the office in the afternoon. But I think it helps time to fly quickly that I make myself busy. So I decided to work hard from September on. I declined the autumn tour. If I do it, I would have to go around Japan from September to 13th of December for four months. It is too long. Maybe I would be in bed again for two weeks after the tour. So instead of the tour, I work on my writing business at the editing company which needs me much more and it keeps me busy.

I am very glad to see Harry again also. And I am excited also for Harry. How wonderful that you will have a peace concert in Hiroshima!! It is a very good idea, especially with youth orchestra on the special day in August. I am very lucky to be able to help as an interpreter when Harry comes to Japan. I will try to do my best.

See you soon.

Love,
Kuny[3]

Hashimoto hadn't seen Bernstein since his trip to Munich over four years earlier, and he may have begun to get somewhat used to not seeing him. And as the nature of his admiration grew into more of a spiritual one, perhaps he had gradually come to accept that their love was not going to take the form of a relationship where they would spend much time together. Yet upon learning of Bernstein's arrival the following year, his yearning to be with him was clearly rekindled. Having Bernstein in Japan would give him a greater sense of reality about their relationship, and that Bernstein was performing a peace concert in Hiroshima must have felt that the maestro was strengthening his ties to the country.

* * *

THE HIROSHIMA PEACE CONCERT was the brainchild of Mitsunori Sano, an Osaka native roughly Hashimoto's age. Just as Bernstein had been a central part of Amano's and Hashimoto's lives since their youth, he had had a special place in Sano's musical and professional development. Sano had been a Bernstein devotee since seeing the film *West Side Story* in the fifth grade and learning that the composer was the same man who hosted the Young People's Concerts series, which he had eagerly watched on television. Although he did not choose to pursue a career as a musician, he had been a member of a youth chorus and was a serious lover of music. After having worked for Kajimoto, the largest artist management company in Japan, Sano ran his own artist management agency in Tokyo. One of the artists on his agency's roster was the conductor Akeo Watanabe, who on Bernstein's sixty-fifth birthday had worn the blue armband sent by Hashimoto.

Since entering the world of artist management, Sano had been dreaming of producing a Bernstein concert. He had strong beliefs about nuclear disarmament and was convinced that the combination of Bernstein's stature as both a composer and a conductor and his political commitments would make him an ideal artist for a peace concert. With an introduction by pianist André Watts, whom he represented in Japan, he flew to New York to meet with Bernstein's publicist, Margaret Carson. Impressed by Sano's enthusiasm and vision, Carson encouraged Bernstein to consider the invitation.

Although Bernstein's commitment to antinuclear advocacy drew him to the proposal, the logistics of producing a concert involving a globetrotting maestro whose schedule was booked years in advance posed practical challenges. Sano's initial proposal was to bring Bernstein to conduct the NHK Symphony and a Japanese chorus to perform a requiem in Hiroshima and Nagasaki and also have Bernstein compose a work for the occasion.[4] But Bernstein's summer of 1985 was already booked with the European Community Youth Orchestra (ECYO) tour. Furthermore, he was already scheduled to perform in Japan with the Israel Philharmonic Orchestra (IPO) in September of that year. Making two trips to Japan in two months was not only inefficient for Bernstein but also caused issues for the presenter of the IPO tour, as it diluted the value of the maestro's visit.

Kraut then suggested making the peace concert part of the ECYO tour.[5] Founded in 1976 and financed by the European Community, the ECYO was comprised of young musicians from EC nations selected by a rigorous audition process; under the leadership of conductor Claudio Abbado, the musicians studied with the world's leading conductors and performed and toured together.[6] In many ways, the spirit of the ECYO was a good match for the idea behind the proposed peace concert. Sano, Kraut, and the representatives of the ECYO gathered at Abbado's home in Milan to discuss the idea. There, the parties agreed that the event be called the Hiroshima Peace Concert and that Bernstein and other musicians would perform without fee and donate the revenues to "an appropriate organization active in the peace and anti-nuclear movement, with emphasis that the organization selected should be international, politically neutral, and, if at all possible, based in Hiroshima."[7]

Why did Bernstein go out of his way—rearranging the existing tour with the ECYO, involving a number of parties from different countries, working with individuals with whom he had no prior connections—to conduct this concert? His commitment to the antinuclear movement and his mounting anger with the accelerating arms race must have been paramount. As was evident in A Quiet Place, his work was becoming increasingly reflective of his battle with the state, which was unresponsive to the voices of the people, and this concert may have felt like a productive outlet for his beliefs. Having seen the effect of his advocacy through his sixty-fifth birthday campaign, he may have felt that he could use his visibility and influence for an important cause. In addition, he was dedicated to working with young musicians—a commitment that became stronger in his later years—and the opportunity to bring the ECYO to Hiroshima must have felt particularly important to him. Furthermore, given his growing frustrations with American corporations and the music industry at large, this project, whose goal was humanitarian and artistic with little involvement of commercial interests or industry politics, might have felt like a chance to return to his core mission as an artist. It was likely a combination of these factors that led Bernstein to prioritize the Hiroshima Peace Concert.

Although Bernstein and Kraut were both enthusiastic about Sano's proposal, Sano had limited English-language skills and no previous contact with Bernstein. It was logical for Kraut to bring in Hashimoto as an intermediary to assist in the overall execution of the project.

During Kraut's trip to Japan in September, Hashimoto accompanied him to all the meetings with the parties involved. They took a trip to Hiroshima and Nagasaki to research possible performance venues and accommodations. It then became clear that Nagasaki had neither adequate concert halls nor hotels large enough to accommodate the entire group. While the cancellation of the Nagasaki concert had to do with practical rather than political considerations, it did reinforce the general tendency of the city to be relegated to a secondary place in the historical memory of the atomic bomb and the nuclear disarmament movement and of Hiroshima to serve as a universal symbol for both.[8]

Even as the Nagasaki concert was dropped, the project expanded considerably in scope with the involvement of Unitel, which had been working with Bernstein on video projects. Given that the principal body of the concert was going to be the ECYO, Europe-based Unitel could bring greater expertise, resources, and international visibility to the project than Sano could. In October 1984, Kraut and Unitel's executive Robert Jungbluth expanded the idea for the peace concert beyond Japan to form an international "Journey for Peace": under this plan, the performers would tour in Japan as well as Athens (the capital of the 1985 European Year of Music and "cradle of democracy"), Budapest (the largest city in the Socialist bloc after Moscow and Leningrad), and Vienna.

The musical content and performers also changed in the course of the planning process. The organizers requested that Toru Takemitsu compose a piece and invited Seiji Ozawa to conduct the first part of the concert.[9] Considering that Ozawa was by far the most successful Japanese protégé of Bernstein and that he played a key role in Bernstein's early Japan tours as well as bringing Takemitsu to Bernstein and the American audience, it made perfect sense for these two men to be part of this event.[10] Yet neither of these ideas came to fruition, as Takemitsu was too busy to take on this new commission and Ozawa declined the invitation. Sano then recommended emerging composer Toshio Hosokawa as an alternative to Takemitsu, but the proposal was rejected by NHK, as the television network considered Hosokawa's work too avant-garde for nationwide broadcast.[11] By November 1984, these initial ideas were replaced by having Eiji Oue, whom Bernstein had brought to the podium on his sixty-fifth birthday concert, conduct the first part of the program, including the world premiere of Hiroshima-born composer Tomiko Kojiba's *Hiroshima Requiem.*

* * *

THE TELEX EXCHANGES between Hashimoto and Kraut between the fall of 1984 and August 1985 show that Hashimoto played a crucial role in managing these complex communications and negotiations among various parties on matters ranging from programming to television broadcasts and sponsors. They reveal a different side of Hashimoto from his personal letters to Bernstein and explain why Kraut and Bernstein trusted him. They are consistently concise and to the point; in itemized lists, he directly answers Kraut's questions while calling attention to any issues that need to be addressed. Even in the impersonal format of telex, both his professionalism and personal rapport with Kraut come through.[12]

Kraut was obviously quite satisfied with Hashimoto's work. Thereafter Hashimoto was officially assigned to be the Japan representative for Amberson.

It made sense for Amberson to have a staff representing Bernstein's interests in Japan long-term. Japan's booming economy in the 1980s was reflected in the country's classical music scene. In May 1983, legendary pianist Vladimir Horowitz made his first tour of Japan at age eighty and performed two recitals in Tokyo. The tickets were priced in the range of 8,000 to 50,000 yen—an unprecedented price for a solo recital, when the tickets for the full opera performances by La Scala or the Vienna State Opera went for around 30,000 yen—and were instantly sold out. All across the country, first-rate concert halls were built using both public and private funding, and Japan came to be widely known for having some of the best halls and acousticians in the world. That Amberson felt the need to appoint a Japan representative and specifically chose Hashimoto for the task shows the growing importance of Japan in Bernstein's work.

Hashimoto's relationship to Bernstein thus went through an extraordinary transformation. The "lovesick" young man who had offered to be his maid, secretary, and doll five years earlier became an arts professional working to help the maestro realize his artistic goals.

What this new role meant for Hashimoto is expressed in his letter that fall. Bernstein had called to invite him to Munich again during his European tour, but Hashimoto had to decline this offer, for a reason that had been unimaginable just a few years earlier. He writes:

> Of course, I wanted to go to Munich so much to listen to your concert, cheer and clap my hands, say "Bravo," and see you. When you invited me to Munich by telephone, I was unbelievably happy and about to say "yes." How wonderful I could come see you again in Munich!
>
> However, I don't regret not saying "yes." Because I am working for you now in Japan, and I am very happy to do it. It is the most precious present in my life, much, much more than gold or diamond. I live for you, I always feel you with me. I feel your face, your voice, your breath, your hands, and your kiss. It gives me a life worth living.—I am happy, Lenny. I can repeat this over many thousand times.
>
> "L'automne est deuxieme printemps." Yes I have a beautiful second spring now. A park is lovely and chic with golden and red leaves. They cover the surface of the earth like a carpet, and wrap our steps softly. I walk around. I touch beauty of nature, and I touch you through them.[13]

It must have been extremely painful for Hashimoto to turn down the invitation, especially after not having seen Bernstein in years. Yet at the same time it probably was an easy decision to make. Now that he was working for Bernstein, his love was much more than personal adoration. He was serving a greater purpose, helping to deliver the maestro's philosophy and art to the people of his own country. Working for Bernstein was a great enough cause for Hashimoto to put aside his personal desire to see him. In his earlier letters, he had expressed his love in ways akin to spiritual faith and a commitment to serving a prophet. Now he was actually getting a chance to play that role for Bernstein.

Convinced of Hashimoto's central role in successfully executing the concert, Kraut wrote firmly in his telex about the organizers' meeting scheduled in New York: "LB and I feel that it is most important you come as well." Thus Hashimoto finally made his first visit to New York in December 1984. The trip was arranged by the Amberson staff; he was picked up at the airport and immediately taken to dinner with Kraut. The following days were filled with meetings with the parties involved in planning the Hiroshima concert. Bernstein was vacationing in the Bahamas during much of his stay, which meant that Hashimoto spent little time with him even as he was working for him.[14] But he arranged to stay for a few days after Bernstein's return and visited him and the family both at the Dakota and in his home in Fairfield, Connecticut. He was now part of Bernstein's main business staff and inner circle.

* * *

HASHIMOTO'S NEW ROLE in Bernstein's work also brought the maestro's two Japanese friends together. Hashimoto and Amano had not been officially introduced, nor did they have other reasons to meet, but Hashimoto's work for Bernstein changed this. After Hashimoto's trip to New York, Kraut wrote to Amano:

Dear Kazuko:

Thanks so much for your card and letter.

I write to let you know that Amberson has a representative in Japan whose name is Kunihiko Hashimoto. His card is enclosed.

I'm sure that he would welcome any help you can give us with the very complex projects of next summer, and I have asked him to telephone you when he returns to Japan after the New Year.

Lenny joins with me in sending you warmest wishes for 1985.

Yours cordially,
Harry[15]

Kraut sent a carbon copy of this letter to Hashimoto, who contacted Amano upon his return. The two met in Tokyo on January 23, 1985, and became close acquaintances. Hashimoto found Amano to be charming, enthusiastic, and sincere; in turn, Amano saw an intelligent, sensitive, thoughtful man in Hashimoto. Their respective relationships to Bernstein were quite different in nature. But they shared a love for Bernstein, whom they both admired as not merely a wonderful musician but a great spirit.

Just two days after his two Japanese friends met in Tokyo, Bernstein gave a sermon at All Souls Unitarian Church in New York. The speech is at once a disarmingly honest confession of his personal struggles with love and his plea for peace, especially nuclear disarmament. He quoted

Albert Schweitzer's phrase "the Will to Love" as "almost a definition of the meaning of [his] life."

> The Will to Love guides my living from day to day, always has, and always has messed it up to a remarkable degree, and still does. Which brings me to my second and final confession: I wish it didn't.
>
> The Will to Love is exhausting. It causes one to love far too many people, and to love them deeply, with commitment. It is obviously very difficult, if not impossible, to honor so many commitments simultaneously, or even one at a time, over a considerable geographic expanse. It is unfair to those I love, especially to those who love me in return, and it therefore causes suffering, which is the opposite of what the Will to Love intends. This is true not only of beloved individuals but of whole families, including my own, and including my orchestra-families around the world, for in conducting one I can obviously not be conducting all the others. Moreover, because love is so demanding of time and energy, it causes my work to suffer, compositions to remain uncomposed, old and new scores to remain unlearned—but all that is <u>my</u> problem, not yours. And as we Juditarians say, it should only be my worst problem.

Pointing out the difficulty of speaking about love without falling into cliché, he concluded:

> And yet I try, today, tomorrow, as long as I live. Probably the best I can have done today is to remind you of what you surely knew already, of the life-or-death importance of living out the Will to Love; to remind you by my personal confession of success or failure in my own struggle to make love a practiced reality; to remind you by nudging your awareness—<u>and</u> my own—of the profound moral imperative we share to make our lives into a moment-by-moment, uninterrupted action of bearing witness. If we can pray, let us pray. I know of only two ways to pray: one is to say Thank You, sing a Psalm, <u>Gratias agimus</u>, Hallelujah. The other is to pray that our boastfully-called Divine Spark, our pilot light, that little blue flame which is our capacity to love, may never be extinguished as long as we inhabit this wonderful earth with one another.[16]

* * *

HASHIMOTO'S NEW PROFESSIONAL role also brought depth to his personal relationship to Bernstein. In a brief message on a postcard sent on February 24, 1985, he writes:

Dearest Lenny,

We have rainy days sometimes in Japan recently. But after the rain, spring is approaching us step by step. Although spring hasn't come, I think of the summer beyond spring. This summer is very special for me. Even in a puddle, I can see the summer with you.

With love,
Kuni[17]

The coming summer meant not only getting to see Bernstein again but also playing a role in realizing Bernstein's work and sharing his Will to Love. The sense of wonder he felt in seeing Bernstein in his mind as he looked down at a puddle on the street in Tokyo must have been of a very different sort than the excitement he felt when he was about to travel to Munich to see Bernstein in previous years.

In late March, after complex negotiations, the representatives of the organizations involved signed a formal agreement about the Hiroshima Peace Concert.[18] Shortly thereafter, Hashimoto wrote again on a postcard:

Indeed spring blossoms. Especially now, cherry trees are in full bloom in Japan.

I thank you so much for your Hiroshima peace concert. On 28th March, Jungbluth and Sano agreed on the contract for this peace concert after a long meeting. It was the best birthday present for me. I am very happy to touch this project. How much can I thank you!!

With love,
Kuni[19]

15

A Summer of Prayer

EARLY IN THE morning on August 6, 1985—long before the crowd gathered for the official peace ceremony—a group of about two hundred formed a circle at a corner of the Peace Memorial Park in Hiroshima. Seiji Ozawa had invited his friends to sing together as a prayer for peace. Many community members joined the chorus, singing a requiem and a series of Japanese and European folk songs that Ozawa had printed. Among them were biwa performer Kinshi Tsuruta and shakuhachi player Katsuya Yokoyama, with whom Ozawa had performed Takemitsu's *November Steps* numerous times.

Bernstein joined the group after laying a wreath at the memorial. Local and national newspapers reported on this beautiful act of prayer with a photo of the two maestros singing together.[1] Yet Ozawa was not on the stage of Bernstein's peace concert held later that day. He had been invited to be part of the concert but had declined.

It was clear that Ozawa was as committed as Bernstein was to peace and the antinuclear movement. He said in a newspaper interview:

> I had been concerned about the issue [of nuclear weapons] before this, but why have I decided to go to Hiroshima and Nagasaki this year in particular? Because I believe that the fortieth anniversary of the atomic bombing is an occasion to remind ourselves and appeal to the world of the seriousness of the issue of nuclear weapons to the future of humankind and of the tragic consequences it can bring. So I am not giving prayers only to those who were killed by the atomic bombs. In the real world, there are many conflicts, not just war. Unless we all strengthen our awareness about the

FIGURE 15.1 Seiji Ozawa conducting a requiem at the Peace Memorial Park in Hiroshima on the morning of August 6, 1983. Published in *Chugoku Shimbun* on August 7, 1983. Courtesy of *Chugoku Shimbun*.

FIGURE 15.2 Seiji Ozawa and Leonard Bernstein at the Peace Memorial Park in Hiroshima. Published in *Chugoku Shimbun* on August 6, 1983. Courtesy of *Chugoku Shimbun*.

importance of not letting those conflicts lead to atomic destruction, there is no way to know what could happen in the future.[2]

If the invitation to be part of the peace concert had come twenty or even ten years earlier, it is quite possible that Ozawa would have graciously and eagerly accepted the invitation from his mentor. But in 1985, Ozawa was himself one of the world's leading conductors. Having spent decades living and working around the world as the first Japanese conductor of Western music to achieve international acclaim, he had formed his own complex historical understandings, political beliefs, and moral convictions. He was particularly wary of organized social movements whose message and actions were often politicized. Thus, when a group of Japanese musicians founded the group, Hankaku Nihon no Ongakuka tachi, or Japanese Musicians against Nukes, in 1982, he chose not to participate.[3] In the same interview, he asserted his preference to act as an individual rather than as a member of an organization:

> I had been urged to participate in these types of movements and organizations, not only from musicians but also writers and others. But I found many of those activists much too radical and did not accept those invitations. Fundamentally, I have a belief that I do not need to join a group in order to act. Even in religion, I believe that one can connect with God without going to church. Just like spiritual faith is not necessarily born out of listening to the minister in a church, one does not need to be part of a group in order to oppose nuclear weapons. Many Japanese people seem to think that one needs to be part of a group to get anything done. I think that is false. Plus, working in groups often leads to conflict over power.

He then explained that he declined Bernstein's invitation to be part of the concert because he wanted to express his commitment to peace in his own way. "One does not need to raise a lot of money to put on a concert in a large hall in order to express one's beliefs [in peace]."

Ozawa did not make any direct criticism of Bernstein's project in the interview. But it is possible that he felt that Bernstein's Peace Concert exuded a certain air of official sanction that he did not want to be associated with. After all, the concert had the support and cooperation of the city of Hiroshima, was sponsored by the Hiroshima Junior Chamber, and was held in a major public hall downtown. The mayor hosted a big reception for Bernstein the day before the concert, and the maestro was an official guest at the Peace Memorial Ceremony. The program book for the concert included messages not only from Japan's Ministry of Health and Welfare (which administers the welfare program for victims of the atomic bombing) but also from the heads of state of European Community member nations, US Senator Howard Metzenbaum, New York City mayor Edward Koch, Jerusalem mayor Teddy Kolleck, and former chancellor of the Federal Republic of Germany Helmut Schmidt. The Hiroshima Junior Chamber had commissioned the prominent Japanese composer Ikuma Dan to write a symphonic work to "leave a cultural legacy for Hiroshima on the occasion of the fortieth anniversary of the atomic bombing."[4] Per the Junior Chamber's request, Dan's score was ceremoniously presented to Bernstein at the Mayor's reception. Things could not get much more official.

Amano was also in the city for Bernstein's concert. Upon his arrival at his hotel, Bernstein found a letter and gift from her. It had been almost three years since her last correspondence, which may be explained by her busy life in publishing. Her Catholic faith had been apparent in her previous letters and seems to have strengthened during these years.

Beloved Lenny,

Thank you for coming! I follow you with my prayers during the whole JOURNEY . . .

The Bishop of Hiroshima will come on the first day. He loves your music and books and looks forward to listening to you, and pray together in his heart. . . . Isn't it wonderful?

With ever lasting LOVE,

Kazuko[5]

The capitalization of the word "journey" shows her understanding of the nature of Bernstein's visit—that it was not simply a concert tour but a journey through which the musicians and the audience reflected upon the meaning of peace by sharing music. Her gift was a *jinbei* (traditional Japanese summer clothing consisting of a loose top and matching pants) and a fan. On another sheet of stationery, she wrote three Chinese characters that phonetically resemble "Bernstein" and translated them as "Heaven of ten thousand glories." These were the characters she had chosen for him when he first came to Japan in 1961. She wanted to have the characters printed on the *jinbei* but could not find a good artisan to do this. She then explains, "with <u>the warmest welcome</u> from all who will gather united in the prayer, and a feverish, ardent musical PRAYER that you will give, you need to <u>be refreshed afterward.</u> . . . I hope you will like both the *jin-bei* and the fan." Summers in Hiroshima are oppressively hot and humid, and Bernstein could certainly use breezy clothing and a fan. Bernstein cherished traditional Japanese art and artifacts and made a point of shopping for them on every visit. He also had a deep love for words and writing, and even though he did not know the Japanese language, he had made efforts to learn phrases and practiced writing some letters and characters. The thoughtful selection of the gift was typical of Amano.

She went to the concerts alone. She was invited to and attended the reception hosted by the Mayor of Hiroshima on August 5 and listened to the concerts on both the sixth and the seventh. But unlike all of Bernstein's previous visits to Japan, she did not see the maestro in his green room after the performances—security around the event was tight, and she did not insist on gaining special access—or spend any personal time with him. She kept a low profile during Bernstein's five days in the city.

Hashimoto, too, was not always at Bernstein's side throughout the visit, but for completely different reasons. As a member of Bernstein's staff, he had been working behind the scenes for a year leading up to the concert. For more than ten days before Bernstein's arrival, he was busily engaged in meetings with various parties involved in the event and serving as a guide for Margaret Carson—Bernstein's publicist who had encouraged him to accept Sano's proposal for the event—who arrived days before the maestro. During Bernstein's stay in Hiroshima, Hashimoto was needed in one meeting after another in addition to attending to the maestro.

In the summer of 1985, Ozawa, Amano, and Hashimoto—the three Japanese people with whom Bernstein was closest—were all gathered in Hiroshima to share Bernstein's prayer for peace. Yet their roles in the event were quite different: one was an observer, one was an audience member, and one was an organizer. Their respective places in the peace concert were reflective of their evolving relationships with Bernstein. It was also a sign of the complex politics involved in the concert.

* * *

PRESIDENT HARRY TRUMAN'S statement delivered sixteen hours after the bombing of Hiroshima on August 6, 1945 had set the tone for the dominant United States narrative about the atomic bomb. Celebrating the

United States' scientific knowledge and the industrial and financial resources that enabled the nation to win "the greatest scientific gamble in
history," he declared the nation's ability to wreak further destruction on
Japan: "We shall destroy their docks, their factories, and their communications. Let there be no mistake; we shall completely destroy Japan's power
to make war." Not only did the statement imply that the targets of the
bombing were military and industrial, obscuring the civilian casualties,
but it also suggested that the bombing was an act of saving the Japanese
from greater destruction. In the postwar decades, the extent of civilian
sacrifice has been widely acknowledged, and the necessity of dropping
the atomic bomb in bringing Japan's surrender has been much debated.
Yet even as the anxiety of the Atomic Age spread rapidly, the dominant
American historical narrative maintained the idea that the atomic bomb
hastened the end of the war, that it spared many American as well as
Japanese lives, and that it symbolized victory in the "Good War" against
fascism.[6]

The Japanese government was complicit in the American narrative
about the atomic bomb. Even long after the end of the US-led occupation
of Japan, during which the press code suppressed the coverage of the impact of the atomic bomb, Japan's mainstream historical narrative evaded
the question of the moral right of the United States' decision to use the
bomb on cities densely populated by civilians, while framing Japan as the
victim and thus obscuring its role as a colonizer and perpetrator of wartime atrocities and erasing non-Japanese citizens who were also victims
of the bomb.[7] The historical narrative was shaped on the local level as
well. As Hiroshima went through rapid urban renewal and economic recovery in the postwar years, it established its identity as a "city of peace,"
formalized in the 1948 Peace Memorial City Construction Law (Heiwa
Kinen Toshi Kensetsuhō). Through the design of the Peace Memorial
Park and waterfront development, sponsoring of municipal festivals, and
tourism campaigns, the city converted the landscape of death into one of
peace, comfort, and prosperity.[8]

Commemorating the fortieth anniversary of the bombing, the Peace
Memorial Ceremony at eight in the morning on August 6, 1985, brought
out fifty-five thousand attendees, the largest in the history of this event.[9]
Seated near Bernstein were actor Jack Lemmon, who had starred in the
film *The China Syndrome* about cover-ups at a nuclear power plant. Also
present were the Quaker peace activist Barbara Reynolds and journalist
and peace advocate Norman Cousins. With such international guests

at the ceremony, the ceremony was the object of worldwide attention, attracting a large number of major international reporters.

At the ceremony, Prime Minister Yasuhiro Nakasone declared that the nation would "protect the invaluable earth from the tragedies of war, especially the atrocities of nuclear weapons." Buried under this antiwar message was the Japanese government's long-standing position, which he reinforced in his statement at the press conference, that the government was already providing assistance to the survivors through existing laws and that no new legislation was necessary. In protest, in the middle of his speech, eight college students seated near the back raised signs reading "Engo-hō wo seitei seyo,"—Enact the Assistance Act—calling for comprehensive assistance for atomic bomb survivors. Police officers instructed them to take the signs down, and the protest lasted only a minute. But in the center of the seating for the general public, six Hiroshima residents also stood up to wave small black flags in protest.[10] These small but visible acts of resistance were overwhelmed by official containment. According to Akira Kinoshita, a photojournalist who covered Bernstein over many years, the 1985 Hiroshima Peace Ceremony was "infuriatingly bureaucratic in its approach, which kept the general public away," and "the ceremony turned into an officially endorsed commodity and a tool of political conflict."[11]

It is unknown where Ozawa was during the ceremony, but he was probably quite content not to be seated as an official guest.

* * *

THE MUSICIANS AND organizers of Bernstein's concert had to carefully navigate these politics surrounding the commemoration.

Kraut understood the high stakes of the issues and the diverse positions that existed even among those who shared a belief in nuclear disarmament. In a memorandum sent to all parties involved in the Journey for Peace, he noted the importance of being "very careful and absolutely consistent" in public statements made by the tour participants. To reinforce the point, he wrote in all caps: "When the overall press coordinator is with us, we should make coordinated public announcements, BUT BE CAREFUL TO MAKE ANNOUNCEMENTS WHICH MUST BE CONSISTENT AND COORDINATED WITH OVERALL POLICY."[12]

Kraut was not being overly sensitive. Bernstein's Peace Concert was questioned not only by Ozawa but also by those on opposite ends of the political spectrum. Upon learning of the Hiroshima concert, a man named

Lee Fleming Reese in San Diego, California, wrote to Bernstein: "Here is something which you should know before your [sic] proceed with your 'Journey for Peace' to Hiroshima." Reese stated that Japan had built atomic bombs and that the US Joint Chiefs of Staff had ordered the research facilities and equipment in Japan be seized. "The military order (Japanese) to develop atom bombs was for the express purpose of dropping them in mainland United States. It is high time that the public know these now-unclassified facts."[13] Although he did not make any direct comment about the concert, the implication was that Bernstein's performance in the city was a misplaced admission of American guilt and absolution of wartime Japanese atrocities. In response, Kraut wrote a letter thanking Reese for the information and enclosed Bernstein's official statement about the journey. He closed the letter: "We do not travel to Hiroshima as an apology, but rather regretting that the use of the atom bomb was necessary 40 years ago, and praying that the bombs dropped on Japan were the last to be used on the human race."[14]

During Bernstein's visit to Hiroshima, his antinuclear message was not just delivered in the form of music played on the stage. For instance, the program book—which emphasizes the prayer for the victims of the atomic bombing, commitment to peace and nuclear disarmament, and the spirit of international cooperation that the event embodied—opens with two messages from Bernstein. The first speaks of his view of the artistic significance of the tour:

> This journey is an act of prayer, personal and profound. For me, as an American who loves both his country and his planetary neighbours, the significance of this occasion is threefold: first, that we come as an international musical body; second, that this body is composed of young people, master musicians of our future; and third, that our main musical statement, Kaddish, is a prayer for the dead, yet one which literally speaks not of death but of life, of peace, and of sublime peace.[15]

Bernstein explicitly acknowledges his role as a citizen of the nation that used the atomic bomb and was currently engaged in a nuclear arms race, but he also speaks of his concern with the well-being of the planet and humanity as a whole. By emphasizing the international body of talented young musicians, he speaks to the power of music in communicating across borders and generations. And by articulating the meaning of the Kaddish, he expresses both his mourning for the victims and his faith in life and peace from both a Jewish and a universal standpoint. This message is followed by a more focused and emphatic statement of protest against the continuing accumulation of nuclear weapons:

> Our nuclear folly has rendered [war] obsolete, so that it now appears to be something like a bad old habit, a ritualistic, quasi-tribalistic obeisance to the arrogance of excessive nationalism, face-saving, bigotry, xenophobia, and above all, greed. Do you not find something reprehensible, even obscene, about the endless and useless stockpiling of nuclear missiles? Isn't there something radically wrong with nation-states' squandering the major portion of their wealth on military strength at the expense of schools, hospitals, libraries, vital research in medicine and energy—to say nothing of preserving the sheer livability of our planetary environment? Why are we behaving in this suicidal fashion?[16]

Here Bernstein does not bother to hide his anger at the military, political, and economic interests driving the arms race, nor does he shy away from naming the forces behind those interests. The combination of the two sets of messages exemplifies Bernstein's dual role as an artist and an advocate, which made him a particularly effective figure in appealing to the many audiences the event was designed to address: residents of Hiroshima, Japanese citizens, political leaders of the Cold War superpowers and the international community, antinuclear activists, and musicians and artists around the world.

Bernstein's message was also delivered at the press conference on the day of his arrival. In his statement, Bernstein evoked the connection between the atomic bombing of Hiroshima and the Holocaust, while noting that he was "not making a comparison between the perpetrators of the Holocaust and those of the Atom Bomb, except that we <u>are</u> commemorating the 40th anniversary of both." He thus linked the victims of two mass tragedies of the war, while rejecting the moral equivalency between the two acts, and he used the word "perpetrators" in referring to those who used the atomic bomb. As an American Jew delivering a message of peace and disarmament in the midst of the Cold War, Bernstein understood the moral and political complexities of the position from which he spoke.

Bernstein also made a pointed remark about the internal conflicts within Japan's antinuclear movement. In Japan, the antinuclear movement began to show signs of internal division in the 1960s over whether the opposition should be directed at all testing of nuclear and hydrogen bombs by any nation or if it should solely target the United States. The debate divided the organization along party lines, with the Communist Party asserting that the USSR was a peaceful power and should not be targeted for protest. By the 1980s, these divisions were exacerbated as the movement expanded to oppose not only nuclear weapons but also nuclear power and waste management plants, and as grassroots organizations and community-based citizens' movements joined the antinuclear voices that had been led by established organizations.[17] Bernstein took care to learn about what was taking place on the ground: he underlined as he read newspaper articles about the issue and kept the clippings. He ended his message at the press conference:

Please, my dear Japanese friends, this is no time for you to be out of luck [in reference to a quote from Natsume Soseki's novel *Grass Pillow*]. It is a time to join hands, especially here, especially this week, and to be a model of unity for the whole world. As an American, of course, I would be the first to defend free speech and the right to public debate; in fact, I underline{insist} on it. But when we are all gathered for a purpose as noble and necessary as this, we must not weaken our movement by disunity. We cannot afford weakness; the forces arrayed against our cause are too strong. We must first of all commit ourselves, and declare ourselves; then, afterwards, there will be time for arguments involving methodologies, ideologies, economic procedures, and all the rest of our differences. But first we must recognize that basically we underline{have} no difference; we are all here to pray together—to whatever God or spirit or humanistic principle we choose—to pray over those who suffered and fell in Hiroshima, in Nagasaki, in Auschwitz, in Dachau—wherever mankind was murdering itself four decades ago; and to pray with all our hearts that the world can soon understand that murder is murder no matter how official; that war is obsolete, and that there can never again be a winner—only losers, and the losers would be nothing less than the whole world: man, beast and vegetable. This must not be allowed to happen; and we are here to make that promise.[18]

While he urged the Japanese activists to overcome disagreements and unite for peace, he clearly marked himself as an American. By making references to Auschwitz and Dachau, he also implicitly spoke as a Jew. His assertion that "murder is murder no matter how official" implicates the United States and suggests that the nation did not "win" as a result of it, the dominant historical narrative notwithstanding.

Bernstein's public statements in Hiroshima were mixed with exchanges that were personally meaningful to both Bernstein and those whom he encountered. On the day after his arrival, Bernstein visited the Hiroshima Peace Memorial Museum, with Eiji Oue as his guide. Turning his head away from the display of figures running away from the fire, he saw a young boy who had come from Kyushu. "I just impulsively grabbed him and kissed him and said to myself a prayer that this should not happen to him, this beautiful little kid," he said in a television interview afterwards. The boy's mother then gave him a necklace strung of origami cranes symbolizing prayer, which he cherished as "the most precious honor of my visit so far."[19]

Bernstein wore the necklace throughout the remainder of his time in Hiroshima, including the rehearsal that afternoon, where he showed it to the orchestra and spoke of its significance. During the rehearsal, Ozawa made an appearance to give his encouragement to Oue. Bernstein greeted him, and the three maestros bonded through their shared commitment to the cause expressed in different ways.

In the middle of the rehearsal, malfunctioning sprinklers began to spray water all over the hall, forcing the rehearsal to be put on hold. With Kraut and Hashimoto in a meeting and Sano on his way to the airport to meet the arriving ECYO staff, chaos lasted for quite some time. As the young orchestra musicians nervously waited while the hall's staff tried to bring matters under control, Bernstein sat down at the piano and began playing boogie-woogie. The musicians gathered around the piano, some of them jamming on their instruments and others dancing to the music. Not only did the jam session lift the anxious mood and keep everyone entertained until the rehearsal could be resumed, but it also brought the young musicians closer to Bernstein: he was no longer the revered maestro on the podium but a human being with whom they played music and laughed.

It was not only the young musicians but also the maestro himself who cherished the moment. The delay in the rehearsal caused by the accident shifted Bernstein's schedule, whose next item was the mayor's reception.

Both exhausted by the already long day and enjoying his time connecting with the young musicians, he suggested to Kraut that he might skip the reception. It was only with Kraut's stern face and words that Bernstein was persuaded to change into formal wear and hurry to the reception. Clearly Bernstein found more meaning in making music with the young musicians than the official event. After changing into his black-tie attire, he put the origami necklace back on and wore it to the reception.

* * *

BERNSTEIN'S HIROSHIMA PEACE CONCERT on the evening of August 6 and 7 drew full houses at Yūbin Chokin Kaikan Hall and was characterized by a serious and somber but hopeful mood. Of approximately 1,800 seats, 150 were sold at 20,000 yen and the remainder at 3,000 yen (approximately $13 in 1985 rate, $30 in 2018) to make the concert accessible to the general public.[20]

The program displayed a rich and complex array of emotions, ideas, and spirits. It opened with Bernstein conducting Beethoven's *Leonore* Overture no. 3, op. 72b. This overture to the opera *Fidelio* is a gallant work that exudes faith, heroism, and triumph. Bernstein took ample time in the music and used his entire body to lead the orchestra in its march to victory. In leading up to the fast finale, he could hardly contain his joy in the act of music making and his union with the orchestra.

The piece was followed by Oue conducting Tomiko Kojiba's *Hiroshima Requiem*. The piece opens with a distant, high dissonance that crescendos until it is cut off by a sharp, loud snap. A dark, unsettling sonority follows, with brooding lines gradually growing into a frenzy of desperation and pain. An abrupt cut is followed by a solo violin that wanders like a woman searching for her children. The texture thickens again into a longer, clearer theme, which then fades to nothingness, out of which the solo violin reappears. The orchestra re-enters, more subdued but still angst-ridden, searching, yet somewhat resigned, eventually yielding to a small, antique cymbal, as though intoning a Buddhist prayer, and then silence. Oue then conducted Mozart's Violin Concerto no. 5 *Turkish*, a piece filled with a broad, majestic, hopeful air that Mozart wrote when he was nineteen. Bernstein's choice of this piece and Midori as the soloist reflected his awe and faith. Midori—who had made a sensational debut with the New York Philharmonic at age eleven just two years earlier—was a symbol of the extraordinary talent of the new generation that bridged Japan and the United States. She stood with her head down and eyes on the floor during the lively orchestral introduction, but as she made her entrance, the grand substance and maturity of the sound she made with her three-quarter-sized violin was immediately clear. That Bernstein trusted Oue to conduct these two pieces that communicated core messages of the concert in drastically contrasting moods and styles showed that he was one of Bernstein's most important protégés of the new generation. In many ways, Oue was in the place that Ozawa occupied two decades earlier, both learning from Bernstein and carrying the maestro's art and spirit to Japan and the world.

In the second half of the concert, Bernstein performed his own Symphony no. 3 *Kaddish*, with the young African American soprano Barbara Hendricks, speaker Michael Wager, and a chorus consisting of the Wiener Jeunesse-Chor, Kyoto Echo, and the Little Singers of Osaka. Bernstein's desire to perform this piece in Hiroshima revealed his arguments with God and the secular world as well as his faith in and prayer for peace. After the haunting opening, the Kaddish prayer is interrupted by angry bursts of brass and percussion. The "Amen"s of the chorus sound more like a provocation to God rather than a prayer. The speaker's pleading and increasingly angry words, the intense blasts of percussion and brass, and the jagged phrases of the strings wrestle with one another as in a battle. The chorus's "Amen"s are intermixed with jazzy tunes and rhythms, as if mocking the prayer, and they reach a chaotic climax. But as the speaker regains his faith, the phrases played by the orchestra gradually morph into a harmonious affirmation of hope. As the speaker addresses God and asks to "believe," he is joined by the beautiful, broad melody of the orchestra and the children's chorus. The uncertain, questioning motive of the opening resolves in a soaring unity of the voices and instruments.[21] Bernstein's buoyant conducting exuded his faith and prayer, and his facial and physical expressions as he wiped his sweat and tears after the last note conveyed the heart and soul he put into the performance.

The audience responded with loud shouts of bravo. As always, even after a physically demanding performance, Bernstein generously spent time autographing, shaking hands, and speaking with fans. Moved and exhilarated by the performance, he stayed up late into the night, socializing with the young musicians of the orchestra who wanted to spend more time with him. Back in his hotel room, he asked Hashimoto to go through all the gifts he received from his fans and to translate the letters. He instructed Hashimoto to carefully store the letters he wanted to reply to and the gifts he wanted to write thank-you letters for.

The concert was widely covered in local and national media. *Yomiuri Shimbun*, the Japanese newspaper with the largest circulation, devoted five columns to the concert, commenting on the youthful energy of the performers and concluding: "The early-morning mini performance and the big evening concert differed in style and form, but all participants and attendants communicated across the boundaries of nation, ethnicity, region, age, and gender, reaffirming the meaning of living in peace."[22]

* * *

THE JOURNEY FOR Peace affirmed the participants' love, faith, and prayer, both on and off the concert stage. The prayer for peace, faith in humanity, and love for music and for Bernstein took many forms. Ozawa, Amano, and Hashimoto each had reached a new stage of their relationship with Bernstein and had found new ways of expressing their love and dedication to the maestro.

By choosing not to be part of the Peace Concert, Ozawa passed on Bernstein's teaching and love in his own way. He watched and listened to his beloved mentor deliver his prayer for peace to the country he had first introduced him to twenty-four years earlier. He expressed his own commitment to peace through the chorus of people who share a love of music. And he enabled the emerging artist Eiji Oue to deliver the world's prayer to his hometown.

Amano's low profile during Bernstein's Hiroshima visit, too, was an expression of her respect and love. She understood not only the maestro's packed schedule but also that the mission of the journey transcended personal relationships. She conveyed her warm welcome and true embrace of Bernstein as she had always done, but she showed her love and support precisely by keeping her distance and staying true to her place as his most dedicated fan.

For Hashimoto, the summer in Hiroshima was the climax of the new chapter in his relationship with Bernstein. Trusted with a key role in a project that was artistically, philosophically, and morally precious to Bernstein, Hashimoto worked to realize the maestro's goals. Unlike the time he spent with Bernstein in Munich, he was not always at the maestro's side. But he was now expressing his love for Bernstein by serving the great artist, in more ways than he had ever imagined.

After five extremely demanding days, Bernstein left Japan for Budapest, the next destination of the Journey for Peace.

16

An Early Autumn

ON HIS BIRTHDAY, August 25, Bernstein was in Tel Aviv for a rehearsal for his forthcoming Japan tour with the Israel Philharmonic Orchestra (IPO). Hashimoto sent a telex to his hotel so that he would receive the greeting on his actual birthday.[1] As an Amberson representative, he now had Bernstein's detailed itinerary and no longer had to send letters to Bernstein's home in New York. He could send letters, telexes, or telegrams while Bernstein was on the road and could also call Bernstein at his hotel when he wanted to speak to him.

Concurrent with the Hiroshima Peace Concert, Hashimoto was assisting in preparations for the IPO tour, which included concerts in Osaka, Nagoya, Matsudo, and Tokyo. The IPO was the orchestra that Hashimoto saw Bernstein conduct on his first trip to Munich in 1979, so it was especially meaningful for him to be able to assist with its tour in Japan. The tour was arranged by the Japan Performing Arts Foundation, which brought the world's best opera companies, orchestras, and maestros to Japan under the helm of the powerful impresario Tadatsugu Sasaki. Japan's classical music fans enthusiastically anticipated Bernstein's arrival with the IPO: aside from the Hiroshima Peace Concert with the ECYO, this was Bernstein's first performance in Japan with an orchestra other than the New York Philharmonic.

Because of the Japan Performing Arts Foundation (NBS) sponsorship, the tour involved fewer tasks for Hashimoto compared to the Hiroshima concert, which had to be organized from the ground up. Yet he served an important function as a liaison between NBS and Amberson on matters including scheduling, programming, transportation, and video recording. The Jewish Sabbath added complications to scheduling rehearsals and performances, and miscommunication—leading to program changes after the tickets had already gone on sale—caused difficult negotiations between Sasaki and Kraut. Furthermore, because Hashimoto was brought in after NBS and Amberson had already reached a basic agreement and NBS had never had an intermediary in negotiating with artist organizations, Hashimoto was put in a somewhat awkward position.[2] Yet he was evidently tactful and persuasive in handling the complex negotiations: he successfully convinced Sasaki to change the programs so that one was a concert of Mahler's Symphony no. 9 and the other was Bernstein's *Halil*, "Symphonic Dances" from *West Side Story*, and Brahms's Symphony no. 1.

Bernstein was met by Hashimoto at the Osaka airport on August 31. Returning to Japan only three weeks after the Hiroshima Peace Concert, Bernstein knew that there were no plans for him to come back to the country for the foreseeable future. He was thus looking forward to enjoying some personal time he did not have on the previous whirlwind trip.

The first task that Bernstein gave Hashimoto upon arrival was to send a birthday telex to Seiji Ozawa. Bernstein expressed his unwavering respect, support, and love for his most cherished Japanese protégé, colleague, and friend, who had introduced him to the country. Hashimoto, now serving as the messenger from one maestro to the other, sent the message: "Dear Seiji, This day in your country, I think of you with deep feelings of love and hope and with prayers for a long and healthy life. Lenny."[3]

The subsequent days Bernstein and Hashimoto spent together were manifestations of their ripening relationship: private time alone and social time with others, sharing Bernstein's appreciation and love for Japan. After the rehearsal and press conference, the two drove to Kyoto and stayed at Tawaraya Inn, a generations-old traditional inn run by Y. Ernest Satow, a dear friend of Bernstein and Amano from her days at the CIE library. They also visited Satow's private residence and the Tofukuji Temple. In Osaka, they saw a noh performance, which Bernstein had come to love over the years. In Tokyo, they went to a kabuki performance. While dining at a trendy restaurant and bar in the Roppongi district, Bernstein enjoyed an unexpected reunion with Kyoko Edo, a pianist and Ozawa's ex-wife. They also went antique shopping in the Kanda district to look for souvenirs for Bernstein's family. On a free evening, Bernstein hosted a private party in his hotel suite, to which Hashimoto invited some of his own friends.

In addition to attending to the maestro, Hashimoto was also responsible for assisting his staff and company. Thus, his days were busy with meetings with Kraut, serving as a tour guide for Bernstein's assistant Phillip Allen and flautist Ransom Wilson (who played a solo in *Halil*), and attending to others' needs as they arose. This trip must have brought Hashimoto the utmost fulfillment, embracing Bernstein's personal love as well as serving an important professional role.

* * *

DURING THE CONCERTS in Osaka and Nagoya, the IPO received a threat from an organization in support of Palestinians. The proximity of Hotel Okura, where Bernstein had usually stayed on previous trips to Tokyo, to the US Embassy led to a last-minute change in accommodation to the Century Hyatt Hotel in Shinjuku. On the day of the concert at NHK Hall, some protesters made speeches in front of the hall criticizing Bernstein's support of Israel.[4]

Although these protests were a reminder of the volatile conflict in the Middle East and its international repercussions, ongoing as the performances took place, the music Bernstein and the IPO delivered to Japanese audiences clearly spoke across those borders. The concerts, especially the performance of Mahler's Symphony no. 9, became legendary. According to a critic, the intensity and density of the music filled the large NHK Hall, and after the last note faded, the audience—often prone to loud ovations even before the conductor's hands were completely lowered—sat in utter silence for a very long time, overcome by emotion.[5] Bernstein told an interviewer that it was "the best Mahler he had ever heard." This wording shows that he saw himself as not a conductor on the podium directing the orchestra but a servant of music and conduit conveying the composer's intentions. Even as he had been in the midst of recording the Mahler cycle with several European orchestras, he described the concert as "an unbelievable performance he had never experienced before."[6]

The *Japan Times* devoted an unusually large amount of space to its review of the September 8 concert, which, according to the reviewer, received "from a capacity audience the biggest and most extended ovations accorded any previous orchestral event I can recall in this city." The reviewer described Bernstein's warm advocacy for the composer and his profound understanding of every detail of the work, which was

> constantly demonstrated in the animating rhythm adopted with each variation of harmony or counterpoint, and in the expressive intensity brought to bear in those contrasting moments in the music's swift changes of mood and atmosphere. Mahler's scoring can never have sounded more subtly (and precisely) imagined. Each sudden

piano in the strings told, so did every horn sforzando, each harp harmonic, each sarcastic nudge and lurch in the Rondo-burleske.

The glowing review concluded with a description of the final movement, in which "human yearnings, earthly strivings and attachments, passions and emotions, evanescence of all desires and final resignation are sublimated in the rapt music of this wonderful Adagio—Mahler's vision of our floating world."[7] Hidekazu Yoshida, Japan's most influential music critic at the time, published a long, effervescent review in *Asahi Shimbun*, describing it as "not a fine performance but rather a great performance, the sort that grants its audience an invaluable enlightenment." He wrote: "The biggest factor that made this a great performance that will remain in historical memory is that Bernstein's approach succeeded in elevating the wondrous spirit inherent in this work to something on the 'spiritual' level. . . . Music is a prayer, a ritual of prayer—that is the ultimate, finest message of this work. Music, in its most primitive form, was a prayer, and in times of crisis music still has the power to serve as prayer. This performance demonstrated this. At times weeping helplessly, at other times sobbing, and yet at other times voicelessly pleading to a corner of the heaven with arms raised, Bernstein shows that there remains a path for a conductor to return to his primordial role as the master of a ritual."[8]

But more than any professional critic, Amano's letter captured the miracle of the performance. Too excited to sleep after attending the Osaka concert, she wrote at 2:30 a.m. on hotel stationery. She was so overwhelmed that she accidentally dated the letter a month ahead.

> Being so touched and excited by your heartbreakingly beautiful and deep rendition of Mahler's 9th, I am unable to sleep and took my pen willing to tell you what I meant to express by words right after the concert in your private room backstage. Lenny, it was really SOMETHING beautiful, touching, innerly rich and quiet at the same time, SOMETHING which goes far beyond my poor and "banal" vocabulary. Thank you so much for what you gave us tonight! I really wanted to tell you so directly but I knew that even after the performance you were still so much involved in the spirit of Mahler's music that I couldn't speak to you, it was a pity to speak to you, it was not possible. . . . To be frank, Lenny, although I adored your former Mahler 9th, I should confess that now,

I much prefer your new rendition of the same symphony. I felt something like a confession of all your feelings about LIFE and LOVE and DEATH, about the sadness and depth of our human lives. For me it was a real PRAYER far beyond the so-called "religion," a sincere and touching CONFESSION of all your sorrows and desires and everything! For me, who is getting older day by day with experiences of all kinds up to now, I quite agree with a heartbreaking understanding of your feelings, if I may say so. This performance will sound forever in my soul and heart, giving me courage and resignation at the same time. And besides I will never forget the sight of my beloved and most brilliant conductor, unable to turn toward the audience immediately after the end of the performance. I knew that you were crying and so I was, and not only me, Lenny, many persons around me, young and old, were apparently sobbing or just wiping their tears in a very Japanese way. Lenny, did you notice the big difference or "progress" on the part of the audience? The last time, many years ago, an enthusiastic applause started even before your baton was quiet and "absolutely down." The applause arose when your both hands were still some ten centimeters from your body! I couldn't forgive that; even my children were upset about it. "Why, but why?" they asked me. . . . And Mr. Oga of CBS Sony told me backstage that he was shocked and frightened. "I hope," said he, "that Lenny won't be angry about the fact!" Yesterday was quite different. The full audience was listening, even without breathing devotedly, and in a communion with you and the orchestra, waiting until the very end, and even when it <u>came</u>, there was a PAUSE, and then the applause started hesitating at first and then bursting most enthusiastically! Thank you so much for what you gave us![9]

Amano's understanding of what Bernstein brought to Mahler's music is deeply moving in itself. Her knowledge of what Bernstein had gone through in recent years, layered with her own experience of "life and love and depth" and "the sadness and depth of our human lives" must have made her particularly sensitive to what he communicated through Mahler's music.

Yet every sign of the audience response shows that one did not have to be personally acquainted with Bernstein to feel the immense power of the performance and grasp his message. One of the letters given by a fan after the concert, which he asked Hashimoto to translate for him and store, was by a college student who enclosed an *orizuru*, a paper crane.

> Dear Mr. Leonard Bernstein who loves peace,
>
> I major in pharmacology at the university and play the oboe in the university orchestra. I often listen to your recordings and am always moved from the bottom of my heart.
>
> Please come to Japan again soon.
>
> Enclosed item is called *orizuru*. In Japan, we believe that when we fold one thousand cranes any wish would come true. You probably saw them in Hiroshima. I fold one every day and pray. This is the one I made today, on September 5. While I folded this crane, I prayed for your health. As you are in an unaccustomed land of Japan, please do take good take care of your health.
>
> From one of your dedicated fans,
> Toshiki Takagi[10]

His address indicates that he must have traveled from Nagano to Nagoya—at least three or four hours by train—to listen to Bernstein's performance. Another fan, an elderly gentleman who came to the Tokyo concert, presented Bernstein with a fan on which, like Amano, he had written Chinese characters phonetically resembling Bernstein's name. Bernstein was deeply touched as Hashimoto explained the meanings of the characters: for "Leonard," the man wrote the characters signifying "beautiful/graceful, sound/chirp, anger," and for the last name he used the two characters for "amber." Although the Japanese word for "amber" does not sound anything like "Bernstein," he clearly knew the German origin of the name Bernstein, which was the namesake for Amberson. These letters and gifts from fans—who never expected to have any personal contact with Bernstein but merely wished to express their admiration and appreciation for his music—show that the Japanese listeners, and perhaps others around the world, felt a personal connection to Bernstein's music, heard his prayers, and shared his faith as well as his anguish.

* * *

THE CENTRALITY OF Hashimoto in Bernstein's summer of 1985 is evidenced not only in business correspondence but also in Bernstein's personal writing. A rare example of Bernstein's direct reference to Hashimoto is dated September 6, 1985. On this day, Bernstein composed three haikus dedicated to Hashimoto:

Haikunihiko;

Weeping cherry bough
Fragile
Tender
Strong as God

Weeping cherry bough
Bowed
Crabapple upright
White
Sunning together

Cherry bent, and mauve.
Apples straight, and white.
Together grafted
Perfectly mated
Ten days every spring.
Once a storm broke—
—Which one? [11]

Bernstein must have composed these poems when he was alone in his hotel room to reflect his appreciation for Hashimoto's work and their love. He wrote them on a notepad in longhand, noting the number of syllables next to each poem, and signed his full name and dated it at the bottom. On the top left corner of the Xerox copy that remains in the archive, Bernstein wrote in red pencil, "For Kunihiko H, 3 Haikus." Bernstein clearly wished to make known the authorship and dedication of the poems.

The three poems—related to each other in a fashion not unlike Japanese *renga*—reveal Bernstein's tender love for, and acute understanding of, Hashimoto. Perhaps in the earlier phase of their relationship Hashimoto came across more as "fragile" and "tender," but now Bernstein sees him also as "strong as God." Perhaps their brief but deeply meaningful time together in Japan made Bernstein see himself as the straight, upright, white apple tree that was "together grafted, perfectly mated" with Hashimoto's weeping, bent cherry for "ten days every spring." But the ending of the poem reveals Bernstein's vulnerable side. With his frequent physical ailments and demanding travel and performance schedule, Bernstein must have been more aware of his own age and mortality as well as Hashimoto's youthful energy. The poem gives a glimpse of Bernstein's deepening affection and appreciation for Hashimoto, whom he not only loved but also came to depend on.

On the very last day of the IPO tour, Bernstein presented Hashimoto with a *shikishi*, a square board made of handmade paper edged with a strip of gold paper on which people write messages and autographs, typically given at farewell parties. He must have received a number of *shikishis* from fans on his previous tours and perhaps learned of its meaning from Ozawa or Amano. On it, he wrote in large, assured handwriting:

For Kunihiko Hashimoto with eternal love, Lenny 14 IX 85.[12]

The changing dynamic in the two men's relationship comes across in Hashimoto's own writing as well. Although Hashimoto's profound love for Bernstein never changed, having a professional role in Bernstein's work did alter the nature of their interactions. After Bernstein's two consecutive trips to Japan, he wrote with a renewed sense of yearning and passion.

Dearest Lenny,

Also the day after you left Japan, we have weeping weather in Tokyo. It is not showering; it continues quietly, solemnly without any sound. The grey sky made a hole in my heart. The hole is the same color—grey, and vacant without any thoughts, just weeping quietly.

In return for passing passionate summer heat, early autumn has just arrived with rain and tomorrow's weather must be weeping again. However, I know that autumn is beautiful. "C'est deuxieme printemps."

After these weeping days, it is sure that high blue sky will come back.

While looking up the beautiful sky, I will remember our memories, imagine of you, think about you.

Love,
Kuny[13]

A week later he followed with a five-page letter overflowing with emotional intensity:

> How cruel hard it is to live without you!
>
> When you said how you could live the rest of your life without me, I thought that you could do it, and I believed that I could live without you. Because I had survived before without you for four years since we had seen each other in Munich for Tristan. But this time is not the same as that time. When I came back from Munich to Tokyo, for 18 hours on the airplane I remembered every moment which we had in Munich. And while remembering, I tried to prepare for the life without you. But this time, suddenly the last day came, and you left me in Japan. Without any preparation, my lonely life has come. It is like a sandglass after sands have fallen down, and I am an empty sandglass now.
>
> I was very busy this time, having meetings, shopping, being a guide and so on. I regret that I could not guide Phillip, Ransom, and you to enough nice places. We were too busy to have free time in Tokyo.
>
> In Munich, I did not need to care about anything, I cared for only you. I was with you every moment there. But in Japan, I had to care about so many things. Japanese language and English made me confused sometimes, and waiting on Japanese people made me nervous. I forgot to count the date because of our too busy schedule, and the day when you left Japan came. Even after you left, I had no time to turn our days around, and I had to have dinner with Mr. Hiro and four other persons of Japan about stuff at the airport.
>
> Now I hardly try to prepare to live without you day by day. I can't take off the earphone of my Walkman listening to your Mahler 9th with Berlin Philharmonic Orchestra again and again. I am afraid of being alone. I remember that you said I was a serious person. I don't think so, but it is for sure that I am serious in loving you. . . .
>
> I wonder when I can turn the sandglass upside down.[14]

Spending time with Bernstein after years of having been apart intensified rather than eased Hashimoto's yearning. The letter shows that his new professional role brought a far greater pleasure and a stronger connection with Bernstein, as well as demands that kept him away from Bernstein. Most importantly, it reveals the transformation of Hashimoto's love for and relationship with Bernstein into something much greater than personal romance.

Just as Bernstein channeled Mahler to elevate a musical performance to a plane of spirituality and prayer, through his work for the maestro Hashimoto put his love into service for a greater being and purpose. Just like the early autumn that came to Japan after Bernstein's departure, their relationship too matured and bore a new, deeper color.

PART III

17

The World According to the Maestro

BERNSTEIN'S PERFORMANCES IN Japan in the summer of 1985 were an index of how he envisioned his role in the world at this mature stage of his life and career.

Organizations globally recognized Bernstein with their highest accolades during this period. Among the honors he was awarded in the mid-1980s were honorary memberships in the Guildhall School of Music in London, New York Philharmonic, Royal Academy of Music in London, and Vienna Philharmonic, and an honorary office as the president of the London Symphony Orchestra and laureate conductor of the Israel Philharmonic Orchestra. For his artistic achievements, he received a Gold Medal from the American Academy of Arts and Letters and an Emmy Award for outstanding individual achievement. His accomplishments and contributions were also honored by civic and national awards beyond the United States. He received the title of *commandeur* in France's Legion of Honor, West Germany's Commander's Cross of the Order of Merit, the Grand Order of Merit of the Italian Republic, and civic awards from Vienna, Schleswig-Holstein, and Venice. He had clearly become a maestro respected and admired by the world.

Indeed, he had achieved immense success in more areas than any other musician of his generation: composition for Broadway and for the classical stage, conducting the world's best orchestras, producing hundreds of notable recordings, and communicating to the wide public about the power of music. He also served as a forceful advocate for a number of causes such as human rights, nuclear disarmament, and AIDS research.

At the same time, Bernstein had experienced his share of frustrations and disappointments. Despite his love of the operatic form, his *Candide* and *A Quiet Place* did not achieve a level of critical or commercial success that matched his artistic investment. Even as he was recognized as one of the world's top conductors, he did not have the opportunity to conduct as many operas as he would have liked. Changes in the recording industry were posing increasing challenges for classical recordings, even those conducted by Bernstein.

The country and the world in which he lived also brought mounting frustration and fury for Bernstein. The Reagan administration and the rise of the New Right undermined the rights of minorities, threatened the social safety net, exacerbated divisions and inequalities, and challenged freedom of speech while failing to address urgent issues such as the AIDS epidemic. Cold War rhetoric was mobilized for the growing arms race, which portended catastrophic consequences.

Amidst these personal, professional, national, and global concerns, Bernstein—now in his late sixties, increasingly aware of his mortality yet afraid to contemplate it—looked ahead at what he wanted to accomplish in whatever time he had left. He had neither a professional nor financial need to take on projects for which he did not have genuine passion. Rather, he needed to be vigilant in his focus so as to secure time and energy for what he cared most about.

Bernstein's activities in the mid-1980s illustrate a clarity about what was most important to him artistically and professionally. The projects he signed on to during this period also indicate his renewed priorities and commitments. Substantial new works like *Jubilee Games* for orchestra and baritone solo (1986, revised in 1988) and *Arias and Barcarolles* (1988) demonstrated his continued productivity and new ideas as a composer. He rededicated himself as a recording artist with European labels, especially the Mahler cycle produced by Deutsche Grammophon.

Among Bernstein's most significant enterprise during this period was the 1985 release of the *West Side Story* recording with Deutsche Grammophon. This was the first time he conducted the work that made Bernstein a household name worldwide. Almost three decades after its first production, this quintessentially American musical was being recorded by a German company, with opera singers including New Zealander soprano Kiri Te Kanawa as the Puerto Rican heroine and Spanish tenor José Carreras as the American hero. This symbolized the global reach of Bernstein's work and its enduring popularity and relevance. It also showed that, despite Deutsche Grammophon's strategy of marketing Bernstein as an intellectual deeply rooted in the European artistic tradition, this popular American work was still at the core of his stardom.

The documentary film of the recording session, *The Making of West Side Story*, portrays Bernstein's joy in revisiting the work and conducting it himself.[1] Rehearsing with the singers in his apartment, he says that he had studied the score—for the first time, since he had never conducted the work himself before—every day and night for ten days. To the female singers who look at him in awe and adoration, he declares excitedly, "I think it's *funky*! I can't get over how *funky* this piece is!"

The film shows that he undertook this project with a pickup orchestra with the same seriousness as when he recorded Beethoven, Brahms, and Mahler with the New York Philharmonic or the Vienna Philharmonic. The viewer sees that he expected and demanded the very best from the singers, orchestra, and recording engineers. It is most evident when he shows overt frustration with Carreras, who had difficulties with elocution and rhythm and at one point storms out of the studio in humiliation and exasperation. Bernstein is honest about the physical and mental toll the recording has on him: after a full day of recording, he speaks to the camera and refers to himself as "a tired, aging maestro"; at a press conference during the recording, he talks about how exhausting it is to listen to many takes repeatedly. But most of all, the film reveals the unfading originality of Bernstein's music, which thrills the musicians and the audiences alike, and his own pride in the composition.

Although in the show the song "Somewhere" is not sung by Maria's character, Bernstein became so enamored of Te Kanawa during the recording session that they made a take of her rendition of the song (it was replaced by Marilyn Horne's singing in the final recording). Both for Bernstein at this particular juncture in his life and for the world of the mid-1980s, the song carried renewed meaning and weight:

> *There's a time for us,*
> *Some day a time for us*
> *Time together with time to spare*
> *Time to look, time to care*
> *Some day*
> *Somewhere*
> *We'll find a new way of living*
> *We'll find a way of forgiving*
> *Somewhere.*

This recording of *West Side Story* turned out to be one of the best-selling releases in Deutsche Grammophon's history, earning the Gold and Platinum Award in England and the Netherlands, respectively.[2] By the end of the decade, the benefit of having Bernstein on Deutsche Grammophon's catalog was fully evident to the company. In 1989 the company offered a renewal of an exclusive five-year contract with generous terms, guaranteeing production of a minimum of fifty CDs (averaging ten CDs per year), an advance of $40,000 for non-copyright-protected symphonic works and concertos, and $20,000 for works under copyright.[3]

Along with his continued commitments as a composer and a conductor, Bernstein decided to prioritize education as his mission during the late period of his career. He had always loved working with young musicians and had done so in various capacities. He was particularly invested in summer music festivals as an educational setting. Bernstein himself had been trained at Tanglewood as a young conductor by Serge Koussevitzky in 1940 and considered the experience instrumental to his musical and professional growth. Carrying on his mentor's legacy, he dedicated summer after summer to working with young musicians in this immersive and intimate educational environment. Tanglewood was where he worked with Seiji Ozawa, to whom he later passed the festival's baton; Ozawa later brought Eiji Oue to Tanglewood and introduced him to Bernstein. Tanglewood was thus an indispensable site where the world's leading conductors were trained through generations of mentoring, where young orchestra musicians studied with the world's best conductors and instrumentalists. Wishing to spread the spirit of Tanglewood to other parts of the globe, in 1987 Bernstein founded the Orchestral Academy of the Schleswig-Holstein Music Festival in the north of Germany. The young Japanese conductor Yutaka Sado, who also studied with Ozawa at Tanglewood in 1987, attended Schleswig-Holstein and became one of Bernstein's beloved pupils.

The documentary film *Leonard Bernstein: Teachers and Teaching*, produced in 1988, begins with him discussing how teaching and learning are one and the same: "When I teach I learn, and when I learn, I teach."[4] The film gives an intimate portrait of the maestro through his commentaries on the influential teachers he studied with, such as Isabella Vengerova, Fritz Reiner, Dimitri Mitropoulos, Serge Koussevitzky, and Aaron Copland. It captures him working with young musicians at Tanglewood and Schleswig-Holstein. His own protégés, including Seiji

Ozawa and Michael Tilson Thomas, speak about Bernstein as a teacher who was at once rigorous, demanding, warm, and compassionate. Most importantly, the film communicates Bernstein's passion for teaching and sharing the joy of music by working with the next generation.

*   *   *

WHILE BERNSTEIN THUS renewed his artistic energy and dedication to teaching, he also used his visibility and influence in his battle with the US government. Enraged by the government's ineptitude and unwillingness to address the AIDS crisis as the decade wore on, he took on leadership roles in a number of musical events for the cause. As a member of the organization's national council, Bernstein helped plan and performed in a benefit for the American Foundation for AIDS Research held at the Public Theatre in December 1986.[5] The following year, he and other leaders of the classical music world organized Music for Life, a benefit concert for the Gay Men's Health Crisis (GMHC)—the largest private agency formed to deal with the AIDS epidemic—held at Carnegie Hall on November 8.[6] With an audience that looked like New York's who's who, the event raised $1.7 million, its success owing considerably to Bernstein's participation.[7] His fame and networks enabled him to conceive and realize genre-crossing events that generated attention from a wide public. In 1988, Bernstein organized and performed in another Carnegie Hall gala event in honor of Mathilde Krim, the cofounder of the American Foundation for AIDS Research, which raised $2.5 million.[8] The following year, he joined his three children and other artists in Children Will Listen, a Carnegie Hall benefit concert for the education and care of children affected by AIDS and their families. At these concerts, Bernstein and his three children together performed a song he co-wrote with Jamie.[9]

His defiance of the US government took on another phase in November 1989, when he received notification that President Bush was awarding him the National Medal for the Arts.[10] The notification took place shortly after the National Endowment for the Arts (NEA) announced that it was withdrawing its sponsorship of the show *Witnesses: Against Our Vanishing* at Artists' Space, a nonprofit gallery in New York. The NEA had awarded the gallery a ten-thousand-dollar grant but withdrew it on the grounds that the show, which dealt with the theme of AIDS, included images of homosexual acts and that the exhibit catalog had text criticizing public figures such as California congressman William E. Dannemeyer and North Carolina senator Jesse Helms, who had led the campaign against government sponsorship of arts they considered obscene. This decision followed the controversy over the NEA's sponsorship of exhibitions of works by Robert Mapplethorpe and Andres Serrano that some critics characterized as sacrilegious and obscene. These instances crystallized the culture warriors' vicious politicization of the debates over the government's role in the arts.[11]

President Bush's seemingly benign invitation led to one of Bernstein's most well-known and influential actions: he rejected the award. In a concise but pointedly worded letter to the president and the first lady, Bernstein wrote:

Thank you very much for your invitation to lunch with you at the White House next Friday in honor of the recipients of the National Medal of Arts. I would have liked to share in the privilege of saluting those artists and patrons, but in the present climate I find I must decline.

I cannot risk that coming to Washington to be officially honored during your administration might imply that I am an "official" artist, content to collect my medal in kind and gentle silence while hoping for less stifling days ahead.[12]

Despite his many years of working with various institutions of the US government, Bernstein refused to be labeled an "official" artist, and "kind and gentle silence" was the opposite of what he wrote and performed. He was replaced by pianist Vladimir Horowitz—who died on November 5 and thus was awarded posthumously—on the list of honorees, which included dancer Katherine Dunham, author John Updike, and trumpeter Dizzy Gillespie.

Bernstein's rejection drew a great deal of media attention, and on November 16 the NEA reversed its decision and returned the grant to Artists' Space. The NEA's reversal showed Bernstein's political and moral influence in American society. A number of people wrote to Bernstein to praise his principled stance against government censorship and prejudice about issues of sexuality and people with AIDS.[13]

Despite the settlement of the immediate issue of the funding for Artists' Space, Bernstein was upset enough by the controversy to sketch a song titled "The NEA Forever March" on November 22, 1989. The lyrics read:

Ev-'ryone got a medal but Bernstein
The President gave twelve medals
Not to Bernstein
Well, actually, there showed up only ten to toast,
'cause one of the dozen couldn't make it,
and the other was just a ghost.
But ten of twelve is better than most,
And the President was a very lovely host.
So ev-'ryone had a great time but Bernstein.
The Lord be praised![14]

The cheeky waltz in C major—Bernstein wrote in "tempo di valse (*leggiero*)" and "*grazioso*" (graceful, elegant) in the score—satirizing the event expresses his anger and refusal to remain silent.

* * *

AS BERNSTEIN FOUGHT the parochialism of American politics, political and social transformations around the world were unsettling the Cold War global order.

President Richard Nixon's visit to the People's Republic of China in 1972 stunned the world. The Cultural Revolution came to a close in 1976, and China appeared to be moving toward political democratization and opening its doors to the West. In 1973, the Philadelphia Orchestra became the first American orchestra to perform in China. With the normalization of US-China relations in 1979, both the Chinese government and American artists and organizations eagerly explored cultural exchanges. Seiji Ozawa—who was born in Shenyang, China, in 1935—led the Boston Symphony Orchestra (BSO) on its tour of China that spring, during which he conducted a joint concert of the BSO and the Central Philharmonic Orchestra of China.

The most famous American musician to visit China during this period was the violinist Isaac Stern, whose tour was depicted in the documentary *From Mao to Mozart*. The film traced the painful history of persecution of musicians during the Cultural Revolution and its consequences for the nation's musical education and culture. At the same time, it also displayed the great talent among the nation's young musicians, the eagerness with which they absorbed Western music, and the discipline with which they studied it. It signaled the country's enormous potential as both a producer and consumer of classical music.

Although Bernstein had already made six trips to Japan and had also performed in South Korea during the 1979 tour with the New York Philharmonic, he had not yet been to China and had a growing desire to do so. He was already a revered maestro in China as in other parts of the world. The effort to bring a production of *West Side Story* to China had failed; in October 1980 the Chinese Ministry of Culture officially invited Bernstein, but the visit did not materialize.[15] Yet the interest in Bernstein's music was clearly growing in China, among the general public, musicians, and music students. The Central Conservatory of Music in Beijing hosted a seminar to study Bernstein's works, giving central attention to *The Unanswered Question*, a book consisting of his lectures given at Harvard.

In the mid-1980s, Bernstein and the Amberson staff began exploring the possibility for a China tour, with the projected goal of the summer of 1990.

18

Turning Point

AFTER THE INTENSE summer of 1985 when Hashimoto poured all of his intellectual, administrative, and physical energy into serving Bernstein's art, his work as Amberson's Japan representative entered a lull. Although Bernstein's ever-growing Japanese fan base was hoping for the maestro's return—they particularly wished to see him conduct the Vienna Philharmonic Orchestra—the schedule given to Hashimoto did not show any plans for a future Japan tour. The schedule indicated tentative plans for a China tour with the London Symphony Orchestra in the summer of 1990, but it was unclear whether Japan would be part of this itinerary. Thus, Hashimoto was brought in only when there were some projects or issues that needed to be handled. He returned to the life focused on his own work as an actor, writer, and editor.

Through the company that he ran, he had numerous writing assignments for various magazines on topics such as travel and theater. This frequently took him to cities and resorts around the world. His correspondence between the winter of 1985 and 1987 reflects his new life. In December 1985, he writes poetically and poignantly:

Dearest Lenny,

This autumn, I was too busy to have a chance to walk around the park while looking at beautiful Japanese maple trees with flaming red leaves. And now, quickly cold winter has come. In spite of coldness, we have a very clear blue sky every day in Tokyo. So at night time the moon and stars are shining like a gem, and during the daytime, this beautiful pure clearness gives me the look of New York and you. It gives me a hallucination—that I have a wing and can fly to you.

I will come to New York. I will be there from Jan 2 through Jan 9. Maybe this clear sky made me decide to fly to New York.

I hope to see you, even if it's only talking by phone.

With love,
Kuny[1]

Although the purpose of his trip was to write reviews of Broadway musicals for an entertainment guide, the prospect of going to the city so strongly identified with Bernstein gave him a vision of New York and Bernstein in Tokyo's clear winter sky. He knew that Bernstein was spending the holidays in Fairfield, so he was sober about his prospects but nonetheless hoped to see him.

By then a trusted member of Bernstein's inner circle, Hashimoto stayed at Kraut's apartment near Lincoln Center. Amberson staff helped him secure the best seats for musicals for which it was impossible to get tickets through regular channels. He did see Bernstein, albeit briefly, in Fairfield. He was clearly in a very different place from when he first met Bernstein six years earlier: no longer an avid amateur lover of the performing arts and a dedicated fan of Bernstein, he was himself part of the performing arts world as an actor and a critic; he was part of Bernstein's business and a close colleague and friend of his executive staff; and he was a family friend of the Bernsteins.

Two months after this New York visit, he writes:

Dearest Lenny,

Although I have not written you for two months, it is not a fact that I forgot you. Rather I think of you more and more now.

Although you have not received any letters from me, it is not a fact that I found somebody instead of you. Rather I can hardly endure my lonely life now.

When you came to Japan last time, you asked me why I had not told you about my friend from New Zealand. That time I could not answer clearly, I remember. And I think I said, "You are very special for me, and if I think about you, he is not a serious passion for me . . ." It is still true now. You are very very special. But since that time, I decided that I would tell you about anybody I had as a boy-friend. However, I didn't tell you, because I did not have anybody. I am alone, I can say that I am living with our wonderful memories. When I visited New York last time, although I saw you only two times, that is one of our beautiful memories, too. I don't want to look back at past things. But with these beautiful memories, and times that we shared, I would like to have a hope to see you again in a future. Yes, indeed, I am living to see you again.

With love,
Kuny[2]

His declaration of love for Bernstein echoes the passion of his earlier correspondence, but the letter also displays the evolution of his life and love. The letter makes it clear that during Bernstein's visit to Japan he introduced him to his "friend from New Zealand." But when Bernstein asked why he had not told him about this new friend, he apparently struggled to find words to explain. Bernstein's question pushed him to reflect on the meanings of the men and relationships in his life. He then came to a clear conclusion: no man whom he had been with was any-where near as special as Bernstein was for him. Having introduced the friend to Bernstein suggests his seriousness about the relationship, yet he is firm that his feelings were of an entirely different sort than his love for Bernstein.

At the same time, his letter gives a glimpse of the transformation of Hashimoto's love. He cherishes the beautiful memories of Bernstein and their time together. Yet he seems to have reached an acceptance of a life in which there would be different kinds of love and relationships. Bernstein would always be the serious, passionate love of his life, and it was the love that he lived for. But he probably understood that there might be other men who would bring different kinds of love and enrich his life in new ways. The cover of the card on which he wrote this message has a photograph of a lotus flower and leaf on the water, which seems to correspond with the sense of serenity and peace he gained after inner reflection.

In the following months, Hashimoto traveled extensively for business and vacation and sent postcards from the Philippines, Hong Kong, and Thailand. He was following Bernstein's whereabouts and activities amidst his own trips, as is evident from his references to the Leonard Bernstein Festival in Vienna and his performance with Midori at Tanglewood.[3] In

September 1986, he mentions that he would be in Holland for two weeks and writes, "I will call you from Amsterdam to Paris or Zurich or Vienna. May I call you? Because I miss hearing your voice." He not only spoke to Bernstein on the phone but visited him in Vienna at the end of his trip. Bernstein was making a live recording of Sibelius's Symphony no. 2 with the Vienna Philharmonic Orchestra at the Musikverein, and Hashimoto attended the rehearsal and the concert. His postcard the following month mentions this visit briefly: "While walking around a park and breathing the autumn air, I remember Wien and you. In spite of the very short days, I had a nice time with you. Thank you very much."[4]

A few months later during the winter holidays, his work took him back to New York, where he saw Bernstein again. During the first years of their relationship, Hashimoto wrote him immediately after his trips, both exhilarated from their time together and sad about being apart again. This letter was sent a full four months after the trip.

> Dearest Lenny,
>
> Four months have passed already since we met in N.Y.C. It is like yesterday, not four months ago. Even when we met first in Japan is like yesterday. The scene appears clearly in front of me, always.
>
> I have been very busy for these four months. I don't remember what I have done.—I worked hard and caught a cold. One week busy vacation with my family. My uncle's death . . . I had no time to go to the park to see cherry blossoms. Now it is gone.
>
> Although I could not see blooming cherries, I feel beautiful spring. Fresh green and air, the sun becomes vital and comfortable, the ground which I step on is tender. I breathe in this beautiful season as much as possible. I breathe this vivid nature.
>
> When I look at nature, I look at you. Nature is yourself, and you are Nature itself. When I touch nature, I touch you. When I feel nature, I feel you. You come to me like spring comes.
>
> I wish you have nice concerts and trip this year.
>
> With love,
Kuny[5]

His love is no less pure or intense than during the first years of their relationship. His identification of nature with Bernstein illustrates the spirituality of his love, which transcends mundane, everyday life.

In October 1987, Hashimoto had another business trip to Europe that allowed him to see Bernstein again, this time in Amsterdam, where Bernstein was recording Mahler's Symphony no. 1 with the Royal Concertgebouw. But there are no letters from him that mention this, either before or after the trip. He must have called Bernstein by phone to let him know about his trip to Amsterdam and arranged to meet him there.

* * *

I have just arrived in Sydney on the 11th of December. Now I am looking for an apartment.

It is real summer here. I went to a beautiful beach yesterday. Sydney has plenty of nice beaches. It is like a resort city, indeed.

But I have never seen before many people walking around without shirts, naked and some people are barefoot. And also I have never seen before so many people with tattoo. They are very rough and too casual. In spite of this being a city, flies are flying around my face!

Do you think that I can survive here?

Let me see anyhow.[6]

This is Hashimoto's next correspondence by mail. It is a Christmas card mailed from Sydney, Australia, dated December 14, 1987. The card has an illustration of koala bears in Christmas attire standing in front of the Sydney Opera House. But Hashimoto's message indicates that this was not like his other postcards. He expresses a mixture of excitement, amusement, and culture shock upon his arrival in the city. In the postscript, he notes that he has kept his place in Tokyo, but that he would send Bernstein his address as soon as he settled into an apartment in Sydney. Clearly, this was not a short-term visit but was intended to be a permanent move.

He must have talked with Bernstein about this when he saw him in Amsterdam two months earlier. He had never mentioned relocation in his previous letters, nor does he provide any explanation for this major life change in his early thirties. He had been quite decisive and unsentimental when he reported to Bernstein about leaving the insurance company to go into theater, which indicates that he is not someone who wavers about making decisions. It is possible that something precipitated this one. Even then, it is unlikely that he would have moved to Australia without having told Bernstein, especially given that his relocation abroad would have made it difficult for him to continue as Amberson's Japan representative.

Why did he move to Australia, a country he never even mentioned having visited before? Why would he give up his role as Bernstein's representative when the work had given him so much joy, fulfillment, sense of purpose, and reason to live? What was it that made him choose this completely new path in life that was presumably more important to him than his work for Bernstein?

Hashimoto's next correspondence was a birthday card in the summer of 1988. This birthday was Bernstein's seventieth. Celebration events were held worldwide, including the New York Philharmonic's yearlong celebration of Bernstein's compositions, the city of Vienna making Bernstein an honorary citizen, the Israel Philharmonic Orchestra installing Bernstein as laureate conductor, and numerous concerts all over the world.

Over the course of four days around August 25, a series of performances under the title Bernstein at 70! were held at Tanglewood, the summer home of the Boston Symphony Orchestra (BSO), of which Ozawa was the Music Director. The performances included a prelude concert of songs commissioned in honor of Bernstein; a concert by the Tanglewood Music Center Orchestra featuring violinist Midori, cellist Yo-Yo Ma, pianist Peter Serkin, and singers Roberta Alexander and Christa Ludwig; a fully staged production of Mass by the Indiana University Opera Theatre; and a BSO concert in which Bernstein himself conducted Haydn's Symphony no. 99, followed by Ozawa conducting A Bernstein Birthday Bouquet, eight variations on Bernstein's "New York, New York" composed by a number of composers, including Takemitsu. In the second half of the concert, Bernstein conducted Tchaikovsky's Symphony no. 5.[7] Over these four days, receptions for over three hundred guests were held by Bernstein's close associates, including a supper hosted by Ozawa and his wife. Ozawa's influence in the classical music world was now comparable to the one Bernstein had when he first became Ozawa's mentor. The fact that he was hosting Bernstein's birthday celebration at Tanglewood said as much about Ozawa's professional and personal journey as Bernstein's.[8]

The Japanese names on the invitation list are telling of the artistic, business, and personal relationships Bernstein had built in Japan over the years: Midori, Eiji Oue, Mitsunori Sano, Akio Morita, and Naoyasu Kajimoto, the founder of Japan's largest artist management company, which had coordinated the Osaka Expo performances.[9] Whereas all these were either musical colleagues or business partners, two other Japanese people on the list of invitees—Amano and Hashimoto—had very different relationships with Bernstein. There was a striking contrast between their places in the festivities.

Marie Carter of Amberson Enterprises helped make arrangements for Amano's travel from Tokyo. While preparing for her trip, Amano wrote to Carter that although she assumed that it would be expensive to use the car service from New York City to Pittsfield, Massachusetts, "with my actual health condition, THIS seems to be worth doing it."[10] She had suffered a stroke a few years earlier and, after a period of rest and rehabilitation, left her job at the publishing house. While she was still her vibrant, audacious, active self, she had to prioritize her physical comfort. After spending a night in New York City and spending time with Helen Coates, she took a limousine to Pittsfield for the celebration.

On the other hand, Hashimoto was in his prime, just beginning an entirely new life in Sydney. Although he was invited, he did not attend the celebration. He sent a simple birthday card instead, along with a T-shirt and a sweatshirt. The card again had pictures of koala bears and played "Happy Birthday" when it was opened. Hashimoto wrote simply, "Can you hear the birthday song for you from Down Under?" at the top of the card, then signed, "Best Day! With Big Love, Kuni" with a drawing of the Australian continent around the word "Big."[11]

At the end of that year, Hashimoto sent a Christmas card with a brief but poignant message, his spelling indicating his adaptation to Australian English: "Dearest Lenny, Merry Christmas!! The sun and a lot of smiles and light in Australia paralyse me. I had a sort of amnesia, but I never forget you. I try to recover in 1989. With love, Kuni."[12] His words indicate the vast distance—geographical, cultural, psychological—between his Australian surroundings and the life he left behind in Japan. The message, "but I never forget you," seems all the more heartfelt for its brevity.

Exploring the Uncharted

AFTER HASHIMOTO MOVED to Sydney, the plan for Bernstein's China tour was expanded into "China/Japan Tour 1990." The idea was that Bernstein and his longtime protégé Michael Tilson Thomas would tour with the London Symphony Orchestra (LSO) in both countries. In order to give form to Bernstein's dedication to teaching, Amberson envisioned this as not merely a performance tour but also an educational program in which the maestros and the LSO would work with young Chinese musicians for a few weeks and then take the Chinese student orchestra to perform in Japan.

Despite the enthusiasm of both the Americans and the Chinese, practical issues bedeviled planning a performance of this scale and caliber in China during this period. For instance, upon visiting the Beijing Concert Hall, reputed to have the best acoustics in the city, the organizers noted that the four-year-old hall already appeared decades old and was inadequate for LSO rehearsals and performances.

But the organizers' biggest concern was building a relationship with the officials of the Communist nation, which was just opening up to the Western world. The involvement of the Center for United States–China Arts Exchange (CUSCAE) was critical in this regard. The organization was established in 1978 in anticipation of the resurgence of the arts in China with the liberalization of the Communist regime. Under the directorship of Chou Wen-Chung, himself an accomplished composer, the CUSCAE was housed at Columbia University and served as an agency for all types of arts exchange programs between the two nations. Chou was instrumental in bringing a number of talented young Chinese composers, including Tan Dun, Chen Yi, and Bright Sheng, to the United States in the 1980s. His connections to the Chinese Ministry of Culture and his knowledge of Chinese political and business protocols were crucial to this phase of the event planning.[1]

The organizing team that was put together for this project—a group that included representatives of Amberson and the LSO as well as Mitsunori Sano and Tadatsugu Sasaki, who worked on Bernstein's 1985 Japan tours—was aware of the complexity of earning the support of the Chinese government. "International cultural exchange" was crucial, both in substance and in rhetoric, in gaining the support of the Chinese officials. From the earliest stages of the planning, Kraut deliberately stressed the professional exchange and the educational nature of the proposed event while downplaying its commercial aspects.[2] Indeed, during the organizers' meeting with representatives of the Chinese Ministry of Culture, the Chinese officials expressed enthusiasm for the event and emphasized "the importance of high quality exchanges and the teaching/learning opportunities" and "China's need to go beyond musical technique to a realm of more artistic, creative understanding" as well as speaking of the "improving conditions in China's music world." These officials were clearly aware of the difficulties faced by musicians in China during the Cultural Revolution and its aftermath. They also wished to overcome the widespread perception that Chinese musicians excel in technique yet lack artistic understanding and creative expression. Their interest demonstrated China's aspiration to make an entry onto the world stage after reopening its doors to the West.

Despite the artistic, intellectual, and political interest in the project, funding loomed as a seemingly insurmountable obstacle. In the late 1980s, various cultural organizations around the world were already vying for a place in China. The officials claimed that most of the relevant part of the Ministry of Culture's budget for 1990 was already allocated to the Asian Games taking place in Beijing that September and the scheduled tour of Britain's Royal Opera Company. In the absence of a tradition of philanthropic fundraising in the country, it was difficult for China to bear the major expenses of the event, they asserted. While proposing a number of ways to help the Chinese government cover some of the expenses, Kraut put pressure on them by stating that the "level of financial support by China indicates value they attach to the project" and suggesting that they might move the event to Hong Kong if the Ministry of Culture failed to make a definite commitment. Yet the Ministry of Culture remained firm about its inability to cover the expenses.[3]

Under these circumstances, Japan proved an economic powerhouse that could enable the project to come to fruition. During this period, bolstered by the Plaza Accord of 1985, which depreciated the US dollar and strengthened the yen, Japan gained unprecedented power in the American market. One Japanese company after another acquired major American corporations and symbolic real estate, including the ABC Headquarters Building, Hyatt Regency Waikiki, Tiffany Building, and Exxon Headquarters Building. Amidst this surge, Sony acquired CBS Records. The company purchased Columbia Pictures the following year. Two decades earlier, the joint venture of CBS/Sony was seen as a large American record company entering Japan's domestic market. In contrast, Sony's outright acquisition of a major American music and film company was depicted by the American media as the return of the "yellow peril," an unwanted invasion of the Japanese into America. The cover of *Newsweek* on October 9, 1989, showed the Statue of Liberty wearing a kimono, with the headline "Japan Invades Hollywood."[4]

Given the unparalleled financial power of Japanese corporations, it was natural that the organizers turned to them for funding of this project. Securing corporate sponsorship in Japan turned out to be more difficult than expected, however. Kraut first approached Sony, counting on the company's longstanding relationship with Bernstein and hoping that it would assume title sponsorship.[5] But Norio Ohga quickly declined, saying that the strong yen was putting the export-oriented company through a difficult period and that they did not have the capacity for sponsorship.[6]

Another possibility was Suntory, an alcoholic beverage company that was one of the most important corporate sponsors of classical music in Japan. The company had established the Suntory Music Foundation in 1969 to support classical music and in 1986 opened Suntory Hall in the heart of Tokyo, which quickly came to be known as one of the world's best classical music performance venues. The company expressed interest in possible sponsorship, not only because of the interest of its president, Keizo Saji, in classical music but also because of China's appeal as a future market for Suntory.[7] The precedent of the Vienna Philharmonic refusing sponsorship by a liquor company kept the organizers from pursuing the possibility, however.[8]

The organizers then approached other possible sponsors in various sectors.[9] The range of companies that the organizers explored—including Asahi Beer, Nippon Tobacco, Seiko, the telecommunications company KDD, the television network Asahi Broadcasting Company, and the Fuji

Sankei Group, another large media company—indicates the level of corporate interest in sponsorship of the arts during this period of Japanese affluence.[10] In these delicate negotiations, the organizers shrewdly marketed Bernstein's celebrity status, charging as much as three hundred thousand dollars for his appearance at events and the use of his photographs.[11]

After complex negotiations, in February 1989 the organizers successfully secured an agreement with Nomura Securities, Japan's oldest stockbrokerage firm, which boasted the largest number of shares in all business divisions of the nation's market. Nomura agreed to pay $2.5 million for sponsorship rights and an additional $2.5 million for promotion rights.[12] Nomura's title sponsorship reflected not only the economic but also the cultural power that the financial sector exerted in the global market at this time and the dominant role Japanese corporations played in it.

After securing title sponsorship, the organizers entered a new phase of subtle and not-so-subtle negotiations of power. Discussing the draft agreement, Amberson agent John Triggle insisted that the rights holders—in this case the LSO, Bernstein, and Tilson Thomas—rather than the sponsor give final approval on any matter requiring judgment.[13] He asserted:

> As ASATSU [the company serving as Nomura's agent] is the promoter in Japan **we must be very vigilant** that ASATSU acting as promoter does not attempt to give Nomura more exposure than they have paid for through the sponsorship contract. Key [Enterprises, Amberson's sponsorship agent] has to approve **ALL** exposure of Nomura. <u>NOTE</u>: make sure that in the promoter's contract the LSO prohibits ASATSU from offering Nomura any exposure, or other benefits that would normally be given to a local sponsor by the local promoter.

Bernstein's staff carefully deliberated a number of issues, such as the precise wording for the title sponsorship, the relative size and positioning of the corporate logo, and the fonts used for the names of the conductors and the LSO.[14]

Nomura sponsorship gave the organizers powerful ammunition in obtaining the Chinese officials' support for the project. The memorandum presented to the Chinese officials in anticipation of the meeting with the vice-minister of culture showcases Kraut's exceptional skills as a businessman and a diplomat. He describes the project as a visit by the LSO, Bernstein, and Tilson Thomas "to assist the young musicians of the PRC in achieving greater knowledge, expertise, and understanding of Western symphonic music, and as part of this purpose to give concerts in Beijing and Shanghai." To stress the educational nature of this tour, Kraut mentioned that all the LSO rehearsals in Beijing would be open to Chinese musicians and students, "so that the complete preparation of several programs by a major Western orchestra with major conductors will be exposed to observation and study." They also expected, Kraut wrote, to discuss plans to organize the Young China Orchestra and for the most promising young conductors to be coached by Bernstein and Tilson Thomas and possibly be given the opportunity to conduct the LSO. Kraut's memo also mentioned the prospects for television coverage and recording activity for the project: "We believe that such television will result in a great deal of positive publicity for China; it will be an artistic, educational project, mounted on a modest investment scale." Kraut noted that family and personal friends would want to travel to China with the party, "paying on a normal touristic basis," and furthermore, "Western companies in the music business will want to accompany us for the purpose of making demonstrations and establishing relationships in fields like instrument manufacture, music publishing, phonograph recording, home video, music television broadcasts, etc.," stressing that the project would bring coveted foreign currency and future business enterprises to China. On the critical matter of expenses and sponsorship, the memo assertively stated that the organizers were voluntarily making various concessions to accommodate the limited budgetary capacity on the Chinese side, and then claimed:

> Based on our discussions with a potential Japanese sponsor, as well as a potential producer of television programs about the activities of this project, we believe that we will be able to conclude agreements which will enable us to absorb more of the costs of this project than we had thought possible. . . . The potential Japanese sponsor will expect maximum, and perhaps exclusive, visibility in the sponsor's role for this project.
>
> The commercial Japanese sponsor we have in mind will wish to make a good impression in China, and will need cooperation from the Ministry of Culture and other agencies. We believe that there is good potential for support for further projects of the Ministry from this sponsor. In addition, we understand that the sponsor

will wish to invite senior government officials and the appropriate ambassadors to receptions following the concerts.

This language achieves multiple goals at once: it gives the impression that the arrangement is quite a generous one; it calls attention to the economic benefits of the sponsorship arrangement for China; it protects and advances Nomura's interests; it appeals to the pride of the Chinese officials; and it solicits the cooperation of the Chinese. In concluding the memorandum, Kraut writes, with a tone that is at once collegial, uncompromising, and quite American:

> Almost two years of discussion have brought us to this point; it seems clear that we all wish to accomplish this project. It also seems clear, at least to me, that this proposal is fair, and should be acceptable to all parties. I fear that any further delay will result in our having to withdraw; unless we have a firm agreement in the immediate future we will be unable to hold the artists' time available.
>
> Let's do it.[15]

* * *

A MONTH AFTER this resolute declaration, Kraut wrote to Hashimoto, asking about his new life in Sydney and reporting on the negotiations about the tour.

> I just got back from Japan, where Mitsunori [Sano] and I missed you—we spoke many times about you and how you are the only Japanese we know who is "easily assimilated." So now you're suddenly Australian? But seriously Japan is not the same without you.
>
> We signed the sponsorship contract for the tour next year today. We all make lots of money, and I think that everyone will get what he wants from the arrangement, so in lots of ways it's ideal.

While reporting on various individuals he met during the trip, he gives his observations of the changes in Japan and China.

> You <u>must</u> come to Tokyo when we're there next year. How could we manage without you? With any translator I've had no one pays attention—I need the elegant accent again! Especially now that

everything (and everyone) has gotten so ritzy in the land of the rising sun. . . .

China was fascinating—the changes in Beijing during the last year are staggering! It's really become a consumer society. And Shanghai is more crowded than any other place I've seen including Tokyo and Mexico City. There are so many of them!

I didn't see any of the friends in Tokyo. . . . Kazuko Amano was in the hospital. She's better now and we just missed seeing each other on the day that I left. Where have all the flowers gone?

Now I must go back to work—please write and tell me about life in Sydney. All the gory details. . . .

Much love,
Harry[16]

Kraut's care for Amano indicates his understanding of the precious place she had in Bernstein's heart. Most of all, the letter expresses Kraut's personal closeness with and professional trust in Hashimoto, and also his desire to get him involved in the project.

* * *

ALL OF THIS careful planning and diplomacy came to an unexpected halt on June 4, 1989. The Chinese government ordered its troops to suppress the student-led popular demonstrations at Tiananmen Square in the heart of Beijing, resulting in a massacre with thousands of casualties. Soon thereafter, the Minister of Culture Wang Meng and Vice Minister Ying Ruocheng—with whom the organizers had been negotiating the tour plans—were removed from their positions. China's *Centre Daily News* reported that Wang was dismissed for "allowing 'bourgeois liberalization' to inundate the country and for failing to steadfastly support the policy of 'arts for the masses' "; Ying incurred the displeasures of the old guard when he allowed Bernardo Bertolucci to shoot the film *The Last Emperor* in the Forbidden City.[17]

Kraut immediately grasped the urgency of the situation. On the day of the Tiananmen massacre, he sent a telex to the organizing team, expressing his grave concerns about the state of affairs and raising questions about the feasibility and desirability of executing the project in China. Kraut and Bernstein spoke later that day and agreed that they had to put all China plans on hold.[18]

The CUSCAE issued a quick response. On June 9, Chou sent a letter to the CUSCAE Advisory Council members expressing sorrow and indignation at the events leading up to the massacre yet also reaffirming his commitment to international cultural exchange. He then announced the postponement of scheduled projects:

> In the meantime, it is with great sorrow and regret that we have had to postpone Center projects planned for this spring and summer. Inasmuch as a popularly supported, peaceful voice in the dialogue on reform and human rights have been stifled; progress toward greater freedom of artistic expression has been disrupted; and there has been a devastating loss of life, the Center feels it would be unproductive and inappropriate to conduct any programs in China at this time.[19]

Kraut called an emergency meeting in Rome, to be held on June 19–20. At the meeting, much of the decision was based on the views and interests of the corporate sponsor. Nomura's staff in China had been evacuated, and they issued a report on the situation: the intellectual classes were being persecuted for the maintenance of the regime, and there was a danger that music could be condemned as a "bourgeois" practice, as it was during the Cultural Revolution; if the planned tour were to be carried out, the Chinese government could use it as a propaganda tool in the face of all the sanctions of major nations against China; and holding concerts in China under the present regime would be equivalent to doing so in apartheid South Africa.[20]

Judging that conducting the tour under these circumstances would serve neither the Chinese people nor the reputation of Nomura and the musicians, the group quickly decided that the China portion of the project had to be canceled. On August 3, the American and British parties of the organizing team sent a joint letter to Vice Minister Ying and Wu Zuqiang of the Chinese Ministry of Culture informing them of their decision to cancel the trip and relocate the project to another venue in Asia:

> It is with very deep regret that we take this decision, both for what has transpired in your country, and for the loss of what might have transpired next year. We nonetheless thank you both personally, as well as your colleagues, for the co-operation and friendship you have shown to all of us during the past year.

When conditions in China have become more conducive to the practice of our gentle art, we will again be interested in trying to arrange a similar trip even though it will be necessary to find a new means of doing so.

Thank you again for all your help. Please be sure that you have our sincerest wishes for all good things personally.[21]

The laborious diplomacy with the Chinese government thus came to naught. Bernstein's dream of working with Chinese students and sharing music with Chinese audiences—and the students' dream of a democratic China—were shattered by political and military suppression.

20

Cultivating New Soil

THE ORGANIZERS COULD not afford to be consumed by their profound disappointment over the failed China tour. Having reserved precious weeks in the packed schedules of Bernstein, Tilson Thomas, and the LSO, and with hard-earned sponsorship in hand, the organizers were unwilling to consider canceling the entire project. During the two-day meeting in Rome, they had to quickly come up with a plan to redirect these resources and Bernstein's dream into a meaningful yet feasible project.

First and foremost, they needed an alternative venue. With the project only a year away, concert halls in major cities such as Tokyo and Osaka were already booked. In brainstorming possible sites, the organizers inquired about Nomura's major international markets. Cities such as London, Seoul, Bangkok, Kuala Lumpur, Singapore, Sydney, Hong Kong, and Vancouver were considered, yet all were dismissed for practical reasons such as weather, season, and availability of appropriate concert halls.

Then the city of Sapporo in Japan's northern island of Hokkaido was raised as a possibility. The physical environment seemed ideal: although June, when the project was scheduled, is the rainy season in most of Japan, rain is far less frequent in Hokkaido at that time of the year. Unlike other Japanese cities, Sapporo is spacious and has an open atmosphere. Having hosted the Winter Olympics in 1972, the city had ample accommodations to house the musicians. A new performance complex, Sapporo Art Park, was being built on the outskirts of the city and would be well suited for the event.

Sano was tasked with investigating this possibility and flew immediately to Sapporo. Through the executive director of a local music promotion agency, the general manager of the Sapporo Symphony Orchestra, and the representative for cultural promotion of the city of Sapporo, he made tentative bookings for various concert halls in and around Sapporo for the summer of 1990.

Yet city officials were not entirely enthusiastic at the outset. Despite the city's pleasant summer weather, Sapporo is better known for its picturesque winters, especially the annual Snow Festival featuring large snow sculptures in Odori Park downtown, and the officials had difficulty envisioning a summer festival. The city had suffered a serious financial loss from a food festival it hosted in 1988, making the officials reluctant to take on another big event.

Although it is the largest city in northern Japan, with a population of approximately 1.6 million at the time, in 1989 Sapporo was still provincial in many ways, especially in terms of its arts scene. Musicians of international renown rarely came to the city, and it was unimaginable to many Sapporo residents that they could see a live performance of artists such as Bernstein and Tilson Thomas in their hometown. The Sapporo Symphony Orchestra was not yet a top-notch professional orchestra that could provide sufficient artistic support for an event of this scale. The facilities at Sapporo Art Park, still under construction, had only squat-style toilets, and Western-style restrooms would have to be quickly installed if it were to host many musicians from abroad.

With the summer of 1990 only a year away, many questions still remained as to whether Bernstein's dream of bringing young Asian musicians together could be realized in Sapporo.

* * *

Kuni, is there any chance that you would be interested in working with us on this project in some respect, either from Australia or back in Tokyo, full-time or part-time? I think that we could find a very useful place for you, and that you'd find it interesting. The concerts for 1990 that I'd like to arrange would include artists from all the Pacific countries (Te Kanawa? Sutherland?) in addition to the London Symphony, Pacific Youth Orchestra, LB and MTT [Michael Tilson Thomas]. The music I'd like to see played should range from the normal classical fare to first-class rock, as well as "native" musics, with an emphasis on things that are pan-Pacific and international, for this peaceful festival. Let me know what you think.[1]

At his new home in Sydney, Hashimoto received this telex from Kraut in August 1989. Kraut's tone shows both friendly familiarity and his professional trust in Hashimoto. Clearly excited by the offer, Hashimoto responded the same day.

> What a fantastic idea we have. . . . Of course, great pleasure to work for this project.
>
> Soon after I received your letter [when China was still part of the plan], I already arranged to take one month off to go to Japan in June or July 1990. However, when that Chinese massacre happened I wondered what was going on with the concerts in China and thought LB may come to Aus[tralia] instead. But this new project is more fun. . . .
>
> I will try to go back to Japan this September for one or two weeks. . . . In 1990 I will be in Japan during this whole project. . . .
>
> I have to go on a diet quick, if I am going back to Japan in September. Tell me the currently fashionable American diet system.[2]

The next day, he notified Kraut that he would travel to Japan and assist him during his trip. "I hope you can recognize fat me," he wrote.[3] Shortly thereafter, he wrote to Marie Carter at the Amberson office, informing her of his travel schedule while humorously expressing his exasperation with labor disputes in Australia that were causing much chaos in air travel.[4]

Hashimoto was thus brought in all the way from Sydney to help realize Bernstein's dream. At the end of September, he flew to Japan for meetings in Tokyo.[5] He accompanied Kraut and other organizers to Sapporo. They inspected concert halls in and around the city; visited Sapporo Art Park, then under construction; and checked possible hotels for the maestros and the LSO, whose union agreement strictly stipulated accommodation details, including the size of the closets in individual rooms.

During these meetings, the organizers produced a plan around Bernstein's commitment to education and his belief in the power of music to unite across boundaries. They envisioned a music festival centered on an educational program for a youth orchestra drawn from Pacific Rim nations, much like the Tanglewood Music Festival but in Asia. The more the representatives of Nomura learned about the spirit of Tanglewood, the more excited they became. "This is exactly what the sponsor had in mind for the future in Japan," they stated. Coincidentally, Tanglewood was about to celebrate its fiftieth anniversary in the summer of 1990. Kraut's first job out of college had been at Tanglewood. Tilson Thomas also had first met Bernstein there as a student. With all these factors converging, the organizers quickly came to a consensus about making the 1990 project into "Tanglewood in Japan." The idea of an international music festival focused on education gradually persuaded the reluctant officials of Sapporo, especially Mayor Takeshi Itagaki.

In the fall of 1989, Sapporo officially announced hosting an international music festival the following summer.[6]

* * *

THE WANING OF the Cold War and its uncertain aftermath were shaking the world far beyond Asia. Mikhail Gorbachev's political liberalization and economic reforms transformed not only the Soviet Union but also nations throughout the Soviet bloc. A series of revolutions in Eastern Europe steadily dismantled the Iron Curtain. On November 9, 1989, the Berlin Wall crumbled.

In December that year, Bernstein performed Beethoven's Ninth Symphony in Berlin, conducting an orchestra and chorus consisting of musicians from East and West Germany, Great Britain, France, the United States, and the Soviet Union. He instructed the singers to use the word *Freiheit* (freedom) in lieu of *Freude* (joy) in Schiller's text. Almost half a century after his sensational debut in the middle of World War II, Bernstein led the international chorus marking the end of the Cold War and celebrating the brotherhood of humanity and the gift of freedom. This moving performance was broadcast all over the world. It further inspired an international music festival as an educational opportunity for young musicians from around the world as well as an act of faith in democracy, freedom, and unity.

* * *

AFTER CONDUCTING THE Berlin concert, Bernstein's physical condition took a turn for the worse. He caught the flu during the *Candide* performance at the Barbican at the end of 1989 and was diagnosed with pneumonia shortly thereafter.

In light of Bernstein's ill health, the organizers had decided to have the maestro stay in a quiet, nature-filled environment away from the city during the festival. The Nidom—a brand new super-luxury golf resort— was just being built about ninety minutes away from Sapporo. The largest lodge was to have five bedrooms spread across three wings surrounding an enormous living room and was to be equipped with a private sauna.

A second lodge had the same setup minus the sauna. Even the standard accommodation would be a two-story cottage with two bedrooms, a spacious living room, and a full kitchen. The setup seemed ideal for Bernstein and his entourage. Although the Nidom was not scheduled to open until August, its president, Shuichi Ishikawa, arranged to accelerate the construction to accommodate Bernstein and company before the official opening of the hotel.

In spring 1990, Hashimoto flew to Japan again for further meetings and inspection of the facilities to prepare for the event. The organizers made concrete plans for the content of the festival, which would consist of several interrelated components. Just as Bernstein, Ozawa, and Oue were taught at Tanglewood, young conductors in residence would to be trained through rehearsals and performances with the student orchestra and coaching by Bernstein. Young orchestra musicians, recruited from around the Pacific Rim and selected through an audition, would study major symphonic works with both the conductors in residence and Bernstein himself and perform those pieces in Sapporo and Tokyo. They would also have section rehearsals with the principals of the LSO. The student orchestra and the LSO would perform together in concert. Bernstein and Tilson Thomas would conduct the LSO in several concerts featuring star soloists such as baritone Thomas Hampson and violinist Midori. To highlight the significance of holding the festival in Asia, artists from the region would be brought in to perform traditional music. To reach out to the wider community, a series of chamber music concerts would be given at various locations in and around Sapporo, and educational programs involving the student orchestra would be brought to local schools. They would also organize the Pacific Composers Conference, which would bring together composers from the Asia-Pacific region for exchange of ideas and performances of their works. The festival was to last for two and a half weeks, beginning with the opening ceremony on June 26, 1990.

The festival thus promised to be a rich, multifaceted educational opportunity not just for the young musicians but for the larger Sapporo community. So that the festival would serve as a venue for both world-class musical training and person-to-person cultural exchange, the organizers decided to recruit musicians from as many nations as possible in the Asia-Pacific region, including countries with few resources for classical music training.

At these meetings, the organizers named the new music festival that would become one of the last and most important projects in Bernstein's career: the Pacific Music Festival (PMF). Posters announcing the PMF were put up all over the city. The copy declared *Kuru hito ga ichiban wakuwaku shiteiru*, or "Those about to come are the most thrilled of all." Indeed, all those preparing to come to Sapporo—Bernstein, Tilson Thomas, the LSO, soloists, conductors in residence, and the young musicians being auditioned—were thrilled by the prospect of the summer ahead.

Despite the city's official endorsement, much work remained to be done in the limited time left before the festival's scheduled opening. The planned outdoor stage at Sapporo Art Park was not large enough to accommodate a full-size orchestra. Under the city's standard operating procedure for design changes and construction, the stage would not be ready in time for the festival. So instead it was decided that a temporary stage would be built in the park. Even with the new plan and the breakneck speed with which the work was undertaken, the construction process—interrupted by snow during the winter months—worried everyone involved. One week before the festival's opening, the audience seating area still had exposed red soil, and the lawn had yet to be laid.

* * *

AFTER MUCH ANTICIPATION and uncertainty, the curtain of the PMF finally rose on June 26, 1990.

The First Harvest

At my very advanced age, I now have to make a choice again of how best to serve music and serve people through it. Should I spend whatever days the good lord gives to me going back to my first love, the piano, and playing all the Beethoven sonatas again? Should I just go on being a conductor and playing all the Brahms symphonies again year after year? Should I devote myself only to being a composer and writing the various kinds of music that I do write? And I've been considering this problem, because when you get to be seventy-one, you consider such problems. And my decision has been, without too much thought, to spend most of the remaining energy and time the lord grants me in education, and in sharing as much as possible with younger people, and especially with very young people, whatever I can share, whatever I know, not only about music but about art, and not only about art but about the relationship between art and life, and being oneself, finding oneself, knowing who you are, and doing the best possible job. If I can communicate some of this to as many people as possible in the years that remain, I will be a very happy man. And the Pacific Music Festival is one very large aspect of this commitment, which I hereby make for the rest of my life.[1]

BERNSTEIN SPOKE SLOWLY, pausing after every few words, at the opening ceremony of the Pacific Music Festival (PMF). The freshly completed outdoor stage of Sapporo Art Park overlooked a packed audience seated upon a beautiful green lawn. Thus began two and a half weeks during which Bernstein would share with the young musicians all he knew about music, art, life, and being the best possible human being.

Prior to the opening ceremony, Bernstein walked into the tent where the press conference was held, with Hashimoto, Kraut, and other staff behind him. He hugged Eiji Oue and Yutaka Sado, two of his Japanese protégés who were selected as conductors in residence, and proudly referred to them as "My babies!" As he sat down, he recognized Amano in the audience and affectionately called out, "Kazuko!" in his throaty

FIGURE 21.1 Leonard Bernstein at the opening ceremony of the Pacific Music Festival, June 26, 1990. Copyright PMF Organizing Committee.

voice. His most loyal Japanese fan sitting in the audience, his most recent Japanese pupils seated beside him, and his beloved and trusted Japanese assistant behind the tent were all there in Sapporo to be part of the realization of Bernstein's long-cherished dream.

* * *

WHILE KRAUT AND the other organizers stayed in Sapporo near the festival site, Hashimoto checked into the Nidom on June 21, five days before the festival's opening. He brought his friend—not a boyfriend—Claude Cainero from Sydney. A 6′3″, rugged, laid-back man who liked to sail in his yacht, Cainero was not a fan of classical music and had little prior knowledge of Bernstein's stature or the significance of the PMF. But at age forty-five he had never traveled abroad and thought it was time to venture outside of Australia. Knowing that Hashimoto was to be put up in a two-bedroom cottage, he decided to tag along. Upon check-in, Hashimoto immediately began preparing for Bernstein's arrival by inspecting the facilities and meeting with the managers and staff. He found that none of the Nidom's staff, including telephone operators, spoke serviceable English.

Bernstein arrived the day after, accompanied by his then-boyfriend Mark "Matt" Taylor, a young aspiring novelist. The president and the entire staff of the Nidom greeted him at his lodge. Although he appreciated the warm and grand welcome, he was exhausted after the long flight and wanted to rest. He met with Kraut first thing the following morning and decided to change the program to reduce the physical toll it would take on him. Bernstein's own *Jubilee Games*, which he was scheduled to perform with the PMF orchestra, was replaced with Schumann's Symphony no. 2; Bruckner's Symphony no. 9, which was planned for the performance with the LSO, was withdrawn. The PMF librarian and the principal players of the LSO were immediately notified of the change in order to prepare the score and to begin coaching each section of the PMF Orchestra.

Bernstein's entourage at the Nidom was larger than usual in part because of Bernstein's frail condition. His assistant Craig Urquhart and housekeeper and cook Patty Pulliam stayed in the maestro's five-bedroom lodge. Tilson Thomas and his manager and partner Joshua Robison were in the other five-bedroom lodge. Bernstein's acupuncturist-doctor and his family were also at the Nidom, staying in the standard two-story cottages like Hashimoto and Cainero. Thomas Hampson, who was performing a recital with Tilson Thomas at the piano and also singing solo in an LSO concert, was also in a cottage. Bernstein was thus surrounded by his musical family and close personal friends in the beautiful natural setting.

The peace and quiet and open air at the Nidom proved therapeutic for Bernstein. Within days of his arrival, he showed a remarkable recovery and regained energy and strength. He was eager to meet and start working with all the musicians at the festival.

* * *

FOR THE PMF, 123 young musicians from eighteen countries were selected out of nine hundred applicants. Many were students, some fresh out of high school; others were recent conservatory graduates who were playing in professional orchestras or preparing for auditions. Spending weeks studying major symphonic works with other top-level musicians from so many countries around the world was in and of itself exciting. For many non-Japanese musicians, not only was this was their first trip to Japan but also their first time abroad. For musicians from Japan, it felt as if the world came to them, bringing endless gifts that opened up their horizons.

But first and foremost, it was the chance to study with Bernstein that made the PMF a once-in-a-lifetime opportunity for the young musicians.

They had grown up listening to his recordings and watching *Young People's Concerts, West Side Story,* and broadcasts of his concerts, but most had never heard him perform live. Many of them had friends who had studied with Bernstein at Tanglewood and gushed about the experience. At "Tanglewood in Japan" they could study with the man whom they typically described with such words as "God," "hero," "legend," "rock star," "great master," and "larger than life."

After three all-day rehearsals, during which Oue prepared the orchestra on Schumann's Symphony no. 2, the students had their first encounter with Bernstein on June 30. He walked into the rehearsal studio, wearing a casual black-and-white-striped shirt over a red turtleneck, while Oue was working with the students on the first movement. The young musicians could feel the air in the studio change the moment Bernstein walked in. They were wowed by the maestro from the minute they laid eyes on him. Bernstein listened to Oue's rehearsal for a while, walking around the perimeters of the orchestra, then raised his hand and called out to stop, and made a comment about the musicians' playing of the triplets. He then stepped onto the podium, took the baton from Oue, and said,

> "First, let me say you sound very good. It's already a potential orchestra. It pleases me very much. And I think after a little work, it will be an orchestra, a real one. And after a lot of work, it may be a *very* good one."

He hit the music stand with his baton as he said "very." Then he continued,

> "It will be. But it takes work."

From the outset, he made it clear that being an orchestra involves much more than dozens of well-trained musicians merely playing together.

Thus began Bernstein's rehearsal with the young musicians. They could instantly hear their own sound change. Bernstein had an aura that they had never experienced before. At the same time, many of the young musicians found Bernstein much shorter than they had imagined. Having watched many of his energetic performances on screen, they had pictured a man of a physical size that matched his character. His actual height, combined with his age and illness, which made him look smaller, surprised them.

Everything from watching him take the chewing gum out of his mouth and stick it under the music stand to being amused by the bright-colored shirt he changed into during a rehearsal break—in other words, Bernstein simply being Bernstein—made the charismatic maestro human and relatable to the students. The festival footage reveals Bernstein casually chatting and affectionately touching the students, as well as the comfortable connection the musicians felt with him.

Yet Bernstein was as serious as he was friendly. Recounting the numerous occasions when he witnessed Bernstein's teaching at Tanglewood, Seiji Ozawa spoke of his amazement that Bernstein applied the same standards in teaching inexperienced young conductors and orchestras as he did to musicians in the New York Philharmonic.[2] The rigor and expectations Bernstein placed on the young musicians were evident at the PMF as well. Although Bernstein welcomed interested individuals as observers at the rehearsals, he got upset when the reporters' cameras made noise and broke his and the musicians' concentration. He spoke in a hoarse voice, coughed frequently in between his comments, and constantly wiped sweat away from his eyes. He often began to lose his voice as he spoke. Watching him take a cough drop out of his mouth and pop another one, concertmaster Takane Funatsu stared at him with a look of grave concern. At one point, Bernstein lost his place in the score and said in frustration: "This is what happens with old fucking age. I hate it! I hate it!" He was literally putting all of his life into the rehearsals.

As Schumann's Symphony no. 2—the work that he performed with the Palestine Symphony Orchestra on his first visit in 1947—had been added to the program at the last minute, many worried whether the young musicians could adequately perform this difficult work. The second movement, the scherzo, was the most worrisome, especially for the violinists, who have long, difficult lines of fast sixteenth notes. As soon as they began rehearsing the movement, Bernstein effectively showed—by singing "n-ba-di-ba-DI-ba-di-ba-di-ba-di-ba-di-ba-di-ba-di, ba-di-ba-DI-ba-di-ba-di-ba-di-ba-di-ba-di-ba-di," leaning in and stomping his foot with "DI" at the top of the phrase for emphasis—how to articulate so that each note is heard more brilliantly and the lines are shaped more musically. The musicians immediately responded with a much more contoured phrase, eliciting "Much better!" "Great!" "Wonderful!" from Bernstein.

FIGURE 21.2 Leonard Bernstein rehearsing with the PMF Orchestra. Copyright PMF Organizing Committee.

Bernstein's power as an artist and a pedagogue was felt especially in the rehearsal of the third movement, the adagio, to which he had especially profound spiritual and emotional attachment. When he began rehearsing this movement, he first commended the musicians' hard work on the other movements, then said quietly, "It may be time for a little, very personal, intimate music making." To convey the emotion of the opening theme—an almost inaudible but burning cantabile that slowly rises and then falls with a resigned sigh, played against a slow, panting pulse—Bernstein sang the line in his raspy voice, grasping his throat as he crescendoed to the top. Emphasizing that the phrase needs to remain soft and that the accents must come from within rather than be attacked, he demonstrated that infusing emotions into a phrase does not mean playing loudly or aggressively. "It's music, not beats," he said. As the orchestra played, he showed his approval by exclaiming, "Yes! From the inside!" Even as he praised the musicians' phrasing, he also demanded accurately executing what the score says, pointing out that a *fortepiano* was not the same as a *forte-diminuendo*. To illustrate the lyricism of a phrase, he told the musicians to think of Chopin's piano music played by Rubinstein or Horowitz; to describe the ensemble among the four winds, he compared it to a scene of a quartet in an opera.

At the end of the rehearsal, Bernstein reminded the orchestra of the demands of being a true musician. "It's hard. And this is only the beginning," he said, raising his finger for emphasis.

It's very hard to do. And *very* easy to be a mediocre musician. It's so easy just to do gigs. And hard to play music. There's all the difference between day and night, between doing that and doing what we just did in these last five minutes. It takes dedication and commitment. There's no words for it.

The young musicians took in his every word.

The PMF was an immersive educational opportunity not only for the orchestra musicians but also for the conductors in residence: Marin Alsop, Leif Bjaland, Eiji Oue, and Yutaka Sado. Between the LSO concerts and rehearsals with the PMF Orchestra, Bernstein diligently attended the rehearsals in which the conductors in residence worked with the orchestra on their respective pieces, while demonstrating the rigorous labor and careful attention required of both the conductor and the players. Sometimes standing behind the conductor and at other times standing among the orchestra members to watch the conductor's movement and hear the sound, and at other times putting one arm around the conductor's shoulder and conducting with the other arm, he conveyed how the conductor communicates with the orchestra.

Alsop described the maestro in an interview: "Bernstein has no inhibitions at all. He's completely free. And that's what we're striving for as artists, to be totally free." Through rehearsals with Bernstein, both the conductors in residence and the young orchestra musicians quickly learned the enormous challenge of being completely free as artists. They also understood the true greatness of those who achieved that freedom.

* * *

THE CONCERT ON July 3 at Sapporo Shimin Kaikan was the highlight of the summer for the young musicians of the PMF Orchestra. This was the hall where Maria Callas—who was among Bernstein's close friends—gave the very last recital of her career in 1974. The hall was packed with an audience of over a thousand who eagerly anticipated the fruits of the PMF. It was an extremely hot day—unusual heat for Sapporo—and the air conditioning in the hall was not working properly. The staff brought a huge block of ice and placed it in Bernstein's dressing room.

Just before the concert, Funatsu, the twenty-one-year-old concert-master, knocked on the door of Bernstein's dressing room. During the dress rehearsal, while putting the final touches to the fiendish accelerating coda of the Schumann's scherzo movement, Bernstein had tried an experiment: he told the violinists to stand up for the last thirty-eight bars. Standing up would force them to play from memory, which would make them look confident, project better sound, and, most importantly, play freely, he said. They did as suggested, laughing and enjoying this unusual practice. The section violinists asked Funatsu whether to stand during the performance as well, but the young concertmaster had never had the experience of making such a decision on her own. She asked the maestro: "Um, do we stand at the end of the scherzo?"

Bernstein paused. Then, looking straight into her eyes, he asked her: "What do *you* think?" He wanted to know whether *she* thought the violins sounded better standing up. She said, frankly, "Yes, I think we sound better standing up." Then, with a serious face, he told her: "If *you* think we sound better that way, then we should do it." She then went back to convey the instruction to the violinists.

The concert program consisted of Marin Alsop conducting Beethoven's Symphony no. 2, Yutaka Sado conducting Tchaikovsky's *Francesca da Rimini*, and Schumann's Symphony no. 2 with Bernstein at the podium. Since Bernstein was not conducting in the first half of the performance, he could have waited in the dressing room or listened to the performance in the hall. Instead, he sat in the back of the orchestra on the stage while Alsop and Sado conducted.

While rehearsing *Francesca da Rimini*, Sado had a difficult time shaping some phrases. To show him how to lead the orchestra, Bernstein took his baton and conducted himself, to which the orchestra responded immediately with a much more clearly shaped line. After the rehearsal, Bernstein worried that this might have hurt Sado's feelings and remorsefully said to Hashimoto, "Poor Yutaka. I shouldn't have done that." Clearly his teaching worked, however. The phrases in question were perfectly shaped in the performance. When the piece was over, Bernstein turned around to the trombone section and said with his thumbs up, "Bravo, kids!" The deep satisfaction was seen on the faces of Bernstein applauding onstage, exhilarated Sado taking a deep bow, and the orchestra musicians who shared Sado's journey in creating the music.

The PMF Orchestra's performance of Schumann's Symphony no. 2 that day turned into one that did not pale even in comparison to some of the world's best orchestras that Bernstein conducted. From the opening of the first movement, the orchestra masterfully expressed the delicate lyricism and manic energy of the piece. The young musicians rose to the challenge of the scherzo, impeccably executing the "n-ba-di-ba-DI-ba-di-ba-di-ba-di-ba-di-ba-di-ba-di,   ba-di-ba-DI-ba-di-ba-di-ba-di-ba-di-ba-di" from the first bar. After the tender and lyrical trio in the middle, Bernstein created a pretense of coolness by putting his left hand in his pocket and conducting with his shoulder and eyebrows and minimal movement of the baton, inviting smiles from the musicians in the know. Then, at the coda, all the violinists stood up. The maestro turned toward them to lead and push them further—and to show off their command performance to the audience. The pure joy shared by the musicians—violinists and others alike, who played brilliantly, confidently, and freely—was contagious. The audience broke into a loud, long applause and bravos at the finish of the movement, even though they knew that there were two more movements remaining. Bernstein blew a kiss to the violinists in wholehearted approval.

After a long pause came the soulful adagio, the contrast in mood embodied by Bernstein's entire being. The violins entered ever so softly, singing with their strings a mournful, yearning melody and sighing with a *fortepiano*, against the quiet, panting pulse of the viola. After the slow rise to the movement's climax embodying the innermost reach for love, the full, passionate voices slowed and softened, *poco a poco*, until the orchestra took its last two breaths. The orchestra shared and expressed Bernstein's every emotion—grief, joy, sadness, exhilaration, longing, and prayer—as he conducted.

In the gallant final movement, Bernstein and the musicians' joy could barely be contained. After the triumphant finale propelled by the timpani, Bernstein wiped the sweat and tears off his face. He walked up to the wind players, who played beautiful solos in the adagio, gave each a standing bow, and kissed the flautist's hand. He then turned around, put his arms around section violinists, and bowed with a look of deep satisfaction and appreciation. The young musicians, now having come together as a bona fide orchestra, looked like they had just experienced what it meant to be part of something larger than themselves.

FIGURE 21.3 Leonard Bernstein conducting the PMF Orchestra at Sapporo Shimin Kaikan, July 3, 1990. Copyright PMF Organizing Committee.

* * *

The most important lesson I learned that summer came from Bernstein's response when I went to ask him about whether to stand at the end of the scherzo movement in the Schumann. He looked me in the eye and said: "In your life, if you want to do something, you've got to do it." I was asking him a very small question about a passage in a piece of music. But in response, he taught me the most important lesson about life: that you have to be true to what you believe and what you want to do.[3]

Takane Funatsu, concertmaster

As soon as Bernstein entered the rehearsal room, every single eyeball turned to him. And before he even said one word, he had every one of us in the palm of his hand. . . .

Many of the people in my current life are from that summer in Sapporo. With the PMF, Bernstein really created something amazing. So many lives were changed.[4]

Richard Bamping, cello

IIe truly wanted us to learn from him, not just in rehearsals and concerts but just by being and talking with him. . . . When he comes on stage, he just makes you think, "I'm going to play my very best ever." And you did![5]

Regina Helcher, flute

It was a whole different level of music making from what I had known. He had powerful ideas, bigger than I ever had been exposed to.[6]

Amy Oshiro, violin

[By studying with Bernstein at the PMF] I understood how much music meant to Bernstein. I understood how much music meant to the world. I understood how much he meant to the world. . . .

He cast his Bernsteinesque spell on everyone to make sense of music. He had an incredible ability to rein in the orchestra in a focused way while letting everyone be very free. We had come from all these different countries and cultures, speaking different languages. And he demonstrated to us how to transcend and connect with everyone, making the music together and making sense of it.[7]

Stuart Chafetz, timpani

When I got to the PMF, I saw all these foreigners, and I barely spoke any English. And everyone played so well, and I was clearly the worst player in my section. I kept thinking, "Oh shucks, oh shucks, what am I going to do?" . . . I just watched and listened to other musicians like nobody's business and tried my best to do what they did myself. And that's how my passion to play in an orchestra was born. . . .

All these years later, after having played with many of the world's best conductors, I have never seen a conductor who makes the musicians' blood flow and heart beat faster the way Bernstein did.[8]

Koichiro Yamamoto, trombone

These are the words of the PMF Orchestra musicians who worked with Bernstein in Sapporo. For them, the PMF was a transformative experience that literally changed their lives. They and countless other musicians who shared the summer in Sapporo have become leading performers and educators throughout the world. They have formed lasting friendships that continue to nourish their professional and personal lives. Almost thirty years later, they vividly talk about the summer of 1990 as if it was yesterday.

* * *

DURING THE TWO and a half weeks in Sapporo, Amano attended every rehearsal and every performance, commuting from her hotel almost two hours away. Yet, as in the summer of 1985, she did not spend any personal time with Bernstein during the festival. She knew how important this festival was to Bernstein, and she understood that he needed rest and quiet when he was not rehearsing or performing. She thus deliberately kept her distance but enjoyed every minute of the festival as his most dedicated fan.

On the other hand, Hashimoto attended to every need of the maestro and his entourage throughout the festival: translating for all of the Nidom staff and drivers, answering telephone calls at all hours of the day and night, ordering every meal for every guest. He served as a guide for Pulliam and Urquhart's shopping and sightseeing trips. When Robison and Pulliam wanted to go horseback riding, he made the arrangements and accompanied them as a translator, riding a horse for the first time. He played tennis with the acupuncturist's wife and swam in the pool with her baby. Even his friend Claude Cainero helped out by driving some of the entourage between the hotel and the festival site. Although Hashimoto was extremely busy catering to everyone's needs and had little time with Bernstein alone, he felt the utmost joy and fulfillment in spending his weeks serving Bernstein and his company.

For Bernstein, the Nidom proved to be a blissful haven, providing much needed rest and rejuvenation with his cherished friends and colleagues. The isolation from the busy life of the city, the privacy afforded by being the only guests at the resort, and the intimacy created by spending weeks together turned all those at the Nidom into a family of sorts.

The hotel staff mistook Pulliam as Bernstein's young wife and presented her a beautiful silk kimono and obi as they gave a men's kimono set to the maestro. Adorned in the kimono with the assistance of a professional stylist, Pulliam in fact looked like she could be Bernstein's spouse. The days at the Nidom were filled with other amusing occurrences. One day Hashimoto, Cainero, Urquhart, and Pulliam went to an open-air hot spring adjacent to Lake Shikotsu. Cainero jumped from the hot spring into the lake and vanished from sight as he swam away. Japanese visitors of the hot spring panicked: while the name "Shikotsu" originates from the indigenous Ainu word for water source, it is a homonym of the Japanese word for "dead bone," and the local legend has it that drowned bodies never reappear from the lake. Urquhart reassured them, "No worries, he is an Aussie, mate!" Cainero emerged from the lake after a leisurely swim.

Bernstein took joy in hearing these stories in his living room, which became a gathering place for all those at the Nidom. The living room had a Boesendorfer grand piano, on which Bernstein played boogie-woogie, as he often did when he was with friends and students. On July 4, Bernstein hosted an Independence Day party at the lodge. Pulliam prepared American-style food, and the group enjoyed Japanese hand-held *hanabi* ("flower fire") in lieu of grand fireworks in the sky. These were weeks of absolute joy and happiness for Bernstein.

* * *

ON JULY 8, Bernstein conducted the LSO in a special matinee concert commemorating the fiftieth anniversary of the Tanglewood Music Festival. The concert symbolized Bernstein's role in the world: the maestro conducting a European orchestra in Sapporo to celebrate the Massachusetts tradition launched by a Russian artist. With the success of this concert, Bernstein completed his mission in Sapporo. The seed he planted in Sapporo bloomed and bore abundant fruit. Although the festival had been organized as a one-time event without any plans for the future, all present witnessed the profound significance of this international festival for the young musicians as well as the Sapporo community.

Bernstein autographed the iron plate of the piano as he checked out of the Nidom, where he had regained his health and energy. After the matinee concert, the maestro and the entourage left Sapporo for Tokyo. Eager audiences were waiting to see Bernstein in his six remaining performances on the main island of Japan.

Discussing the PMF in a television interview, Bernstein calmly said:

I love two things: music and people. I don't know which I like better. I make music because I love people, and I love to work with them, and I love to play for them and communicate with them on the deepest level, which is the musical level. And it all has to do with love. Loving people and loving music, it's the same.

22

The Last Japan Tour

BEGINNING WITH HIS first tour with the New York Philharmonic in 1961 and three subsequent visits, along with the two summer tours in 1985, the 1990 tour marked Bernstein's seventh time performing for the Japanese audience. In conjunction with the PMF, he was also leading the tour of the LSO and was to perform in Tokyo, Kyoto, and Osaka. He was scheduled to conduct a joint performance of the LSO and the PMF Orchestra in Yokohama. Although the announced change in program disappointed some, the Japanese audience eagerly waited to see him onstage and experience his music.

Bernstein too was looking forward to the performances and all the things he had come to love about Japan: old friends, kabuki and noh performances, and antique shopping. He was also excited about going to Kyoto and staying at his friend Ernest Satow's Tawaraya Inn.

On July 9, he took his company—some of whom were visiting Japan for the first time—to a kabuki performance. Hashimoto served as an experienced guide for the group, showing them around the bustling districts of Ginza and Harajuku. While the company was generally enjoying their time in Tokyo, one of them was decidedly unhappy. Over the weeks, Bernstein's boyfriend Mark Taylor had become jealous of the maestro's obvious affection for Hashimoto and acted poorly toward both Hashimoto and Bernstein. Seeing the great stress this was causing Bernstein, the staff encouraged Taylor to leave. He acquiesced and left Japan before his scheduled departure.

On July 10, Bernstein conducted the first concert in Tokyo at Suntory Hall, with the emperor and empress in attendance. The audience's excitement, combined with a miscommunication about when the royal party was to leave, resulted in over fifteen minutes of applause during which neither the maestro nor the orchestra could leave the stage due to royal protocol.[1]

Although Bernstein's physical condition was far from perfect, the success of the Suntory Hall concert energized him enough that he joined Sony's Akio Morita for dinner at his residence, but the following day he had to cancel the dinner engagement after his second concert. He spent the next day resting at the hotel while the others went antique shopping. After the whole entourage had dinner together in Bernstein's suite, Hashimoto took Urquhart to enjoy Tokyo's nightlife. Bernstein was too exhausted to join them and stayed behind, and Cainero offered to keep him company.

Although Bernstein had never met or even heard of Cainero until arriving in Sapporo and had little idea what this Aussie was doing at the PMF, he had become quite fond of him during their time in Sapporo. When Bernstein felt too tired to attend Thomas Hampson's recital at the beginning of the festival, he sent Cainero to represent all the guests at the Nidom. Cainero, who had been to few classical music concerts before, was extremely moved by the performance and enthusiastically attended many rehearsals and performances for the remainder of the festival. He quickly became a beloved member of Team PMF.

Sitting with Bernstein in his opulent hotel suite, Cainero asked cheekily, "Why are you always so flamboyant?"

Bernstein replied, "I can't help it. I want to make people happy."

Contemplating this answer and seeing how tired the maestro looked, Cainero said, point blank, "It will kill you one day."

"I am not ready to die yet. I have lots of things to do," said Bernstein quietly.

Bernstein's response made Cainero think of his father, who immigrated to Australia from northern Italy and died when Cainero was young. He began sharing memories of his father while holding Bernstein's hand. He was surprised by his own tears as he talked. When he finished his story, he looked up at Bernstein and asked, "What about *your* father?"

After a moment of silence, Bernstein burst into tears. He then wept so uncontrollably that Cainero could not say a word and simply let him be. After a while, Bernstein left for his bedroom, still in tears. Cainero stayed in the living room until Hashimoto and Urquhart returned.

The next day, July 14, Bernstein was found collapsed on the floor of his suite. The medical representative of the insurance company immediately flew in from New York and was met by Hashimoto at the airport. Arrangements were made to fly Bernstein home at once. The concert presenters promptly announced that Tilson Thomas and Oue would replace him in the remaining concerts in Tokyo, Kyoto, and Osaka, as well as the joint concert of the PMF Orchestra and the LSO in Yokohama.

Bernstein left Japan on the 4:55 p.m. flight from Narita airport on July 16. With Urquhart handling the many suitcases, Hashimoto and Cainero rode in the limousine alone with Bernstein. During their last moments at the airport, Bernstein said to Hashimoto: "Take care of the rest of the concerts and look after the conductors."

After seeing Bernstein off, Hashimoto went straight from the airport to the concert at NHK Hall, where Oue conducted in Bernstein's place. After Tilson Thomas conducted the concert the following evening, Hashimoto accompanied him to Kyoto and Osaka for the remaining performances. He attended to Tilson Thomas's needs and took him sightseeing, and the two stayed at Tawaraya, where he stayed with Bernstein five years earlier.

With the heroic determination of the conductors and the orchestra, all of the scheduled concerts were completed. However, some audience members were upset by the last-minute changes in conductors and loudly protested to the presenters after the concert. The severity of Bernstein's illness had not been disclosed, and some media coverage also expressed criticism of his cancellation.

* * *

AFTER BERNSTEIN'S HASTY departure from Japan, Amano sent him a letter. In it her deep concern about his health is mixed with happy news about the kindness with which his friends treated her after his departure and her emerging friendship with Yutaka Sado. She then closes the letter:

> Tonight there was a program on the TV of your concert with Wiener Philharmonic with Mahler's 9th at Berlin Philharmonic Hall. It is my favorite music from many many years ago and I have already decided several years ago that this music, performed by you, the last movement, will be the music for my funeral, after the Requiem Mass, as I am a Catholic. This movement is like a "résumé" of my whole life. I cannot listen to it without tears, and I know that you were crying too. Music is wonderful. Lenny, you are not only wonderful but great, warm, honest like a child, sometimes. I will treasure the words you said to me in Sapporo, in Tokyo, about my life. But if I dare to be praised for my courage and all, it is because YOU

ARE WITH ME. Happy birthday again and please take the utmost care of your health. Je vous embrasse très tendrement, bien à vous, votre Kazuko[2]

Even as she worries about Bernstein's health, it is her own funeral that she is thinking about. This was not an expression of self-absorption; she had suffered a stroke several years earlier and must have thought seriously about her own mortality. But perhaps more importantly, it was probably easier for her to think about her own funeral than contemplate Bernstein's death. Her deepening Catholic faith and her references to Bernstein and his music indicate that for her, too, the love for Bernstein had acquired a spiritual dimension beyond personal admiration and friendship.

Later that summer, Bernstein conducted Beethoven's Symphony no. 7 at Tanglewood. In the midst of the performance, he had a coughing fit that terrified the musicians and the audience alike. Having heard this news from a friend, Amano wrote:

I was just terrified. Poor Beloved Lenny, how hard, very hard it must have been for you, both physically and mentally, caught between a terrible wish to take a complete rest due to such pains and weakness, and an ardent desire to go on your wonderful dream in life, your wonderful vocation. Although I am not a woman of your level, because of my late sickness and my devoted love toward you, I understand your inner struggles and pains together with the physical ones. Because you are greater, yes, really greater than others, you have to fight more than the average people. The sad destiny of a genius. How glamorous it looks, but how painful it is in reality! But Lenny, you are a chosen and blessed one from God. It is my belief, my firm belief. So Beloved Lenny, please take the utmost care of yourself and be happy.[3]

With his condition worsening, in early October Bernstein officially announced his retirement from the stage. As soon as she heard the news, Amano sent him a fax from her home. That she sent a fax instead of mailing a letter or a card suggests that she sensed the gravity of his condition. Although she might not have admitted it even to herself, she may have instinctively felt that an air mail letter might not reach Bernstein in time. As if to make a point about the immediacy with which she was writing, she not only dated but time-stamped her message, "October 11, 1990, 6:00 AM."

> Beloved Lenny!
>
> With a broken heart did I hear just now (5:45 AM) (with the TV direct from New York) your sad but brave decision to . . . retire from . . . "conducting." . . . Nothing is more heartbreaking for Kazuko, her children and all your true friends here. How great you are and . . . how <u>brave</u> you were to come to this decision.
>
> I pray for your <u>quick recovery</u> and your solace and satisfaction to come from now on . . .
>
> Be Blessed Beloved Lenny. Please recover at the earliest. How I wish I could take your illness upon me, so that you could be your old self. Lenny, you remain the greatest Conductor, forever and ever.
>
> With love and fond embrace,
>
> Kazuko[4]

She puts quotation marks around the word "conducting" as if in disbelief, like she is trying to process what she just heard on television but is unable to fully comprehend it. Although she prays for his quick recovery—what else could one say, really, under the circumstances?—she probably knew deep down that he was not going to "be [his] old self" again. She understood what it meant for Bernstein to retire from conducting.

Whereas Amano wrote several times to express her concern for Bernstein's condition after his departure from Japan, Hashimoto never wrote to him after seeing him off at Narita airport.

The last letter from Hashimoto to Bernstein is dated June 2, 1990, a few weeks before the opening of the PMF. Aside from his telexes, this is the only letter he sent to Bernstein that is typed. But just like all of his earlier letters, this too begins with "Dearest Lenny":

> Recently, almost every night, I have seen you in my dream. It is such a sweet dream, my heart throbs with the dreams, and when I wake up, a strange sensation remains.
>
> The sensation must come from my memories. Even though I do not touch you in my dreams, the sensation I had when I touched your face, stroked your hair, cuddled with you tightly . . . has stayed

with me strongly. Now, when I am about to see you after three years, the sensation just came back and rose faster and stronger than in my memory. How strange!

The letters you wrote to me in response to the letters I kept sending you, the pictures I took in Munich, Positano, Amsterdam, and the presents you gave me . . . I have kept all of them and locked them in a briefcase. Just like you keep my letters in New York. But I try not to open the briefcase to see them. Because, if I opened it, the wonderful, great memories will burst out and make me miss you so much. I am afraid for that to happen. I know that I will burn with love again, too seriously, if I opened it. Even without opening the briefcase, it has happened to me sometimes and I have longed for you. Although I try not to touch our memories, now my sensation brings up those memories. It is like Ondine longing for something when she touches water, or an angel who comes down to earth looking up at the sky for no reason. Now I am flapping the wings and flying to the sky!

The time when I loved you was the most brilliant time of my life. That kind of love may never happen in my life again. When I loved you, I never wished for the realization of our love. I may have had a small hope for it, but I was very happy just to love you. I just kept loving you without caring about what happened to our relationship. I found the great happiness of pure love, the act of loving someone, not the happiness of fulfilled love. But I was in Japan, and you went around the world. . . .

It is true that I loved Terry, but it was different from my love for you. For you, I feel not only love but also respect and awe, like one feels for a master. But Terry and I were equal.

During my days with Terry, I still kept loving you and even now I have not changed in loving you. . . . However, I gradually started thinking about changing my life and decided to go to Australia. . . . Indeed, Australia is a suitable place for me, on the other side of the earth, a new continent isolated from both western and eastern world.

But now, I am about to fly to the sky, to find once again the memory and glory of heaven. And just like an angel, I will come down again with the memories after finding wisdom.

Here, in Australia, I have never forgotten you. I still continue loving you. This love may be different from that painful, too serious, too passionate love that I had before. But I still look up at the sky and extend my arms to the sun.

How many times I listened to your recording of *Tristan* after I went to the terrible performance of *Tristan* at the Sydney Opera House! How much I miss you when I listen to your new recordings, like Beethoven's Ninth Symphony which you conducted in Berlin.

The final sentence of this letter—which turned out to be the last sentence Hashimoto wrote to Bernstein—is: "But Lenny, I can see you soon."[5]

Bernstein died at his home on October 14, 1990.

23

Making the Garden Grow

AT BERNSTEIN'S MEMORIAL concert at the Cathedral of Saint John the Divine in New York in December 1990, an orchestra consisting of students from the three music festivals he founded or cultivated in different parts of the world—Tanglewood, Schleswig-Holstein, and the PMF—performed to honor the maestro's commitment to education. Inspired by Bernstein's spirit, Sapporo mayor Takeshi Itagaki declared at the concert that the PMF would continue as an annual festival.

Bernstein's dream of bringing young musicians from around the world to study and share music was thus realized in Sapporo, not just in the summer of 1990 but every year that followed. The festival administration was reorganized under the auspices of the city of Sapporo; the facilities at Sapporo Art Park expanded with a larger and permanent outdoor stage, rehearsal halls, and studios; and many of the performances came to be held at Kitara, the new world-class concert hall in downtown Sapporo. With the steadily growing number of applicants auditioning from around the world, the PMF became not only an important cultural event for the Sapporo community but also one of the most coveted opportunities for young classical musicians around the world.

The PMF also allowed Amano and Hashimoto to keep their love of Bernstein alive and continue to serve him in their own ways.

Amano kept attending the festival every year after Bernstein's death. She became a devoted fan of Tilson Thomas, following him in his performances and attending to him as she had done for Bernstein. She enthusiastically joined the PMF Friends, a membership organization that supports the education of young musicians at the festival. She also served as a resident advisor at the accommodations for the orchestra members, using her multilingual skills and international experience to assist the young musicians, for many of whom the PMF was their first trip abroad.

Bernstein's death did not end Hashimoto's commitment to serving him. Although he was no longer officially Amberson's Japan representative, he was called upon to assist when major issues arose with regard to licensing and other matters. But more than any administrative assistance he gave to Amberson, his continued involvement in the PMF embodied his true dedication to Bernstein's goals and dreams.

Bernstein had asked Hashimoto to "look after the conductors." Hashimoto took this to heart and did exactly that. He earned the trust and affection of subsequent music directors of the PMF, all conductors of worldwide renown: Michael Tilson Thomas, Christoph Eschenbach, and Charles Dutoit. He also built a close rapport with Bernstein's Japanese protégés Eiji Oue and Yutaka Sado, both of whom oversaw the auditions and conducted the PMF Orchestra. For many years, Hashimoto would not only take care of these artists' needs related to the PMF but also spend personal time with them when they visited Sydney for performances and other business. His friend Claude Cainero became a beloved member of the PMF family, and he took the maestros sailing on his yacht in Sydney Harbour.

Hashimoto also came to play a much more substantial role in the PMF. Almost every year from 1994 to 2002, he participated in the festival as an artist in his own right. By then a seasoned actor and voiceover artist, Hashimoto narrated such works as the concert performance of Mozart's *Cosi fan tutte* and Stravinsky's *L'histoire du soldat*. But what most effectively demonstrated his talent, creativity, and understanding of Bernstein's spirit—what Bernstein would have been most proud of and delighted by—was his translation of Bernstein's *Candide*.

Candide had never been performed in Japan. Hashimoto made it happen. To commemorate the fifth anniversary of the PMF in 1994, Kraut requested that Hashimoto translate the libretto and text of the concert version.

Translating lyrics requires special insight and skill. A literal translation from English to Japanese would have resulted in many more syllables and hence musical notes. Beyond conveying the meaning of the text, the translation needed to fit the notes in a musical phrase and be singable for the vocalists and intelligible to the listeners. Entrusting Hashimoto with this challenge demonstrated Kraut's judgment about his literary and musical skills and, perhaps most importantly, his grasp of Bernstein's spirit in the original work. As Hashimoto himself later wrote: "The most important thing is comprehending the concept and intentions of the writer of song and lyric and express it in Japanese without losing any of the intended meaning of mood for the piece. The work attempts to show the entire Milky Way. It is like selecting suitable constellations from the Milky Way, arranging, disposing and scattering them on a celestial body so that Japanese speakers can understand the beauty and expanse of the entire Milky Way."[1]

He must have listened to the work over and over as he followed the score. The overture to *Candide* had been performed as the finale of the memorial concert at Carnegie Hall a month after Bernstein's passing. The conductorless performance by an international orchestra, with an empty podium lit up, had left all in attendance, including Hashimoto, in tears and utter silence. Although the overture has no vocal text, Hashimoto must have studied the music carefully, as it crystallizes the essence for the entire work. Each listen would have brought back the visceral memory of the concert but also reminded him of Bernstein's spirit, driving him forward with the bursting syncopated opening and throughout the piece. No doubt he studied Voltaire's original novella and pored over the book by Hugh Wheeler. He would have perused the lyrics—written by Richard Wilbur, Stephen Sondheim, John LaTouche, Dorothy Parker, Lillian Hellman, and Bernstein himself—while listening and singing along to its catchy melodies and jovial rhythms. As he wrote down various possible translations for each phrase, considering effective expressions and clever puns, he must have felt like Bernstein's mischievous collaborator.

Hashimoto's translation is a masterpiece whose ingenuity matches the brilliant wit of the original. Rather than trying to provide a literal translation of the lyrics, Hashimoto often changed the meaning of the text considerably for the sake of capturing the spirit of the scene, characters, ideas, and morals. He also "translated" the slapstick humor of the original into the comic effect through a clever use of the Japanese language. His craft is showcased most effectively in numbers sung by the heroine Cunegonde and the Old Lady. For Cunegonde's aria, "Glitter and Be Gay"—a showpiece of comic performance and extreme virtuosic singing in which the heroine sings of using jewels and laughter to conceal her misery—Hashimoto's text combines old-fashioned poetic language to dramatize the tragedy in the opening ballad and the clever use of rhyme in the fast coloratura section. In the Old Lady's "I Am Easily Assimilated," he adapts the idea of cultural mixing and assimilation to comically create a rhyme between the words *gracias* (which is not in the original lyrics) and *okoshiyasu* (Kyoto dialect for "welcome") and between *somaru* (to be influenced, assimilated) and *namaru* (to speak with an accent). The result is an effective rendition of the sassy, indomitable character who survives her travails by appropriating cultures and assimilating to the environment. Cunegonde and the Old Lady's duet "We Are Women" similarly uses plays on words to convey the tongue-in-cheek commentary on feminine wiles.

The Japanese premiere of *Candide* at the PMF was conducted by Bernstein's last Japanese protégé, Yutaka Sado, with Hashimoto himself in the role of the narrator. After the PMF, the work was performed in Tokyo in September, with Sado conducting the New Japan Philharmonic Orchestra founded by Seiji Ozawa. The *Japan Times* reviewer's reference to the production said it all: "The Voltaire/Bernstein/Hashimoto Japanese 'Candide'—of the Japanese, by the Japanese and for the Japanese."[2]

Hashimoto repeated the creative project the following year by translating the concert version of Bernstein's *On the Town*. The work was performed at the 1995 PMF, again with Yutaka Sado conducting.

In 1999, Hashimoto again played an important part in carrying on Bernstein's legacy. Using Bernstein's Young People's Concerts as a model, the maestro's protégé Michael Barrett and daughter Jamie Bernstein Thomas developed the idea for the Bernstein Beat, an educational concert to introduce Bernstein's music to young audiences.[3] Hashimoto adapted this idea for the Japanese audiences at the PMF, writing the script and hosting the show himself.

In a concert titled What Makes Music Dance? Hashimoto seamlessly interwove the account of Bernstein's life and work with lessons on rhythm and beat as a key component of music. In his final words before the Sapporo Symphony Orchestra's performance of "America" from *West Side Story*, Hashimoto talked about the mingling of different races that made up America and connected it to the spirit of the PMF, where musicians of different backgrounds gathered in Sapporo to make music together. "Leonard Bernstein loved diverse music from around the world," Hashimoto told the young audience in his deep, calming voice. He closed his commentary with these reminders:

> He gathered all these different music from the world together. And he turned it into his own, new compositions, and presented them to all of us, and the entire world, as his gift. That is what this music is about. And that is what the Pacific Music Festival is about.[4]

Bernstein's gift to the world is crystallized in "Make Our Garden Grow," the finale number of *Candide*, sung by the entire cast. The song is moving for its simple humanity. The phrasing, characteristic of musical theater, is set to Richard Wilbur's lyrics:

> *Let dreamers dream what worlds they please;*
> *Those Edens can't be found.*
> *The sweetest flow'rs, the fairest trees*
> *Are grown in solid ground.*
> *We're neither pure nor wise nor good;*
> *We'll do the best we know.*
> *We'll build our house, and chop our wood,*
> *And make our garden grow,*
> *And make our garden grow.*

Hashimoto's Japanese translation, composed to match the linguistic and musical phrases, translates back into English as: "Beautiful flowers and leaves, blue sky; trees are born and grow in this robust ground. Humans too shall live our best, aspiring to the heavens. We'll build our house, and chop our wood. With our forces together, we shall live. And make our farm grow."[5]

Bernstein's dream that flowered and bore fruit in Sapporo in 1990 kept growing for many years after his passing. At the opening ceremony for the PMF's tenth anniversary in 1999, the artistic director Tilson Thomas concluded his speech with the remark: "Maestro Bernstein, your dream is fulfilled. Now watch us grow."[6]

Coda
Emails from Honolulu and the Making of *Dearest Lenny*

MY JOURNEY ON this project began in the summer of 2013, when I accidentally discovered Amano's and Hashimoto's letters in the Leonard Bernstein Collection at the Library of Congress while doing research for a completely different topic.

Moved and intrigued by the letters, I first searched for information on Hashimoto, believing that as an actor and writer he would be easier to locate. Indeed, it did not take me long to find that Hashimoto was still living and working in Sydney. Upon conceiving the outline for the book, I inquired with the Library of Congress about the use of his letters. The archivist consulted the staff at the Leonard Bernstein Office, who in turn passed my unexpected request on to Hashimoto. They then suggested that I contact him directly to describe my project and seek his permission. I carefully composed an email in Japanese, explaining how I came to read his letters and what I wished to do with them in my proposed book.

To my amazement, I received a reply from him within twenty-four hours. He apologized for not responding sooner—he had been in a remote area with limited internet access—and sent a seven-page letter expressing his shock at receiving my email. He had shared his stories of Bernstein with only a very few people in his life and had intended to have his letters sealed until his death. He had also put away Bernstein's letters in a locked trunk, his emotions too raw to this day to open it. Nonetheless, he considered my request seriously and carefully, and gave me permission to move forward with my research and writing under one condition: that the Bernstein family approve the project. I therefore sent my proposal to the Leonard Bernstein Office, and the family discussed it and gave me support for the project.

I spent the next four years researching as much as I could at the Bernstein Collection and other archives, including the New York Philharmonic Digital Archives and the Houston Grand Opera Archives, as well as researching and interviewing sources in Japan. Coincidentally, I was invited to teach an intensive summer session at Hokkaido University in Sapporo and decided to teach a course on the political economy of the arts, using the Pacific Music Festival as a primary case study. For three consecutive summers, as part of the course I took the students to the PMF rehearsals and concerts, talked with the members of the organizing committee, hosted an educational seminar for the general public where I interviewed the guest conductors, and moderated special sessions where the PMF academy members and the students of Hokkaido University engaged in discussions. I thus witnessed Bernstein's legacy on the ground in Sapporo almost three decades after his passing. I also spent a night at the beautiful and peaceful Nidom, in the two-bedroom cottage with the same setup as the one where Hashimoto and Cainero stayed in 1990, and walked through Bernstein's suite, which has now been converted into a wedding chapel.

In May 2017, having finished the first draft of the manuscript, I went to meet Hashimoto in Sydney.

Hashimoto has continued to work in a range of creative fields as an actor, writer, director, and producer in Australia and Japan. His work for Bernstein resulted in other projects that broadened his artistic horizons. His translation of *Candide* led to him being hired to translate the libretto for Stephen Sondheim's *Pacific Overtures*, directed and choreographed by Amon Miyamoto, Japan's foremost director of musical theater, and produced at the New National Theatre Tokyo in 2000.[1] Sondheim saw the performance in Tokyo and was so impressed by the production that he convinced the Lincoln Center in New York and the Kennedy Center in Washington to host the same production in 2002. Thus the Japanese version of *Pacific Overtures*, with Hashimoto's translation, was performed at two of America's most prestigious performing arts venues—two halls that Bernstein had helped establish and remained closely connected to. Hashimoto's involvement in Sondheim's work continued, as he was hired to translate the lyrics for *Into the Woods*, performed at the New National Theatre Tokyo under Miyamoto's direction in June 2004.

Hashimoto is the sensitive, articulate, bold, and kind man that one imagines from the letters he wrote decades ago. He lives with his partner and a dog he named Amber. He welcomed me into his life and generously spent time with me, sharing memories of Bernstein and thoughts about what I had written. He also took me to meet Claude Cainero at his waterfront mansion, where he told me moving stories of his time with Bernstein in the summer of 1990.

Amano's long friendship with Bernstein is not my original discovery, as it had been covered in a few Japanese magazines in the 1990s. But because the people I met who knew Amano—including Hashimoto—all told me that they had not heard from her in many years, I assumed that she had passed away. It was Hashimoto who tried to help me find Kikuko's whereabouts—I wanted to get the family's permission to write about Kazuko's letters—by calling, from Sydney, the Tokyo number he had in his old address book. To his surprise and mine, both mother and daughter were still living in the same condominium where Kazuko wrote many letters to Bernstein.

I went to meet them in Tokyo in July 2017. I got lost in the confusing streets typical of Japan's residential neighborhoods, and Kikuko came to find me on her bicycle despite the heat and humidity. Kazuko met me at her home with a big smile, wearing a PMF T-shirt. She is the vivacious, thoughtful, and perceptive woman that I had pictured her to be from her letters. As she shared her memories, she showed me Bernstein's photographs and Helen Coates's letters she has cherished over the decades. Her love of music and passion for Bernstein's work has been a primary source of her vitality and positive outlook throughout her seventies and eighties, even after she injured her back and lost much of her mobility. Her unwavering dedication to family is evident in her relationship with her children and grandchildren.

My understanding of Amano's and Hashimoto's characters and the nature of their love for Bernstein was not betrayed by meeting them. But my direct communication with them—in person, on the phone, and through correspondence—filled in some critical gaps in the story and gave me a more multidimensional sense of their lives, reminding me of both the power and limits of research based on extant papers.

As I write this coda in the summer of 2018, there are countless events taking place around the world in honor of Bernstein centenary: concerts, exhibits, and lectures revisiting his works and reflecting on the world he lived through and made his mark in. Indeed, Bernstein embodied the turbulence of the twentieth century: born at the end of World War I and making a sensational debut during World War II, he lived through the Cold War and passed away having witnessed the fall of the Iron Curtain. He produced original and exciting music out of a profound understanding of European traditions and serious engagement with other cultures. He pioneered new ways of sharing the joy of music during the period when the means of musical experience expanded beyond the concert halls to radio and television broadcasts, LP recordings and then CDs, and films and videos. While he adroitly navigated these changes in technology, media, and industry as one of the foremost musicians of the century, his power as a human being lay not only in his musical talents but also in his deep, uncompromising engagement with the world. More than any other musician of his time—or perhaps any time—Bernstein was involved in the political, social, and ethical issues of the real world and tirelessly acted on them. Out of that embedded engagement came the freedom as an artist and an individual that empowered him to reach across borders. He made every decision in art and life in service of his pursuit of truth, faith in humanity, and love of people.

The more I probed into Amano's and Hashimoto's relationships with Bernstein, the more I realized that they spoke to my scholarly interests in the cultural history of US-Japan relations. Amano's encounter with Bernstein was enabled by the cultural diplomacy of the US occupation of postwar Japan; Hashimoto met the maestro when Japan's economic power made it an indispensable market for classical music. Many of the key moments in the two individuals' evolving relationship with the maestro were linked to the changes in global economy and politics, the places of the United States and Japan within them, and the relations between the two nations, even as their love and devotion transcended those factors.

The history of Bernstein's connection to Japan and these two individuals deeply resonated with my personal history as well. My parents, who grew up during the war in different parts of Japan, met each other when my mother placed a "pen pal wanted" ad in a magazine for young Japanese students of English and my father was one of many who responded to the ad. Their relationship emerged in the early 1950s through their correspondence in English, a language they both labored to learn. After their marriage, my father was sent to set up the New York office of the Japanese trading firm he worked for. I was born in New York in 1968, on the day that the New York Philharmonic's executive director sent a letter to the presenter of the upcoming Japan tour, asserting that Seiji Ozawa was no longer Bernstein's assistant but an internationally respected maestro in his own right. My family moved back to Tokyo shortly thereafter, and I became a serious student of piano. When I was eleven, we moved to California, again for my father's job. Upon returning to Tokyo a few years later, I continued to study music but later became a student of American studies, building on my cross-cultural experience. Graduating from university at the tail end of Japan's "bubble economy," I left for the United States to pursue graduate study and then landed a job in Hawai'i teaching US-Asian relations. Thus, my birth originated in the English-language letter writing between two Japanese youths, while my upbringing and musical and intellectual development were very much tied to US-Japan relations during the period of Japan's rise as a global economic power.

Unlike the countless handwritten letters that Amano and Hashimoto sent to Bernstein, my correspondence with them mostly took the form of emails across the Pacific: Hashimoto in Sydney, Amano in Tokyo, and me in Honolulu and, during the final phase of writing, Los Angeles. Amano—eighty-nine years old when I met her—does not send emails herself, so I communicated through Kikuko and through phone calls. With Hashimoto, both before and after my visit to Sydney, I exchanged literally hundreds of emails, debating ideas about my manuscript as well as sharing stories unrelated to the book. As an actor and writer, he has been a fountain of insights about storytelling, and his involvement in my writing turned out to be much bigger than what I had initially expected. Far beyond being a protagonist and an informant, he took on the role of an intellectual and editorial collaborator and pushed me to think beyond conventional academic writing and to tell a human story.

In contrast to the days when the letter writer anxiously waited weeks or months to get replies, my email correspondence with Amano and Hashimoto has been quick and efficient. Sometimes I received replies even before I was mentally ready to receive them; on a number of occasions there were many intense exchanges in a single day. The speedy communication deepened my appreciation for these two individuals and facilitated the writing of this book.

And yet the numerous emails across the Pacific that led to the making of *Dearest Lenny* do not have the same resonance as the letters Amano and Hashimoto wrote—on stationery with the print of Mount Fuji, postcards from cities around the world, pages and pages of thin airmail paper—and mailed with beautiful stamps carefully chosen for Bernstein. During the period in which their relationship with Bernstein unfolded, the modes of correspondence across distances also changed, from sea mail to air mail, with the addition of telex and fax, all of which Amano and Hashimoto used deftly to express their devotion to the maestro. But the depth and beauty of their love were inextricably tied to the particular form of communication that shaped their special relationships with Bernstein—letters written by hand and sent via what is today colloquially called "snail mail"—which is rapidly disappearing from our world.

Acknowledgments

THE RESEARCH, WRITING, and editing of this book have been a journey unlike any other I have made. First and foremost, my deepest gratitude goes to Kazuko Amano and Kunihiko Hashimoto, who have trusted me to write about intensely private and precious parts of their lives. Through their profound, continuing love for Bernstein and their faith in this project, I have learned about the true meaning of devotion. I am especially grateful to Kunihiko Hashimoto for his endless patience and generosity in sharing his thoughts on many versions of the manuscript.

Having the support of the Bernstein family and the Leonard Bernstein Office from the beginning of the project has been greatly reassuring. I appreciate Marie Carter's assistance and support on practical matters in addition to her careful reading of the manuscript. Craig Urquhart and Garth Sunderland also provided important assistance during the preparation of the book.

Many of the archival sources come from the Leonard Bernstein Collection housed at the Library of Congress. Like other researchers who have used this incredible collection, I am indebted to Mark Horowitz for his extensive knowledge of its contents. During all my trips to Washington, Theodore Gonzalves and Charita Castro hosted me in their beautiful home, and I enjoyed every minute I got to spend with them. Gabryel Smith of the New York Philharmonic Leon Levy Digital Archives always promptly answered my questions and helped me acquire images and permissions. Brian Mitchell and James Carter assisted me in obtaining materials at the Houston Grand Opera Archives when it was difficult for me to make the trip there. The archivists at the John F. Kennedy Presidential Library and the Lyndon B. Johnson Presidential Library helped me navigate the otherwise overwhelming and bewildering archives. Noriko Shibaki, Fumiko Watanabe, and others at the PMF Organizing Committee provided critical assistance in researching the festival. Hiromi Morita at Chūgoku Shimbun helped me on my research in Hiroshima. Eri Kato and Tomoe Seita gathered some Japanese sources for me at short notice. Alicia Kopfstein-Penk helped obtain images that add texture to the book.

As immensely rich as archival research turned out to be, I also learned much about the limits of relying solely on extant documents, especially in putting together a story about the human act of music making. A number of people have shared personal stories that have been critical in my understanding of the human dimensions of the story. Kikuko Amano not only helped me understand her mother but also shared her own precious memories of Bernstein. Mitsunori Sano spent an entire day talking with me about the Hiroshima Peace Concert and the Pacific Music Festival and continued to answer my many questions in the months that followed. Claude Cainero welcomed me in his beautiful home in Sydney and shared a moving story of Bernstein at the PMF. Noriko Shibaki's stories of attending the PMF in 1990 shed light on the transformative impact of the festival on young musicians. Richard Bamping, Stuart Chafetz, Takane Funatsu, Amy Oshiro-Morales, Koichiro Yamamoto, and Regina Helcher Yost all generously shared their memories of the PMF and helped me understand what Bernstein meant to them and to the world.

My research on the PMF would likely have remained an archive-based one if not for Professor Eijun Senaha's invitation to teach at the Hokkaido Summer Institute. Having the opportunity to be involved in the PMF for three consecutive years through the course added immensely to my appreciation for the branch of Bernstein's legacy that has taken root in Sapporo. I am grateful to Kazuko Morioka for all the administrative assistance related to the course. Yujin Yaguchi not only was my co-instructor for the course but also went with me to experience the Nidom's spectacular setting and gave me a Sapporo native's perspective on the PMF.

Like my previous books, this one was made possible by the intellectual and moral support of my wonderful writing group, whose members commented on early drafts of key chapters: Elizabeth Colwill, Monisha Das Gupta, Cynthia Franklin, Candace Fujikane, Linda Lierheimer, Laura Lyons, Kieko Matteson, and Naoko Shibusawa. I am blessed by their love and friendship through all the ups and downs of the journey.

Through many incarnations of the manuscript, friends and colleagues have read and commented on its various parts and gave me precious encouragement: Scott Anderson, Brad Arington, Kathleen Sands, Barry Schlachter, and Willamarie Moore. Bianet Castellanos, Mariko Iijima, Brian Roberts, and Yujin Yaguchi gave me opportunities to share my work with their colleagues and students, whose feedback has informed my thinking. The support and faith of many friends and colleagues—especially Ken Foster, Lon Kurashige, Josephine Lee, Carol Oja, Nayan Shah, Allen Shawn, Lisa Yoneyama, and Natasha Zaretsky—have meant so much at different stages of the project.

As I encountered serious unexpected challenges, a number of friends and colleagues literally came to the rescue with their incredible generosity, intellect, and wisdom. Katherine Baber, Shiro Kawai, Lon Kurashige, Brian Locke, David Thomas, Judy Tzu-Chun Wu, Yujin Yaguchi, and Christine Yano read the entire manuscript and offered thoughtful and constructive suggestions. Sasha Margolis not only read and commented on the manuscript but also gave me friendship, love, family, and understanding which I cannot even describe.

Having a musical life in addition to a scholarly one—and having a different set of keyboards to tackle—has shaped my thinking and writing in important ways. Whatever technical and musical development I have achieved as a pianist is the patient work of Thomas Yee. My life has been enriched by participating in the Aloha International Piano Festival, Cliburn International Amateur Piano Competition (formerly International Piano Competition for Outstanding Amateurs), and PianoTexas International Festival and Academy, all of which have given me opportunities to learn from renowned artists and nurture enduring friendships with fellow music lovers. Makiko Hirata has been a special friend and teacher who has seen me through the good times and the bad. I cherish the support of Christopher Yomei Blasdell and Mika Kimula, who not only have shown great interest in this project since its early phases but also took a gamble on my piano skills on the professional stage. I am especially grateful to all my friends who have come to my recitals over the years and shared in my music making.

I hope that witnessing my own process through this book has made my graduate students understand that endless rewrites are simply part of our chosen craft. My proud shout-out goes to those who have bravely endured that process, many of them through our writing workshop: Eriza Bareng, Keiko Fukunishi, Jeanette Hall, Yujung Lee, Kevin Lim, Yihung Liu, Yanli Luo, Sanae Nakatani, Stacy Nojima, Eriko Ohga, Yuka Polovina, Yohei Sekiguchi, and Sean Trundle.

Just as I began working on this book, I took on the position of editor of *American Quarterly*. Thanks to the American Studies Association for trusting me with this role. I would not have been able to handle the editorial responsibilities of this important journal while continuing to work on my own research if it were not for the exceptional professionalism of my editorial staff. Katherine Achacoso, Jeanette Hall, Billie Lee, Sanae Nakatani, Logan Narikawa, Brooke Newell, and Stacy Nojima have all demonstrated their administrative, problem-solving, and people skills far above and beyond my imagination. The often unacknowledged labor of the associate editors—Hokulani Aikau, Monisha Das Gupta, Vernadette Gonzalez, Min-Jung Kim, Christopher Lee, Suzanna Reiss, and Yujin Yaguchi—and all members of the board of managing editors has made the editorial work intellectually stimulating and professionally rewarding.

With a better understanding of editorial work, I am all the more in awe of Susan Ferber's brilliance and meticulousness as an editor. I am eternally grateful for her faith and patience through what has turned out to be a unique and complicated project and for her always sound judgment and careful attention. I thank Ben Sadock for his sharp eyes, Damian Penfold for his deft management the project, and all the other staff at Oxford University Press for their professionalism and guidance in turning this manuscript into an actual book.

My everyday life at the Department of American Studies at the University of Hawai'i at Mānoa is made easier by the administrative assistance of Lori Mina and Rumi Yoshida. Over twenty-some years, my departmental comrades have heard me speak my mind on matters big and small, and they shall continue to do so.

I am blessed with the love and support of friends in different contexts of my life. Having Elizabeth Colwill next door is the best reason to go to the office every day. Having Kathleen Sands two doors down makes things even better. Although Jonna Eagle's office is all the way on the other side, she shares my professional and personal travails, commiserates over drinks, lets me play with the kids, and sometimes listens to my advice. I am sad that Heather Diamond and Fred Lau are no longer my neighbors, but I am determined that we will share more fun times and good food in different parts of the globe. Despite all the bad things about Facebook, it has played a critical role in fostering my friendship with Momoko Kawakami, whose intellect and interests always inspire me. Perhaps more than anyone, Yasuko Sato understands both the joys and challenges this project has brought to me, not only as a friend but also as a creative artist. During the years I was working on this project, my BFF Akiko Zama went through challenges far beyond the ones I have ever experienced. The depth and strength of her character through it all has been humbling and inspiring. I send my love to her and her family. To my longtime co-conspirator Yujin Yaguchi: thank you always.

With his love—and meals and drinks and music—Jun Fujimoto has given me the security and confidence that helped me get up and take the next step even during the most difficult times. I am glad that we got to experience Sydney—and so much more—together. Now that he understands what it means to be with someone writing a book, he is well equipped to deal with me writing the next book.

I dedicate this book to the memory of Steve Dinion. He told me that he decided to become a musician when he saw Bernstein conduct at the Kennedy Center. His love of music and commitment to justice inform this book and my life. I think he would have been happy about and proud of this book. I miss him dearly.

Notes

INTRODUCTION

1. Serge Koussevitzky to Leonard Bernstein, December 23, 1946, Leonard Bernstein Collection (hereafter LBC), box 33, folder 17.
2. Isaac Stern to Leonard Bernstein, December 10, 1947, LBC, box 53, folder 34.
3. Yo-Yo Ma to Leonard Bernstein, December 21, 1965, LBC, box 37, folder 20.
4. Nigel Simeone, ed., *The Leonard Bernstein Letters* (New Haven, CT: Yale University Press, 2013).
5. Humphrey Burton, *Leonard Bernstein* (New York: Doubleday, 1994), 323, 519. Charlie Harmon's recent memoir mentions Hashimoto's role as Bernstein's translator during the Hiroshima tour of 1985. Charlie Harmon, *On the Road and Off the Record with Leonard Bernstein: My Years with the Exasperating Genius* (Watertown, MA: Charlesbridge, 2018), chaps. 31, 32.
6. He is no relation to the early twentieth-century composer, violinist, and conductor of the same name.

CHAPTER 1

1. *New York Times*, November 15, 1943.
2. Carol J. Oja, *Bernstein Meets Broadway: Collaborative Art in a Time of War* (New York: Oxford University Press, 2014).
3. Allen Shawn, *Leonard Bernstein: An American Musician* (New Haven, CT: Yale University Press, 2014), 85–89.
4. Geraldine Merken, Office of War Information, to Bernstein, January 19, 1945, LBC, box 1019, folder 20.
5. Barry Seldes, *Leonard Bernstein: The Political Life of an American Musician* (Berkeley: University of California Press, 2009), 70.

6. Oliver J. Caldwell, Department of State, to Leonard Bernstein, October 5, 1948, LBC, box 1019, folder 14.

7. Fumiko Fujita, *Amerika bunka gaikō to nihon—Reisen-ki no bunka to hito no kōryū* (Tokyo: Tokyo daigaku shuppankai, 2015), 40–45; Takeshi Matsuda, *Sengo nihon ni okeru amerika no sofuto pawā—Han eikyū-teki izon no kigen* (Tokyo: Iwanami shoten, 2008), 34–36

8. Leonard Bernstein, "The Essence of Music Study," *Etude 65* (April 1947): 204, 233.

9. Kazuko Amano, "Shirarezaru renii no yokogao," *Ongaku gendai* (July 1998).

10. Carol J. Oja, *Bernstein Meets Broadway: Collaborative Art in a Time of War* (New York: Oxford University Press, 2014), chap. 4.

11. Kazuko Ueno to Leonard Bernstein, February 10, 1949, LBC, box 2, folder 5. Here and elsewhere, some minor grammatical errors in her original letters have been corrected in my transcription.

12. Andre Millard, *America on Record: A History of Recorded Sound*, 2nd ed. (New York: Cambridge University Press, 2005), 189–222, 285–366; David L. Morton, Jr., *Sound Recording: The Life Story of a Technology* (Baltimore: Johns Hopkins University Press, 2004), 129–174.

13. Columbia Records, Inc., to Leonard Bernstein, November 10, 1949, LBC, box 1035, folder 5; Schuyler Chapin, *Leonard Bernstein: Notes from a Friend* (New York: Walker, 1992), 33–36.

14. Satow was no relation to the British diplomat and Japanologist of the same name.

15. Danielle Fosler-Lussier, *Music in America's Cold War Diplomacy* (Berkeley: University of California Press, 2015), chaps 1–2.

16. Kazuko Ueno to Leonard Bernstein, March 29, 1950, LBC, box 2, folder 5.

17. Kazuko Ueno to Leonard Bernstein, August 25, 1950, LBC, box 2, folder 5.

18. On meaning of fandom, see, for instance, Daniel Cavicchi, *Tramps Like Us: Music and Meaning among Springsteen Fans* (New York: Oxford University Press, 1998).

19. Kazuko Ueno to [Jamie] Bernstein, September 1952, LBC, box 2, folder 5.

20. Alicia Kopfstein-Penk, *Leonard Bernstein and His Young People's Concerts* (New York: Rowman & Littlefield, 2015).

21. Leonard Bernstein—Columbia Records Summary of Columbia Records Semi-Annual Statements of Royalty Earnings & Charges for the Six Year from July 1, 1959 to June 30, 1965, LBC, box 1041, folder 6.

22. Humphrey Burton, *Leonard Bernstein* (New York: Doubleday, 1994), 315.

23. Kazuko Amano to Leonard Bernstein, November 18, 1957, LBC, box 2, folder 5.

24. Kazuko Amano to Leonard Bernstein, December 22, 1960, LBC, box 2, folder 5.

CHAPTER 2

1. "Eastern U.S. Tour 1958: Washington, D.C.," "Tour of Europe and the Near East 1959: Publicity," "Tour of Europe and the Near East 1959: State Department Sponsorship and Publicity Material," "Coast Tour 1960: Berlin," "Tour Invitations,

Correspondence of Mosely, Carlos 1968–69," New York Philharmonic Digital Archives.

2. Robert H. Thayer, Special Assistant to the Secretary of State, to Leonard Bernstein, n.d. [October 1959?], LBC, box 1019, folder 14.

3. Christian A. Herter, Assistant Secretary of State, to Leonard Bernstein, December 26, 1961, LBC, box 1019, folder 14.

4. Nicholas J. Cull, *The Cold War and the United States Information Agency: American Propaganda and Public Diplomacy, 1945–1989* (Cambridge: Cambridge University Press, 2008).

5. Walter Nichols, United States Information Agency, to Leonard Bernstein, January 29, 1959. LBC, box 1019, folder 17.

6. Richard Nixon to Leonard Bernstein, April 7, 1960, LBC, box 42, folder 9.

7. East-West Music Encounter pamphlet, April 17–May 6, 1961, New York Philharmonic Archives, RG Communications/Public Relations, Folder Spring Tour 1961: Japan Press Pamphlets.

8. New York Philharmonic Archives, Executive RG, Tour of Japan, Alaska, Canada and Southern U.S. 1961: Concert Logistics and Program Planning, Nov. 1, 1960– Feb. 24, 1961.

9. Vincent Giroud, *Nicolas Nabokov: A Life in Freedom and Music* (New York: Oxford University Press, 2015); Miki Yamamoto, "Sengo no nihon ni okeru kokusai ongakusai no juyō ni kansuru ichi kōsatsu," *Bunka keizaigaku* 3.3 (2003), 68–69.

10. Ginji Yamane, "Wareware no ongakusai wa dou aru beki ka—Kensetsu-teki na men kara kangaete mitai," *Yomiuri Shimbun*, May 3, 1961, 5, evening edition.

11. "New York Philharmonic Returns Home after Tour of Japan, Alaska, and Canada," News from CBS Radio, May 15, 1961, New York Philharmonic Archives, Executive RG, Tour of Japan, Canada, Alaska and Southern U.S. 1961: Program Planning and Concert Logistics, 62–63.

12. Silas Edman to Nabunosuke Saito, June 7, 1961, New York Philharmonic Archives, Finance & Personnel RG, Spring Tour 1961: Budget and Orchestra Wages, Apr 7, 1961–Apr 9, 1962, 82.

13. "Japan Hits Tour by U.S. Orchestra," *New York Times*, March 31, 1960.

14. Ian Hunter to George Judd, December 20, 1960, New York Philharmonic Archives, Executive RG, Tour of Japan, Alaska, Canada and Southern U.S. 1961: Tokyo, Press, Correspondence, Programming, 51; Carlos Mosley to Ian Hunter, January 6, 1961, ibid., 57–58.

15. Ian Hunter to George Judd, Jr., December 20, 1960, New York Philharmonic Archives, Executive RG, Spring Tour 1961: Japan Operations Correspondence, Oct 12, 1959 – May 20, 1961, 108; Nicolas Nabokov to Leonard Bernstein, March 26, 1961, New York Philharmonic Archives, Executive RG, Tour of Japan, Alaska, Canada and Southern U.S. 1961: Tokyo, Press, Correspondence, Programming, 126.

16. Katsujiro Bando to George Judd, Jr., January 10, 1961, New York Philharmonic Archives, Executive RG, Tour of Japan, Alaska, Canada and Southern U.S. 1961: Tokyo, Press, Correspondence, Programming, 65–66; Carlos Moseley to Nicolas Nabokov, April 3, 1961, ibid., 128.

17. Program notes, New York Philharmonic, subscription concert, April 16, 1961, New York Philharmonic Archives.

18. Prior to leaving for Europe, Ozawa studied French conversation with Amano's sister, and Amano herself took over a couple of sessions when her sister was not available. Kazuko Amano to Leonard Bernstein, December 22, 1960, LBC, box 2, folder 5.

19. Carlos Moseley to Seiji Ozawa, December 28, 1960, New York Philharmonic Archives, Executive RG, Tour of Japan, Alaska, Canada and Southern U.S. 1961: Tokyo, Press, Correspondence, Programming, 53.

20. *Ongaku geijutsu*, July 1961, 59. All translations of Japanese sources are mine unless otherwise noted.

21. Ozawa Seiji, *Boku no ongaku musha shugyo* (Tokyo: Ongaku no tomo sha, [1962] 1970).

22. David M. Keiser letter from tour, Japan, May 9-10, 1961, New York Philharmonic Archives, RG Board of Directors, Series President, Folder David M. Keiser letter from tour, Japan, 1961, 4.

23. Naoko Shibusawa, *America's Geisha Ally: Reimagining the Japanese Enemy* (Cambridge, MA: Harvard University Press, 2010).

24. Leonard Bernstein to Felicia Bernstein, April 30, 1961, quoted in Humphrey Burton, *Leonard Bernstein* (New York: Doubleday, 1991), 322–323.

25. *Ongaku geijutsu*, July 1961, 33–34.

26. David M. Keiser letter from tour, Japan, May 910, 1961, New York Philharmonic Archives, RG Board of Directors, Series President, Folder David M. Keiser letter from tour, Japan, 1961, 5.

27. Ibid., 13–14.

28. New York Philharmonic program, 1961 Tokyo East-West Music Encounter, New York Philharmonic Archives, Programs, 1960–61 Season, Tour, ID 3950.

29. Sekio Tojo, "Maesutoro e no omāju—Leonard Bernstein," *ArtGaia CLUB MAGAZINE TC*, March 2007.

30. Kazuko Amano to Leonard Bernstein, April 22, 1961, LBC, box 2, folder 5.

31. Kazuko Amano, "Shirarezaru renii no yokogao," *Ongaku gendai*, July 1998.

32. Kazuko Amano to Leonard Bernstein, May 5, 1961, LBC, box 2, folder 5.

33. Kazuko Amano, "Shirarezaru renii no yokogao," *Ongaku gendai*, July 1998.

34. Kazuko Amano to Leonard Bernstein, May 22, 1961, LBC, box 2, folder 5.

CHAPTER 3

1. Program, Sep 23, 1962 Subscription Season, New York Philharmonic Digital Archives.

2. Julia L. Foulkes, *A Place for Us: West Side Story and New York* (Chicago: University of Chicago Press, 2016); Samuel Zipp, *Manhattan Projects: The Rise and Fall of Urban Renewal in Cold War New York* (New York: Oxford University Press, 2012).

3. Alicia Kopfstein-Penk, *Leonard Bernstein and His Young People's Concerts* (Lanham, MD: Rowman & Littlefield, 2015).

4. John F. Kennedy to LB, January 12, 1961, LBC, box 32, folder 1.

5. Lyndon Johnson to LB, January 15, 1965, LBC, box 30, folder 33.

6. *Report on the John F. Kennedy Center for the Performing Arts for the Period July 1, 1963 through June 30, 1964* (Washington: US Government Printing Office, 1965), 247–256.

7. Arthur Schlesinger, Jr. to Leonard Bernstein, January 20, 1966, LBC, box 1003, folder 7.

8. Roger L. Stevens to Lyndon Johnson, May 18, 1966, Lyndon B. Johnson Presidential Library (hereafter LBJ), Ex FG 284-1 box 308.

9. Harry C. McPherson to Lyndon Johnson, May 20, 1966, LBJ, Ex FG 284-1 box 308.

10. Schuyler G. Chapin, "Memorandum on Administrative Procedures" (n.d. [1969]), LBC, box 784, folder 1.

11. CBS Records earning statement for Leonard Bernstein, June 30, 1969, LBC, box 658, folder 12.

12. Top Selling Records (Jan–Jun 1972), LBC, box 661, folder 1.

13. CBS Masterworks press release, January 1988, LBC, box 792, folder 21.

14. Schuyler Chapin memo on conversation with Columbia Records, June 3, 1969, LBC, box 658, folder 14.

CHAPTER 4

1. Kazuko Amano to Leonard Bernstein, August 26, 1970, LBC, box 2, folder 5.

2. Kazuko Amano to Leonard Bernstein, December 25, 1964, LBC, box 2, folder 5.

3. Kazuko Amano to Leonard Bernstein, January 1, 1969, LBC, box 2, folder 5.

4. Shunya Yoshimi, *Banpaku gensō—Sengo seiji no jubaku* (Tokyo: Chikuma shinsho, 2005), 37–100.

5. Noboru Yoshida to Carlos Mosley, August 2, 1967, New York Philharmonic Archives, Operations/Orchestra Services RG, Japan Tour 1970: Background Material and Preliminary Correspondence, Feb 21, 1966–May 31, 1970, 12.

6. Reo Nagasaki, *"Tsunagari" no sengo bunkashi—Rō-on, soshite takarazuka, banpaku* (Tokyo: Kawade shobō shinsha, 2013).

7. John Nathan, *Sony: The Private Life* (Boston: Houghton Mifflin, 1999); Norio Ohga, *Doing It Our Way: A Sony Memoir*, trans. Brian Miller (Tokyo: International House of Japan, 2008).

8. The name "Sony" is derived from the Latin *sonus* signifying sound and the youthful, energetic image of the English *sonny boy*.

9. [Moseley?] to Bernstein, June 12, 1970, New York Philharmonic Archives, Executive RG, Papers of Leonard Bernstein, 1969–1977, 30.

10. Schuyler G. Chapin to Norio Ohga, July 20, 1970; Schuyler G. Chapin to Norio Ohga, September 23, 1970, LBC, Amberson Business Papers, box 870, folder 7.

11. Frank Milburn to Moseley, Webster, DeWindt, August 17, 1970, New York Philharmonic Archives, Executive RG, Japan Tour 1970: Planning Correspondence, May 28, 1968–Nov 27, 1970, 99; Carlos Moseley to Norio Ohga, September 14, 1970, ibid., 117–118.

12. New York Philharmonic Archives, Visual Collections, Bernstein, Leonard Bernstein, 1970 Tour of Japan and Southern U.S., September 7, 1970. ID: 800-148-26-011, 800-148-26-008.

13. Carlos Moseley to Noboru Yoshida, May 28, 1968, New York Philharmonic Archives, Executive RG, Japan Tour 1970: Planning Correspondence, May 28, 1968–Nov 27, 1970, 3.

14. Program notes, August 29, 1970, New York Philharmonic Archives, 21.

15. The commission fee was $3,000 plus $1,000 for preparation of the material and initial performance fee. Carlos Moseley to Seiji Ozawa, August 5, 1966, New York Philharmonic Archives, Operations/Orchestra Services RG, Seiji Ozawa, 1; Carlos Moseley to Toru Takemitsu, October 19, 1966, New York Philharmonic Archives, Executive RG, Toru Takemitsu, July 24, 1944–Nov 15, 1967, 9, 11–12

16. Toru Takemitsu, "Sound of East, Sound of West," in *Confronting Silence: Selected Writings* (Lanham, MD: Fallen Leaf Press, 1989), 62–63.

17. Kei Samiya, *Sawari* (Tokyo: Shōgakukan, 2011), 221–239.

18. Kazuko Amano, "Shirarezaru renii no yokogao," *Ongaku gendai*, July 1998.

19. Kazuko Amano to Leonard Bernstein, September 7, 1970, LBC, box 2, folder 5.

20. This account is based on the personal stories she shared with the author as well as Kazuko Amano, "Shirarezaru renii no yokogao," *Ongaku gendai*, July 1998.

CHAPTER 5

1. Humphrey Burton, *Leonard Bernstein* (New York: Doubleday, 1994), 411–412.

2. Ambergis Corporation, Minutes of the First Meeting of Board of Directors, April 20, 1973, LBC, Box 608, folder 8.

3. Amberson Enterprises Music Income Analysis 1/1/88–12/31/88, LBC, box 704, folder 2.

4. Amberson Enterprises, Inc., Minutes of a Special Meeting of the Board of Directors held February 24, 1972, LBC, box 609, folder 13; Michael Palma to Edward Murphy, March 24, 1981; Michael Palma to Harry Kraut, August 26, 1981, LBC, box 863 folder 13.

5. W. Stuart Pope to Harry Kraut, April 26, 1972, LBC, box 644 folder 2; W. Stuart Pope to Harry Kraut, June 13, 1973, LBC, box 644, folder 1.

6. Harry Kraut to W. Stuart Pope, June 19, 1975; Harry Kraut Memorandum, April 4, 1975, LBC, box 644, folder 2.

7. Jalni Publications, Inc., agreement with Boosey & Hawkes, May 30, 1979, LBC, box 644, folder 7.

8. Amberson Enterprises, Inc., Minutes of the Executive Committee, September 17, 1976, LBC, box 687, folder 1; Memorandum from Louis Landerson to Harry Kraut, Paul Epstein, Jeffrey Schreier, Mike Palma, Gerry Duerr, Seymour Straus, November 18, 1982, LBC, box 863, folder 14.

9. Schuyler Chapin to Hans Hirsch, December 9, 1969, LBC, box 699, folder 2.

10. Andre Millard, *America on Record: A History of Recorded Sound* 2nd ed. (Cambridge: Cambridge University Press, 2005), 334. http://history. deutschegrammophon.com/en_GB/home, accessed October 2016.

11. Günther Breest and Hanno Rinke to Leonard Bernstein, April 19, 1978, LBC, box 796, folder 8.

12. Columbia Record Sales letter to customers, n.d. [ca. 1974], LBC, folder 658, folder 12.

13. Dorothee Koehler to John Epstein, November 10, 1977, LBC, box 699, folder 4.

14. Schuyler Chapin, *Leonard Bernstein: Notes from a Friend* (New York: Walker & Co., 1992), 161.

15. "Major projects to be accomplished 1977–1982," LBC, box 792, folder 16.

16. Robert Lantz to Leonard Bernstein, June 29, 1970, LBC, box 658, folder 8.

17. Amberson-Unitel contract, January 17, 1971, LBC, box 895, folder 6.

18. Amberson Enterprises, Inc., Minutes of Executive Committee, October 1, 1976, LBC, box 687, folder 1.

19. Herbert Kloiber to Leonard Bernstein, January 26, 1976, LBC, box 896, folder 1; Harry Kraut to Amberson Board, June 16, 1977; 1977 Unitel-Bernstein contract, box 893, folder 1.

20. Schuyler Chapin, *Leonard Bernstein: Notes from a Friend* (New York: Walker & Co., 1992), 120–121.

21. Robert Lantz to Leonard Bernstein, June 29, 1970, LBC, box 658, folder 8.

22. Minutes of Meeting of Board of Directors of Amberson Enterprises, Inc., October 9, 1980, LBC, box 608, folder 12.

CHAPTER 6

1. Kazuko Amano to Leonard Bernstein, August 20, 1971, LBC, Box 2, Folder 5.

2. Kazuko Amano to Leonard Bernstein, December 1972, LBC, box 2, folder 5.

3. *Bernstein in Vienna*, dir. Humphrey Burton, prod. Humphrey Burton, James Krayer (Kultur Video, 1970).

4. Kazuko Amano to Leonard Bernstein, December 1973, LBC, box 2, folder 5.

5. Kazuko Amano to Leonard Bernstein, August 31, 1974, LBC, box 2, folder 5. Translated from French by the author.

6. CBS/Sony ad, program book, the New York Philharmonic 1974 Japan tour. NYP Digital Archives.

7. Akio Morita to Leonard Bernstein, June 28, 1974, LBC, box 40, folder 48.

8. "Parties and Receptions," August 7, 1974; Reception guest list, September 3, 1974, LBC, box 775, folder 6.

9. Norio Ohga to Leonard Bernstein, October 2, 1974, LBC, box 42, folder 37.

10. Kazuko Amano to Leonard Bernstein, December 12, 1976, LBC, box 2, folder 5.

CHAPTER 7

1. Felicia Bernstein to Leonard Bernstein, n.d. 1951 or 1952, LBC, box 60A, folder 16.

2. Humphrey Burton, *Leonard Bernstein* (New York: Doubleday, 1994), 434–447.

3. Kazuko Amano to Leonard Bernstein, May 16, 1978, LBC, box 2, folder 5.

4. Kazuko Amano to Leonard Bernstein, August 1978, LBC, box 2, folder 5.

5. Kikuko Amano to Leonard Bernstein, August 1978, LBC, box 2, folder 5.

6. Humphrey Burton, *Leonard Bernstein* (New York: Doubleday, 1994), 454.

CHAPTER 8

1. New York Philharmonic 1979 Japan tour program, LBC, box 777, folder 7. New York Philharmonic press release, May 10, 1979; New York Philharmonic tour of the United States, Japan and Korea, June 11–July 7, 1979, tour brochure, LBC, box 777, folder 9.

2. Mari Yoshihara, *Musicians from a Different Shore: Asians and Asian Americans in Classical Music* (Philadelphia: Temple University Press, 2007), 35–37.

3. Ezra F. Vogel, *Japan as Number One: Lessons for America* (Cambridge, MA: Harvard University Press, 1979).

4. John Nathan, *Sony: The Private Life* (Boston: Houghton Mifflin, 1999), 153–155.

5. Harry Kraut to Norio Ohga, August 13, 1979, LBC, Amberson Business Papers, box 777, folder 7.

6. CBS/Sony ad for Maestro 1800, tour program book, 1979, LBC Amberson Business Papers, box 777, folder 7.

7. Telex from Nobuaki Arai to Harry Kraut, March 20, 1979, LBC, Amberson Business Papers, box 723, folder 7.

8. Harry Kraut to Namihiko Sasaki, December 18, 1977, LBC, Amberson Business Papers, box 723, folder 9.

9. Yuko Ijichi to Harry Kraut, November 1, 1977, LBC, Amberson Business Papers, box 723, folder 10; Yuko Ijichi to Harry Kraut, February 26, 1978, LBC, Amberson Business Papers, box 723, folder 9.

10. Nobuaki Arai to John McClure, June 29, 1979; Nobuaki Arai to Albert Webster, August 27, 1979, LBC, Amberson Business Papers, box 777, folder 7.

11. Amberson organization and staff chart, December 1979, LBC, box 784, folder 1.

12. Minutes of Special Meeting of Board of Directors of Springate Corporation, May 31, 1979, LBC, box 608, folder 11.

13. "Jack Gottlieb: Work Activities," March 16, 1978, LBC, box 608, folder 11.

14. "James McAndrew, Personal Assistant to L. B." job description, LBC, box 608, folder 11.

15. "John Epstein, Public Affairs Coordinator—Amberson" job description, LBC, box 608, folder 11.

16. "Public Affairs Coordinator—Carson Office," LBC, box 608, folder 11.

17. Memorandum from Jack Gottlieb to Harry Kraut, October 20, 1977, LBC, box 863, folder 10.

18. Amberson organization and staff chart, December 1979, LBC, box 784, folder 1.

19. Amberson personnel job descriptions, LBC, box 608, folder 11.

20. Minutes of Meeting of Board of Directors of Amberson Enterprises, Inc., November 23, 1982, LBC, box 608, folder 13.

21. Telegram from Harry Kraut to Tim Harrold, September 9 [1983], LBC, box 793, folder 4.

22. Timothy D. Taylor, *Music and Capitalism: A History of the Present* (Chicago: University of Chicago Press, 2016), chapter 2.

23. Andre Millard, *America on Record: A History of Recorded Sound*, 2nd ed. (Cambridge: Cambridge University Press, 2005), 342, 354.

CHAPTER 9

1. Kunihiko Hashimoto to Leonard Bernstein, July 8, 1979, LBC, box 60F. I have made some small changes to Hashimoto's letters when the errors of grammar and usage would have interfered with the reader's comprehension, while keeping the overall quality of his language and tone.

2. Kunihiko Hashimoto to Leonard Bernstein, July 14, 1979, LBC, box 60F.

3. Kunihiko Hashimoto to Leonard Bernstein, July 9, 1979, LBC, box 60F.

4. Kunihiko Hashimoto to Leonard Bernstein, July 10, 1979, LBC, box 60F.

5. Kunihiko Hashimoto to Leonard Bernstein, July 11, 1979, LBC, box 60F.

6. Kunihiko Hashimoto to Leonard Bernstein, September 19, 1979, LBC, box 60F.

7. Kunihiko Hashimoto to Leonard Bernstein, July 30, 1979, LBC, box 60F.

8. Kunihiko Hashimoto to Leonard Bernstein, July 14, 1979, LBC, box 60F.

9. Kunihiko Hashimoto to Leonard Bernstein, July 18, 1979, LBC, box 60F.

10. Mark McLelland, *Queer Japan from the Pacific War to the Internet Age* (Lanham, MD: Rowman & Littlefield, 2005); Noriaki Fushimi, *Gei to iu keiken*, rev. ed. (Tokyo: Potto shuppan, 2004), Hideki Sunakawa, *Shinjuku ni-chome no bunka jinruigaku—Gei komyuniti kara toshi wo manazasu* (Tokyo: Taro-jiro-sha editas, 2015); Bungaku Ito, *"Barazoku" no hitobito—Sono sugao to butaiura* (Tokyo: Kawade shobō shinsha, 2006).

11. Kunihiko Hashimoto to Leonard Bernstein, July 21, 1979, LBC, box 60F.

12. Kunihiko Hashimoto to Leonard Bernstein, August 1, 1979, LBC, box 60F.

CHAPTER 10

1. Kunihiko Hashimoto to Leonard Bernstein, September 2, 1979. LBC, Box 60F.
2. Kunihiko Hashimoto to Leonard Bernstein, September 12, 1979, LBC, box 60F.
3. Kunihiko Hashimoto to Leonard Bernstein, September 30, 1979, LBC, box 60F.
4. Kunihiko Hashimoto to Leonard Bernstein, April 28, 1980, LBC, box 60F.
5. Kunihiko Hashimoto to Leonard Bernstein, December 20, 1980, LBC, box 60F.
6. Humphrey Burton, *Leonard Bernstein* (New York: Doubleday, 1994), 463.
7. Kunihiko Hashimoto to Leonard Bernstein, January 27, 1981, LBC, box 60F.
8. Kunihiko Hashimoto to Leonard Bernstein, June 21, 1981, LBC, box 60F.

CHAPTER 11

1. Kazuko Amano to Leonard Bernstein, December [n.d.] 1979, LBC, box 2, folder 5.
2. Kazuko Amano to Leonard Bernstein, October 4, 1980, LBC, box 2, folder 5.
3. Kazuko Amano to Leonard Bernstein, October 21, 1980, LBC, box 2, folder 5.
4. Holograph piano score, Leonard Bernstein, *Touches for Solo Piano*, 1980, LBC, box 1074, folder 19.
5. Holograph piano score, Leonard Bernstein, "Virgo Blues," September 8, 1978, LBC, box 1076, folder 15.
6. Allen Shawn, *Leonard Bernstein: An American Musician* (New Haven, CT: Yale University Press, 2014), 245–246.
7. Kazuko Amano to Leonard Bernstein, December 1980, LBC, box 2, folder 5.
8. Kazuko Amano to Leonard Bernstein, October 4, 1981; Kazuko Amano to Leonard Bernstein; May 11, 1982, Kazuko Amano to Leonard Bernstein, October 3, 1982, LBC, box 2, folder 5.
9. Kazuko Amano to Leonard Bernstein, October 23, 1981, LBC, box 2, folder 5.
10. Kazuko Amano to Leonard Bernstein, December 1981, LBC, box 2, folder 5.
11. Kazuko Amano to Leonard Bernstein, October 3, 1982, LBC, box 2, folder 5.
12. Kunihiko Hashimoto to Leonard Bernstein, November 29, 1979, LBC, box 60F.
13. Kunihiko Hashimoto to Leonard Bernstein, May 25, 1981, LBC, box 60F.
14. Kunihiko Hashimoto to Leonard Bernstein, July 2, 1981, LBC, box 60F.
15. Kunihiko Hashimoto to Leonard Bernstein, December 17, 1981, LBC, box 60F.
16. Kunihiko Hashimoto to Leonard Bernstein, January 22, 1982, LBC, box 60F.
17. Kunihiko Hashimoto to Leonard Bernstein, March 1, 1982, LBC, box 60F.
18. Kunihiko Hashimoto to Leonard Bernstein, June 22, 1982, LBC, box 60F.
19. Kunihiko Hashimoto to Leonard Bernstein, November 3, 1982, LBC, box 60F.
20. Kunihiko Hashimoto to Leonard Bernstein, January 17, 1983, LBC, box 60F, folder 4.
21. Kunihiko Hashimoto to Leonard Bernstein, March 6, 1983; May 24, 1983, LBC, box 60F.
22. Kunihiko Hashimoto to Leonard Bernstein, October 2, 1983, LBC, box 60F.
23. Kunihiko Hashimoto to Leonard Bernstein, October 31, 1983, LBC, box 60F.
24. Kunihiko Hashimoto to Leonard Bernstein, March 20, 1984, LBC, box 60F.

CHAPTER 12

1. Houston Grand Opera news release, May 12 (?), 1982, LBC, Amberson Business Papers, box 804, folder 1. At the initial stage the parties involved were also exploring the possibility of including Vienna and Berlin in the commission, but for logistical reasons—including the availability of Vienna's music director, Lorin Maazel—they did not become part of the commission. Telex communication between Harry Kraut, Lorin Maazel, and Egon Seefehlner, August 1981(?), LBC, Amberson Business Papers, box 889, folder 13.

2. Contract among Leonard Bernstein, Stephen Wadsworth, Jalni Publications, Houston Grand Opera, the John F. Kennedy Center for the Performing Arts, January 27, 1982, p. 5, LBC, Amberson Business Papers, box 804, folder 7. Contract among Leonard Bernstein, Stephen Wadsworth, Jalni Productions, and Teatro alla Scala, LBC, Amberson Business Papers, box 889, folder 14; John F. Kennedy for the Performing Arts, Draft of estimated expenses for *Trouble in Tahiti* and *A Quiet Place*, June 27, 1983, LBC, Amberson Business Papers, box 804, folder 7.

3. Houston Grand Opera news release on David Gockley, LBC, Amberson Business Papers, box 804, folder 5.

4. The process of writing and producing *A Quiet Place* is detailed in Charlie Harmon, *On the Road and Off the Record with Leonard Bernstein: My Years with the Exasperating Genius* (Watertown, MA: Charlesbridge, 2018), as well as Jamie Bernstein, *Famous Father Girl: A Memoir of Growing Up Bernstein* (New York: HarperCollins, 2018), chap. 16.

5. Stephen Wadsworth, Librettist's Notes for the recording of *A Quiet Place*, Deutsche Grammophon, 1987, 12–13.

6. Note on *T in T II*, n.d. (typewritten version dated September 2, 1981), LBC, box 93, folder 29.

7. Bernstein's handwritten note on sequel to *Tahiti*, n.d, LBC, box 104, folder 26.

8. *A Quiet Place*, act I, Sam's aria.

9. Memorandum from David Gockley to Leonard Bernstein, Stephen Wadsworth, John DeMain, and Peter Schifter, June 8, 1983, LBC, Amberson Business Papers, box 804, folder 4. Bernstein's notes on run-through, June 10, 1984[3?], LBC, box 96, folder 6.

10. Robert O. Self, *All in the Family: The Realignment of America* (New York: Hill & Wang, 2012).

11. "Benton for Mayor" letter, n.d, LBC, Amberson Business Papers, box 804, folder 3. This unsigned, undated letter appears to be printed on a paper with the phrase "Benton for Mayor" stamped at the top. Yet the only Benton who ran for Houston's mayoral race in 1982 was Nicholas F. Benton, an anti-Vietnam War activist and a cofounder of the Berkeley Gay Liberation Front. It is possible that the author of this text used it as a smear campaign against Benton or that Benton picked up this letter and used it for his own campaign to fight against the homophobic ideologues.

12. Cindy Patton, *Sex and Germs: The Politics of AIDS* (Boston: South End, 1985), 99.

13. Notes on telephone conversation, May 10, 1983, Houston Grand Opera Archives (hereafter HGO), box PR-9.

14. Houston Grand Opera news release on May 26, 1983 press release, LBC, Amberson Business Papers, box 804, folder 5.

15. J. A. Elkins, Jr., to Harry Kraut, May 13, 1983, LBC, Amberson Business Papers, box 804, folder 5.

16. Transcript of news conference, May 26, 1983; Memo to Stephen Wadsworth, June 14, 1983, HGO, box PR-9.

17. Bernstein's message to an AIDS benefit event, June 1983, LBC, box 95, folder 14.

18. Midnight supper menu, LBC, Amberson Business Papers, box 804, folder 3.

19. Jamie Lerner to the Houston Grand Opera, June 17, 1983, LBC, Amberson Business Papers, box 804, folder 3.

20. Arrival and departure times of national press; Antje Henneking to Harry Kraut, June 3, 1983, LBC, Amberson Business Papers, box 804, folder 3.

21. Alan Rich, "Lenny's Soap Opera," *Newsweek* June 27, 1983, 97.

22. Kunihiko Hashimoto to Leonard Bernstein, July 14, 1983, LBC, box 60F, folder 5.

CHAPTER 13

1. SANE to Leonard Bernstein, March 2, 1960; SANE to Leonard Bernstein, June 15, 1962; SANE to Leonard Bernstein, December 19, 1962, LBC, box 1008, folder 7.

2. SANE to Leonard Bernstein, September 11, 1961, LBC, box 1008, folder 7.

3. SANE to Leonard Bernstein, December 8, 1961; Leonard Bernstein to friends, June 5, 1962, LBC, box 1008, folder 7.

4. Letter of resignation from SANE, October 10, 1967, LBC, box 1008, folder 7; William J. Butler to Leonard Bernstein, December 21, 1967, LBC, box 1008, folder 7.

5. Edward Kennedy to Leonard Bernstein, March 10, 1982, LBC, box 32, folder 1.

6. Barry Seldes, *Leonard Bernstein: The Political Life of an American Musician* (Berkeley: University of California Press, 2009), 161.

7. Lawrence S. Wittner, *Toward Nuclear Abolition: A History of the World Nuclear Disarmament Movement, 1971 to the Present* (Stanford, CA: Stanford University Press, 2003), 169–333.

8. Letter from the Leonard Bernstein 65th Birthday Committee, July 29, 1983, Kunihiko Hashimoto personal collection.

9. Speech re nuclear disarmament, August 25, 1983, LBC, box 95, folder 15.

10. Kunihiko Hashimoto to Leonard Bernstein, November 25, 1983, LBC, box 60F, folder 6.

11. Yuko Shibata, "Dissociative Entanglement: U.S.-Japan Atomic Bomb Discourses by John Hershey and Nagai Takashi," *Inter-Asia Cultural Studies* 13.1 (2012): 122–137.

CHAPTER 14

1. Nicholas Davies to Kunihiko Hashimoto, August 6, 1984, LBC, box 708, folder 6.
2. Telex from Harry Kraut to Kunihiko Hashimoto, August 24, 1984, LBC, box 708, folder 6.
3. Kunihiko Hashimoto to Leonard Bernstein, August 31, 1984, LBC, box 60F.
4. Mitsunori Sano to Leonard Bernstein, January 13, 1984, LBC, box 702, folder 5.
5. Telex from Harry Kraut to Mitsunori Sano, January 25, 1984, LBC box 702, folder 5.
6. 1985 ECYO Program Book, p. 40, LBC, box 791, folder 3.
7. Memorandum on the Hiroshima Peace Concert, p. 2, June 4, 1984, LBC, box 702, folder 5.
8. Hiroko Okuda, *Genbaku no kioku—Hiroshima•Nagasaki no shisō* (Tokyo: Keio daigaku shuppankai, 2010), 108–111, 164–171.
9. Telex from Harry Kraut to Seiji Ozawa, July 10, 1984, LBC, box 702, folder 5; Memorandum on the Hiroshima Peace Concert, p. 2, June 7, 1984, LBC, box 702, folder 5.
10. Memorandum on Journey for Peace, March 29, 1985, LBC, box 791, folder 7; Hans Landesmann to Shimpei Matsuoka, May 23, 1984, LBC, box 702, folder 5; Memorandum on Hiroshima Peace Concert, June 7, 1984, LBC, box 702, folder 5.
11. Author interview with Mitsunori Sano, July 12, 2016; Telex from Kunihiko Hashimoto to Harry Kraut, November 11, 1984.
12. Telex from Kunihiko Hashimoto to Harry Kraut, March 29, 1985, LBC, box 883, folder 4; Telex from Kunihiko Hashimoto to Harry Kraut and Ken Richer, July 23, 1985, LBC, box 791, folder 1; Telex from Kunihiko Hashimoto to Harry Kraut, August 22, 1985, LBC, box 883, folder 6.; Telex from Kunihiko Hashimoto to Harry Kraut, July 16, 1985; Telex from Kunihiko Hashimoto to Harry Kraut, July 17, 1985; Telex from Harry Kraut to Kunihiko Hashimoto, July 17, 1985, LBC, box 721, folder 3.
13. Kunihiko Hashimoto to Leonard Bernstein, November 18, 1984, LBC, box 60F.
14. Telex from Kunihiko Hashimoto to Harry Kraut, November 11, 1984; Telex from Kunihiko Hashimoto to Harry Kraut, November 25, 1984; Telex from Harry Kraut to Kunihiko Hashimoto, November 29, 1984; Telex from Harry Kraut to Kunihiko Hashimoto, November 29, 1984; Telex from Kunihiko Hashimoto to Harry Kraut, December 3, 1984; Telex from Harry Kraut to Kunihiko Hashimoto, December 7, 1984; Telex from Kunihiko Hashimoto to Harry Kraut, December 10, 1984, LBC, box 708, folder 6.
15. Harry Kraut to Kazuko Amano, December 28, 1984, LBC, box 721, folder 2.
16. Sermon re political involvement at All Souls Unitarian Church, NYC January 25, 1985, LBC box 96, folder 29.
17. Kunihiko Hashimoto to Leonard Bernstein, February 24, 1985, LBC, box 60F, folder 6.

18. Hiroshima Peace Concert agreement, LBC, box 721, folder 3.
19. Kunihiko Hashimoto to Leonard Bernstein, April 6, 1985, LBC, box 60F.

CHAPTER 15

1. *Chūgoku Shimbun*, August 6, 1985, evening ed., 3; *Asahi Shimbun* August 6, 1985, evening ed., 11; *Yomiuri Shimbun* August 9, 1985, evening ed., 5.
2. *Yomiuri Shimbun*, July 31, 1985, evening ed., 11.
3. Yumi Notohara, *"Hiroshima" ga narihibiku toki* (Tokyo: Shunjūsha, 2015), 149–153.
4. *Chūgoku Shimbun*, August 6, 1985, 20.
5. Kazuko Amano to Leonard Bernstein, n.d. [August 1985], LBC, box 2, folder 5.
6. Laura Hein and Mark Selden, "Commemoration and Silence: Fifty Years of Remembering the Bomb in America and Japan," in *Living with the Bomb: American and Japanese Cultural Conflicts in the Nuclear Age*, ed. Laura Hein and Mark Selden (London: Routledge, 1997), 3–34; Paul Boyer, *By the Bomb's Early Light: American Thought and Culture at the Dawn of the Atomic Age* (New York: Pantheon, 1985), 181–195.
7. Peter Schwenger and John Whittier Treat, "America's Hiroshima, Hiroshima's America," *boundary 2* 21, no. 1 (1994): 233–253; Lisa Yoneyama, *Hiroshima Traces: Time, Space, and the Dialectics of Memory* (Berkeley: University of California Press, 1999); Laura Hein and Mark Selden, "Commemoration and Silence: Fifty Years of Remembering the Bomb in America and Japan," in *Living with the Bomb: American and Japanese Cultural Conflicts in the Nuclear Age*, ed. Laura Hein and Mark Selden (London and New York: Routledge, 1997), 11.
8. Lisa Yoneyama, *Hiroshima Traces: Time, Space, and the Dialectics of Memory* (Berkeley: University of California Press, 1999), 43–65.
9. Hiroshima Schedule, August 4, 1985, LBC, box 791, folder 1.
10. *Asahi Shimbun*, August 6, 1985, evening ed., 11.
11. Akira Kinoshita, "Bernstein no Hiroshima," *Chūō kōron*, October 1985.
12. Harry Kraut, "Memorandum on Journey for Peace," March 29, 1985, 3–4, LBC, box 791, folder 7.
13. Lee Fleming Reese to Leonard Bernstein, June 1, 1985, LBC, box 791, folder 6.
14. Harry Kraut to Lee Fleming Reese, June 25, 1985, LBC, box 791, folder 6.
15. Hiroshima Peace Concert program book, August 6, 1985, personal collection of Mitsunori Sano.
16. Statement to the press, August 4, 1985, LBC, box 98, folder 7.
17. Hiroko Okuda, *Genbaku no kioku—Hiroshima Nagasaki no shisō* (Tokyo: Keio daigaku shuppankai, 2010), 210, 232.
18. Statement to the press, August 4, 1985, LBC, box 98, folder 7.
19. References to the tour come from "Hiroshima Peace Concert—Bernstein heiwa e no tabi," NHK, originally broadcast on August 10, 1985.

20. *Chūgoku Shimbun*, June 28, 1985, 23.

21. Allen Shawn, *Leonard Bernstein: An American Musician* (New Haven, CT: Yale University Press, 2014), 185–190.

22. *Yomiuri Shimbun*, August 9, 1985, 5.

CHAPTER 16

1. Telex from Kunihiko Hashimoto to Leonard Bernstein, August 25, 1985, LBC, box 60G.

2. Telex from Tadatsugu Sasaki to Harry Kraut, March 29, 1985; Telex from Harry Kraut to Tadatsugu Sasaki, March 29, 1985; Telex from Kunihiko Hashimoto to Harry Kraut, March 29, 1985; Telex from Tadatsugu Sasaki to Harry Kraut, March 30, 1985; Telex from Tadatsugu Sasaki to Harry Kraut, April 2, 1985, LBC, box 721, folder 1.

3. Telex from Leonard Bernstein to Seiji Ozawa, September 1, 1985, Kunihiko Hashimoto personal collection.

4. *Asahi Journal*, October 4, 1985.

5. *Record Geijutsu*, June 2000, 33.

6. "Leonard Bernstein," *Record Geijutsu*, November 1985, reprinted in September 2000.

7. Marcel Grilli, "Profoundly Moving Mahler Ninth," *The Japan Times*, September 15, 1985, 11.

8. Hidekazu Yoshida, "Yomigaetta 'inori no saigï'—Bernstein no Israel Phil idai na meien Mahler no daiku," *Asahi Shimbun*, September 7, 1985, evening ed.

9. Kazuko Amano to Leonard Bernstein, October [September?] 4, 1985, LBC, box 2, folder 5.

10. Toshiki Takagi to Leonard Bernstein, n.d. [September 5, 1985], LBC, box 721, folder 3.

11. Three haikus for Kunihiko Hashimoto, September 6, 1985, LBC, box 98, folder 10.

12. Leonard Bernstein to Kunihiko Hashimoto, September 14, 1985. Kunihiko Hashimoto personal collection.

13. Kunihiko Hashimoto to Leonard Bernstein, September 16, 1985, LBC, box 60G.

14. Kunihiko Hashimoto to Leonard Bernstein, September 22, 1985, LBC, box 60G.

CHAPTER 17

1. *The Making of West Side Story*, dir. Christopher Swann (BBC, 1984).

2. Deutsche Grammophon website, http://history.deutschegrammophon.com/en_GB/home, accessed September 26, 2016.

3. Christoph Schmökel and Aman Pedersen to Harry Kraut, April 7, 1989, LBC, box 794, folder 13.

4. *Leonard Bernstein: Teachers and Teaching*, dir. Humphrey Burton (UNITEL, 1988).

5. Humphrey Burton, *Leonard Bernstein* (New York: Doubleday, 1994), 489; "A Classic Evening for AIDS Research," notes and program, LBC, box 99, folder 13.

6. Yo-Yo Ma to Leonard Bernstein, August 5, 1987; Harry Kraut to Yo-Yo Ma, October 2, 1987; Minutes of the steering committee meeting for Music for Life, July 8, 1987, LBC, Amberson Business Papers, box 728, folder 4.

7. Bernard Holland, "Concert: 'Music for Life,' a Benefit," *New York Times*, November 9, 1987.

8. AmFAR news release and fact sheet for "Serenade: A Musical Tribute to Dr. Mathilde Krim"; Sally Morrison to Leonard Bernstein, December 19, 1988, LBC, Amberson Business Papers, box 681, folder 7.

9. "Children Will Listen" correspondence and lineup, LBC, Amberson Business Papers, box 607, folder 7; Jamie Bernstein, *Famous Father Girl: A Memoir of Growing Up Bernstein* (New York: HarperCollins, 2018), chap. 19.

10. John E. Frohnmayer to Leonard Bernstein, November 3, 1989, LBC, box 41, folder 28.

11. James Davison Hunter, *Culture Wars: The Struggle to Define America*, repr. (New York: Basic Books, 1992).

12. Leonard Bernstein to President Bush and Mrs. Bush, November 10, 1989, LBC, box 41, folder 28.

13. Barry Douglas to Leonard Bernstein, November 16, 1989, LBC, box 41, folder 28; Chou Wen-chung to Leonard Bernstein, November 17, 1989, LBC, box 41, folder 28; Richard Carter to Leonard Bernstein, November 17, 1989, LBC, box 41, folder 28.

14. "The NEA Forever March," November 22, 1989, LBC, box 103, folder 2.

15. Chou Wen-chung to Leonard Bernstein, October 16, 1980, LBC, box 608, folder 13.

CHAPTER 18

1. Kunihiko Hashimoto to Leonard Bernstein, December 20, 1985, LBC, box 60G.

2. Kunihiko Hashimoto to Leonard Bernstein, March 4, 1986, LBC, box 60G.

3. Kunihiko Hashimoto to Leonard Bernstein, March 26, 1986; Kunihiko Hashimoto to Leonard Bernstein, August 6, 1986, LBC, box 60G.

4. Kunihiko Hashimoto to Leonard Bernstein, November 7, 1986, LBC, box 60G.

5. Kunihiko Hashimoto to Leonard Bernstein, April 19, 1987, LBC, box 60G.

6. Hashimoto to Bernstein, December 14, 1987, LBC, box 60G.

7. Boston Symphony Orchestra concert program, Tanglewood Series, Summer 1988, Week 9, Sunday Concert, 38–39. Boston Symphony Orchestra Archives, Symphony Hall, Boston, MA, available online at https://cdm15982.contentdm. oclc.org/digital/collection/PROG/id/603491/rec/1, accessed on July 23, 2018.

8. Invitation by Mr. and Mrs. Seiji Ozawa, LBC, Amberson Business Papers, box 639, folder 1.

9. Guest lists, LBC, Amberson Business Papers box 639, folder 2.

10. Kazuko Amano to Mary [*sic*] Carter, July 29, 1988, LBC, Amberson Business Papers, box 639, folder 4.

11. Kunihiko Hashimoto to Leonard Bernstein, August 25, 1988, LBC, box 60G.

12. Kunihiko Hashimoto to Leonard Bernstein, December [n.d.], 1988, LBC, box 60G.

CHAPTER 19

1. Memorandum from Andrew J. Andreasen and Susan L. Rhodes to Harry Kraut, May 10, 1989, LBC, Amberson Business Papers, box 624, folder 4.

2. Memo from Harry Kraut to Clive Gillinson, "Re: China/Japan Trip 1990," January 13, 1988, LBC, Amberson Business Papers, box 624, folder 1; Letter from Song Chengjiu to Clive Gillinson, Dec. 25, 1987, LBC, Amberson Business Papers, box 729, folder 6; Memo from Harry Kraut to Clive Gillinson, February 18, 1988, LBC, Amberson Business Papers, box 729, folder 5.

3. Memo from Andrew J. Andreasen to Harry Kraut, January 13, 198[9], LBC, Amberson Business Papers, box 624, folder 2.

4. *Newsweek*, October 9, 1989; Andrew G. McKevitt, *Consuming Japan: Popular Culture and the Globalizing of 1980s America* (Chapel Hill: University of North Carolina Press, 2017).

5. Telex from Harry Kraut to Norio Ohga, January 18, 1988, LBC, Amberson Business Papers, box 624, folder 1.

6. Telex from Norio Ohga to Harry Kraut, January 19, 1988, LBC, Amberson Business Papers, box 624, folder 1.

7. Letter from Mitsunori Sano to John Triggle, January 31, 1989, LBC, Amberson Business Papers, box 624, folder 3.

8. Telex from Karin Wylach to Harry Kraut, December 19, 1988, LBC, Amberson Business Papers, box 624, folder 1.

9. Status report by John Triggle, September 6, 1988, LBC, Amberson Business Papers, box 624, folder 1.

10. Mitsunori Sano to John Triggle, January 31, 1989, LBC, Amberson Business Papers, box 624, folder 3.

11. John Triggle to Clive Gillinson, September 8, 1988, LBC, Amberson Business Papers, box 624, folder 1.

12. Mitsunori Sano to John Triggle, February 1, 1989; Mitsunori Sano to John Triggle, February 14, 1989, LBC, Amberson Business Papers, box 624, folder 3.

13. Fax cover sheet from John Triggle to Mitsunori Sano, March 29, 1989, LBC, Amberson Business Papers, box 624, folder 3.

14. Telefax from Harry Kraut to Clive Gillinson, et al., November 1, 1989, LBC, Amberson Business Papers, box 624, folder 5.

15. Harry J. Kraut, "Memorandum—China 1990," March 16, 1989, LBC, Amberson Business Papers, box 624, folder 3.

16. Harry Kraut to Kunihiko Hashimoto, April 14, 1989, Kunihiko Hashimoto personal collection.

17. Summary translation of the article on Wang Meng and Ying Ruocheng in the *Centre Daily News*, August 14, 1989, LBC, Amberson Business Papers, box 624, folder 5.

18. Telex from Harry Kraut to Clive Gillinson, et al., June 4, 1989, LBC, Amberson Business Papers, box 624, folder 5.

19. Chou Weng-Chung to the CUSCAE Advisory Council members, June 9, 1989, LBC, Amberson Business Papers, box 624, folder 5.

20. Report by the Nomura Securities China Section, June 1989, LBC, Amberson Business Papers, box 624, folder 5.

21. Clive Gillinson and Harry Kraut to Minister Ying and Wu Zuqiang, August 3, 1989, LBC, Amberson Business Papers, box 624, folder 5.

CHAPTER 20

1. Telex from Harry Kraut to Kunihiko Hashimoto, August 17, 1989, LBC, Amberson Business Papers, box 624, folder 5.

2. Telex from Kunihiko Hashimoto to Harry Kraut, August 17, 1989, LBC, Amberson Business Papers, box 624, folder 5.

3. Telex from Kunihiko Hashimoto to Harry Kraut, August 18, [1989], LBC, Amberson Business Papers, box 624, folder 4.

4. Telex from Kunihiko Hashimoto to Marie Carter, September 13, 1989, LBC, Amberson Business Papers, box 624, folder 4.

5. Telex from Kunihiko Hashimoto to Marie Carter, September 12, 1989, LBC, Amberson Business Papers, box 624, folder 5.

6. *PMF—20 Years* (Sapporo: Pacific Music Festival Organizing Committee, 2009), 40–44.

CHAPTER 21

1. The video footage used in this chapter comes from *The Joy of Sharing: Leonard Bernstein in Japan* (Kultur Video, 2011) as well as "Pacific Music Festival 1990 [Bernstein and Friends in Japan] Vol.1," https://www.youtube.com/watch?v=F7ZTWnMMtII and "Pacific Music Festival 1990 [The Rehearsal Bernstein and Young Musicians]," https://www.youtube.com/watch?v=Ty4kc9t_1j4, last accessed January 11, 2018.

2. *Teachers and Teaching: An Autobiographical Essay by Leonard Bernstein*, directed by Humphrey Burton (UNITEL, 1998).
3. Skype interview with Takane Funatsu, January 10, 2018.
4. Skype interview with Richard Bamping, January 22, 2018.
5. Telephone interview with Regina Helcher Yost, January 11, 2018.
6. Telephone interview with Amy Oshiro-Morales, January 12, 2018.
7. Telephone interview with Stuart Chafetz, January 9, 2018.
8. Telephone interview with Koichiro Yamamoto, January 18, 2018.

CHAPTER 22

1. Humphrey Burton, *Leonard Bernstein* (New York: Doubleday, 1994), 519.
2. Kazuko Amano to Leonard Bernstein, August 25, 1990, LBC, box 2, folder 5.
3. Kazuko Amano to Leonard Bernstein, September 12, 1990, LBC, box 2, folder 5.
4. Kazuko Amano to Leonard Bernstein, October 11, 1990, LBC, box 2, folder 5.
5. Kunihiko Hashimoto to Leonard Bernstein, June 2, 1990, LBC, box 60G.

CHAPTER 23

1. Kuni Hashimoto, "A Japanese CANDIDE," *prelude, fugue, & riffs*, Spring/Summer 1995, 4.
2. Robert Ryker, "Bernstein's Spoof of Candide Opera Translated into Hysterical Slapstick," *Japan Times*, September 11, 1994.
3. Jamie Bernstein, *Famous Father Girl: A Memoir of Growing Up Bernstein* (New York: HarperCollins, 2018), chaps. 21, 22.
4. Kuni Hashimoto, "The Bernstein Beat: What Makes Music Dance?" developed by Michael Barrett and Jaime Bernstein Thomas, written by Jamie Bernstein Thomas, PMF 1999 Sapporo version.
5. Kuni Hashimoto, trans., *Candide*, Scottish Opera Edition of the Opera-House Version [1989], 1994.
6. *PMF—20 Years* (Sapporo: Pacific Music Festival Organizing Committee, 2009), 82.

CODA

1. Gary Perlman, "Pacific Overtures Makes a Spectacular Debut in Tokyo," *The Sondheim Review* 7, no. 2 (Fall 2000), n.p.; Gary Perlman, "Translating When 'Sondheim' is 6 Syllables," *The Sondheim Review* 7, no. 3 (Winter 2001), n.p.

Index